Oral History Theory

Oral history is increasingly acknowledged as a key tool for anyone studying the history of the recent past. This book is the first to provide a comprehensive and systematic overview of oral history theory in an accessible format.

The book is structured around key themes, including the peculiarities of oral history, the study of the self, subjectivity and intersubjectivity, memory, narrative, performance and power. Each chapter provides a clear and user-friendly explanation of the various theoretical approaches, illustrates them with examples from the rich field of published oral history and makes suggestions for the practising oral historian. There is also a glossary of key terms and concepts.

Combining the study of theoreticians with the observations of practitioners, and including extensive examples of oral history work from around the world, this book constitutes the first integrated explanation of oral history theory. It will be invaluable to experienced and novice oral historians and professionals and to students who are new to the discipline.

Lynn Abrams is Professor of Gender History at the University of Glasgow. She has published widely in the field of women's, gender and oral history, including *The Making of Modern Woman: Europe 1789–1918* (2002) and *Myth and Materiality in a Woman's World: Shetland 1800–2000* (2005).

Oral History Theory

Lynn Abrams

Routledge
Taylor & Francis Group

LONDON AND NEW YORK

First published 2010
by Routledge
2 Park Square, Milton Park, Abingdon, Oxon OX14 4RN

Simultaneously published in the USA and Canada
by Routledge
270 Madison Ave, New York, NY 10016

Routledge is an imprint of the Taylor & Francis Group, an informa business

© 2010 Lynn Abrams

Typeset in Times New Roman by
Taylor and Francis Books Ltd
Printed and bound in Great Britain by
TJ International, Padstow, Cornwall

British Library Cataloguing in Publication Data
A catalogue record for this book is available from the British Library

Library of Congress Catalog-in-Publication Data
Abrams, Lynn.
   Oral history theory/Lynn Abrams.
   p. cm.
   "Simultaneously published in the USA and Canada"–T.p. verso.
   Includes bibliographical references and index.
   1. Oral history–Philosophy.   I. Title.
   D16.14.A25 2010
   901–dc22

ISBN10: 0-415-42754-1 (hbk)
ISBN10: 0-415-42755-X (pbk)
ISBN10: 0-203-84903-5 (ebk)

ISBN13: 978-0-415-42754-8 (hbk)
ISBN13: 978-0-415-42755-5 (pbk)
ISBN13: 978-0-203-84903-3 (ebk)

Contents

Acknowledgements

This book has its origins in a course I teach to undergraduate students at Glasgow University which combines the practical application of oral history techniques with theoretical analysis of the results. Notwithstanding the huge range of texts on oral history available, none seemed to provide a user-friendly guide to theory; so, this is my contribution. The book has also grown out of my own oral history research over a number of years. My first foray into this methodology was interviewing people about their experiences of the Scottish child-welfare system, a moving and sometimes humbling experience. My next project took me to Shetland where I collected personal testimonies from women in those islands for a project that combined the methodologies of history and ethnology. And as I completed the manuscript for this book, I started a new research project on women in the 1950s and 1960s. I have drawn on material from each of those projects in what follows. There is really nothing better than getting out in the field, getting up close and personal – this is what oral history is all about. And my students have responded similarly to this challenge, excited by the opportunity to speak to real people, to create their own sources and to conduct some original analysis.

Many people have helped this book along. Angela Bartie, Sarah Browne, Linda Fleming, Yvonne McFadden, Amy Murphy, Andrew Perchard, Francesca Stella, Penny Tinkler and Ulrike Thieme all took the time to comment on parts of the manuscript and exchanged ideas and experiences about their oral history adventures. I have learned a great deal from them – practising oral historians all – and I hope they will find something useful here. Nigel Fabb introduced me a long time ago to the insights of linguistic analysis for the oral historian. Callum Brown read the entire text twice, corrected my grievous errors and made me see more clearly through the thicket of theory. Any mistakes that remain are, of course, my responsibility.

This book is dedicated to all those who have talked into my microphone in the past. They have contributed more to my research projects and to my thinking on oral history theory than they imagine.

Lynn Abrams
Argaty, by Doune
November 2009

1 Introduction
Turning practice into theory

Introduction

Oral history is a practice, a method of research. It is the act of recording the speech of people with something interesting to say and then analysing their memories of the past. But like any historical practice its theoretical aspects need to be considered.

As a research practice, oral history is engulfed by issues which make it controversial, exiting and endlessly promising. These are well spelt out by the oral historian Alessandro Portelli who starts one of his studies by noting that he is trying to:

> convey the sense of fluidity, of unfinishedness, of an inexhaustible work in progress, which is inherent to the fascination and frustration of oral history – floating as it does in time between the present and an ever-changing past, oscillating in the dialogue between the narrator and the interviewer, and melting and coalescing in the no-man's land from orality to writing and back.[1]

Portelli points to the poetic in oral history, to its permeability, its ability to cross disciplinary boundaries, and also to its ephemeral nature. He sums up what makes this method of finding out about the past so alluring and challenging for the historian.

This book proceeds on the assumption that in oral history research, practice and theory – doing and interpreting – are entwined. Conducting an interview is a practical means of obtaining information about the past. But in the process of eliciting and analysing the material, one is confronted by the oral history interview as an event of communication which demands that we find ways of comprehending not just *what* is said, but also *how* it is said, *why* it is said and *what* it means. Oral history practice then demands that one thinks about theory; indeed it is the practice, the doing of oral history, that leads to theoretical innovation. In this book we approach the oral history interview as a means of accessing not just information but also signification, interpretation and meaning.

This chapter will introduce the book in a number of ways. It will clarify some of the key terminology in the field, place oral history methodology within the wider field of personal-testimony research used by historians, sketch out the history of oral history as it relates to the turn to theory and outline some of the practical considerations encountered by all oral historians.

What is oral history?

Oral history is a catch-all term applied to two things. It refers to the process of conducting and recording interviews with people in order to elicit information from them about the past. But an oral history is also the product of that interview, the narrative account of past events. It is then both a research methodology (a means of conducting an investigation) and the result of the research process; in other words, it is both the act of recording and the record that is produced. Many other terms may also be used interchangeably with oral history, such as personal-testimony research and life-story research, and these will be used in this book. But historians seem to be most comfortable with 'oral history' as an umbrella term that incorporates both the practice and the output.

Such has been the success of oral history that it is now a tried and tested research practice, embedded not only in historical research but also in a wide range of disciplines including ethnology, anthropology, sociology, health-care studies and psychology. Oral history has also been employed outside the academic world as an evidential tool in the legal environment (in war-crimes trials for instance), by medical practitioners and those working in the caring professions. It is also a popular research tool deployed in community and educational projects, practised by young and old, volunteers and paid researchers, and is to be found in use in most countries of the world. Oral history has become a crossover methodology, an octopus with tentacles reaching into a wide range of disciplinary, practice-led and community enterprises. It is used by academics, by governments and during regime change – as in the officially sanctioned Truth and Reconciliation Commission after the collapse of apartheid in South Africa. But it is also used in social work, community enterprises and volunteer-led local-heritage projects. It is thus widespread and highly adaptable, being practical, political or historical in aim.

This success has had a number of consequences. The meaning of the term 'oral history' has been diluted so that almost any interview conducted with an individual may be labelled 'oral history', and historians can now no longer lay claim to oral history methodology as distinctive to their profession. It is important here though to make the distinction between oral history and other forms of data collection using the interview process. Qualitative research which may collect data via an interview can be a close cousin of oral history but may not have the distinctive character of specifically engaging with the past. Likewise, participant observation methods, where the researcher joins people in a social activity and which may incorporate interviews as an element of the research practice, are not always focused on the act of remembering the past.

But oral history's very success across the humanities and social sciences as well as outside academia has had the hugely beneficial effect of bringing together practitioners and theorists from a variety of perspectives. They each bring their own expertise to bear. The result is a vibrant and constantly evolving research practice that draws upon innovative findings from across the disciplinary spectrum. For this reason, this book cites examples from many of these contexts outside the history discipline. Historians who conduct and use oral history have learned to be promiscuous in their use of theoretical perspectives and borrow analytical techniques from literature and linguistics, psychology and anthropology, folklore studies and the performance arts to name a few. As Portelli so aptly says, oral history is permeable and borderless, a 'composite genre' which requires that we think flexibly, across and between disciplinary boundaries, in order to make the most of this rich and complex source.[2]

Yet there is a need for the historian to think in a distinctive way about oral history. This book is designed primarily for historians and also for researchers with their feet in other disciplines and non-academic contexts who use oral history sources; for those who may already have experience of conducting interviews but who require an introduction to the interpretive approaches to analysis. This book does not provide a 'how to' guide to the practical issues concerned with carrying out oral history projects or interviews; it assumes readers will refer to the many excellent print and web-based resources designed for this purpose, some of which are listed in the guide to further reading at the end of the book. However, at the heart of this book is the belief that practice and analysis cannot be separated; that the process of interviewing cannot be disaggregated from the outcome (the oral history narrative and the interpretation of that narrative).

Some clarity is needed at this point in respect of the terminology to be used in this book. 'Oral history' refers to both the practice of conducting interviews and all the subsequent stages of transcription and interpretation. The 'interviewer' will also, for the sake of variety, be referred to as the 'researcher'; likewise, the 'interviewee' may also be referred to as the respondent or narrator. The 'interview' refers to the process of engaging a living witness in an in-depth conversation about the past. The 'recording' refers to the aural or aural-visual product deriving from the interview whether it be on tape or in digital format. The 'transcript' is the written form of the recorded interview. Definitions of the various theoretical terms are to be found in the relevant chapters and in the Glossary.

Fact-finding and theory-bagging

Oral history has changed enormously in a few decades. The international, multidisciplinary, multi-vocal, confident and mature oral history movement of the twenty-first century is a distant relative of the post-Second World War oral history field which struggled to find legitimacy within hide-bound disciplinary traditions.[3] In the 1940s, 1950s and 1960s in the USA, the UK and Scandinavia in particular, oral history occupied a particular and circumscribed place within scholarly research. In America two early initiatives represented the two faces of oral history in that country. In the late 1930s, the New Deal Federal Writer's Project (FWP; a project designed to give work to unemployed artists and writers during the Depression years) began to collect the life stories of ordinary Americans. The result was a comprehensive documenting, without the aid of tape-recorders, of the everyday circumstances of thousands of Americans. It has been described as 'one of the most massive oral history projects ever undertaken'; more than 6,000 writers were employed at its peak and more than 10,000 men and women from all walks of life were interviewed.[4] By contrast, the post-war Columbia University oral history project was initiated in 1948 by historian Allan Nevins with the aim of documenting with the aid of tape-recorders the memoirs of those who 'contributed significantly to society or who were close affiliates of world leaders', what might be called the 'great men' approach.[5]

Britain and the Nordic countries followed a different trajectory. The rediscovery of oral history in the 1950s and 1960s, following decades during which the oral source was shunned in favour of the written record, was informed in part by the European tradition of ethnology and folklore collection which had always privileged the spoken voice as a repository of tradition, and then by the emergence of social history and historical sociology which employed oral history as a means of rescuing the voices of the labouring people.[6] By the 1980s, oral history had become the methodology of choice (and necessity) amongst scholars of the twentieth century seeking to uncover the experiences of a number of groups who had traditionally been disregarded by conventional histories: women, gays and lesbians, minority ethnic groups and the physically and learning disabled to name the most prominent.

These were important developments on both sides of the Atlantic, essentially marking the beginning of the oral history discipline we recognise today. But the early practitioners often worked on the margins of their respective academic disciplines or outside them altogether. Early oral historians were frequently famous figures. In the USA, the writer and broadcaster Studs Terkel took oral history to the masses via his radio programmes (*The Studs Terkel Show* ran for forty-five years from 1952 on WFMT in Chicago and interviewed countless celebrities) and books on subjects ranging from the Depression, the Second World War, working life and race relations which featured conversations with ordinary Americans.[7] In Britain, one of the most influential oral history publications in those early years was Ronald Blythe's *Akenfield,* a portrait of East Anglian village life based on conversations with rural folk published in 1969. Blythe was a writer, not a historian, and he later admitted he was not at all familiar with the practice of what became known as oral history.[8] Similarly, George Ewart Evans's studies of English rural life, notably *Ask the Fellows Who Cut the Hay* (1956), were based on what he called 'spoken history'; but Evans was a writer first and foremost, never a professional historian, and only later was he regarded as a founding father of British oral history.[9]

Moreover, in many countries, oral history has emerged from, and found a foothold in, disciplines and departments other than history. Indeed, the historical profession kept oral history at arm's length for some time, not quite trusting it as a legitimate historical source. At the same time, historians were wary of its practitioners, many of whom were located outside the academy or whose political stance – often sympathetic to the left and working within social, labour history and later feminist history – made them uncomfortable bedfellows with the discipline's gatekeepers. The combination of the political stance of oral history's adherents and the uses to which oral history was put consigned it to a place on the edge of professional practice. In order to establish some kind of academic legitimacy at that time, oral history could be summed up in Ron Grele's definition as 'the interviewing of eye-witness participants in the events of the past for the purpose of historical reconstruction'.[10] Oral history as 'recovery history', the practice of interviewing people to provide evidence about past events which could not be retrieved from conventional historical sources, usually written ones, or to uncover the hidden histories of individuals or groups which had gone unremarked upon in mainstream accounts, was the dominant trend within oral history practice in the 1970s and 1980s. Though this definition of oral history would now be regarded as somewhat limiting, the reconstructive agenda still remains a prime motivation (and a legitimate one at that) for many oral history research projects today.

Despite its narrow role, even the 'recovery history' mode of oral history was mistrusted by many historians and social scientists because it rested upon memory, and memory they regarded as unreliable. In an era when historical research was dominated by the document, oral history did not, in the main, produce data which could be verified and counted. It was not an objective, social-scientific methodology which could be rigorously tested. Thus cornered, pioneering oral historians went to great efforts to justify their practice to the critics. Verification of evidence obtained from oral interviews was one way of doing this, cross-checking with documentary sources in order to separate truth from fiction as well as setting the oral evidence in the wider context and checking for internal consistency in order that oral material could stand up to scrutiny. Oral historians working predominantly within a social-science framework were also concerned about the representative nature of their data, recommending the use of scientific sampling methods and making strenuous attempts to obtain a representative sample of interviewees. Respondents were given numbers to denote scientific tags, and an aura of pseudo-science pervaded much of what oral historians did.[11] Interestingly, Blythe's *Akenfield* fell victim on both counts, criticised by non-historians for not containing sufficient 'facts' for readers to feel comfortable with what they were being told and even more harshly critiqued by historians from the social-science tradition for its 'artistry'. The social historian Howard Newby, himself an expert on English rural life remarked: 'If all oral historians were allowed such artistic licence, what then for oral history? More enjoyable, more plea-surable to read, perhaps, but certainly not history.'[12] And Paul Thompson, generally acknowledged as the father of British oral history, doubted the authenticity and reliability of the oral evidence Blythe cited, describing it as 'less careful scholarship', largely it seems because the author approached his material in a literary and creative fashion rather than adhering to the rules of oral history practice as they were being laid down at that time.[13] Unless the sheen of social science was added to oral history practice, including the care-ful and accurate transcription of interviews and faithful representation of the spoken voice, then the method was depicted as literary and creative rather than as historical and reliable.

The infighting and criticisms of oral history's validity and reliability, and concerns about the representativeness of interview subjects, are still to be heard today. But rather than trying to meet the critics on the same ground (by testing and validating and recruiting huge samples of respondents), oral his-tory researchers since the 1980s have exuded much more confidence in what they do. They feel sure of the distinctive elements of their practice, acknowl-edging that oral history is a subjective methodology, celebrating its orality, recognising that memory stories are contingent and often fluid, and in short arguing that oral sources must be judged differently from conventional docu-mentary materials, but that this in no way detracts from their veracity and utility.[14] In the process, oral historians have become both intuitive and ima-ginative interpreters of their materials.

If one was to identify a point when oral historians began to leave behind their defensiveness and started to redefine oral history as an analytical prac-tice as opposed to a method of recovery it was the 1979 publication of Italian historian Luisa Passerini's critical article, 'Work, Ideology and Consensus under Italian Fascism'.[15] In this seminal piece Passerini acknowledged that oral history had been successful on two counts: in countering the critics' charges about the validity of oral sources, and in expanding the boundaries of historical research by focusing on hitherto-ignored areas of historical experi-ence. But she warned against the tendency to what she termed a 'facile democratisation' whereby oral history could be seen as giving a voice to the oppressed, and cautioned against replacing an 'open mind with demagogy'.[16] Such developments, she argued, risked turning oral history into 'an alter-native ghetto'.[17] Passerini urged the oral history community to go much further than the mining of oral sources for their factual information, not-withstanding the contribution this has made to the process of historical reconstruction. What was important was to understand the real import of oral narratives. 'Above all', she wrote, 'we should not ignore that the raw material of oral history consists not just of factual statements, but is pre-eminently an expression and representation of culture, and therefore includes not only literal narrations but also the dimensions of memory, ideology and subconscious desires.'[18]

This heralded the move of oral history from social science to cultural history. Passerini's clarion call for a new kind of oral history derived from her own life-story interviews with two generations of Italian workers born before 1910 and between 1910 and 1925. The historiographical context was a debate about the stance of the Italian working class towards Fascism. Her interviews threw up some surprising findings, notably that when asked questions about the Fascist era interviewees responded with what she calls 'irrelevant or inconsistent answers'.[19] The irrelevant responses were characterised by silence on the topic of Fascism, particularly in the period of Fascist-led peacetime. The inconsistent responses narrated lives which appeared discrepant with the known historical events; stories were told of everyday lives apparently disconnected from the structures of the Fascist state. In order to explain these surprising results, Passerini made the point that oral sources derive from subjectivity – they are not static recollections of the past but are memories reworked in the context of the respondent's own experience and politics. If one accepts this point then the oral historian is obliged to think hard about how and why those memory stories are produced – about the cultural environments of memory (when things happened) and of remembering (as they are recalled).[20]

Very quickly this new turn in oral history towards reflecting on how memory stories are constructed came to dominate academic practice and debate. Historians at the forefront of this second wave adhered to a revised definition of what we were all doing. In the words of Schrager: 'Talk about events is much more than data for the derivation of history: it is also a cultural production in its own right, a mode of communicating, a surfacing of meaningfulness that binds past and present together.'[21] In other words, whilst oral history produces useful evidential material in the form of description and factual information, the oral history narrative itself has considerable significance in that it is a way by which people articulate subjective experiences about the past through the prism of the present. Ron Grele puts it like this: interviews tell us 'not just what happened but what people thought happened and how they have internalised and interpreted what happened'.[22] The personal testimony produced in the interview mediates between personal memory and the social world. It was at this point in the 1980s that historians realised that they needed to draw on interpretive frameworks largely drawn from other disciplines in order to understand what is going on in an oral history interview. The history discipline was singularly ill equipped with theory to appreciate this developing discipline of oral history interviewing that saw researchers go off into the field to create their own sources via a conversation with a live subject. To get to grips with all the different elements that surfaced in an oral history encounter, oral historians came to other people's theories. These included subjectivity, memory, use of language, structures of narrative and modes of communication as well as issues concerning power and ethics. These are the things we shall be exploring in later chapters.

Since the 1960s, oral history has been transformed from a practice largely undertaken as a means of gathering material about the past to a sophisticated theoretical discipline in its own right. Exemplars from both ends of the spectrum illustrate the distance travelled. British women's historian Elizabeth Roberts' *A Woman's Place: An Oral History of Working-Class Women, 1890– 1940,* published in 1984, is a fine example of 'recovery history'. It is an examination of women's lives in northern England based on interviews with more than 100 respondents, using the rich qualitative material as primary evidence to illustrate and interpret the lives of ordinary women and supporting the argument that women themselves did not perceive their poverty and lack of opportunity to be the result of gender oppression.[23] Roberts was a skilled and path-breaking oral historian who turned to this method as a means of investigating the lives of working-class women who rarely featured in standard accounts and whose everyday lives had left few traces in the documentary record, but she pays no attention to issues concerning the ways in which her respondents constructed their narratives apart from noting in the sequel, *Women and Families,* that all sources contain bias.[24] Roberts' work is a prime example of recovery oral history used to full advantage.

In contrast, Daniel James's *Doña María's Story: Life History, Memory and Political Identity,* published in 2000, is a study of a working-class community in modern Argentina, pivoting around the testimony of one woman and comprising a series of interpretive essays, all of which engage with key theoretical problematics that provide insight into individual agency, gendered experience and labour politics in that country. James manages to convey new empirical information about the meatpacking community at the centre of the study, unionism and Peronism in Latin America, with a sophisticated analysis of oral history as a distinctive methodology. For James:

> life stories are cultural constructs that draw on a public discourse structured by class and gender conventions. They also make use of a wide spectrum of possible roles, self-representations, and available narratives. As such, we have to learn to read these stories and the symbols and logic embedded in them if we are to attend to their deeper meaning and do justice to the complexity found in the lives and historical experiences of those who recount them.[25]

James's work is a masterclass in the use of oral history to uncover new evidence, but it also exemplifies the ways in which sensitive analysis of personal testimony can lead to a deeper and richer understanding of how the past is remembered, reworked and reconstructed by people in the present.

But Roberts and James are part of the same oral history discipline, and although their modes of analysis might not have much in common, they share a commitment to the value of oral testimony and to the practical techniques of oral history. Oral history today is a 'broad church' encompassing a huge diversity of practitioners, from academics to community activists, from health workers to volunteers in the developing world. It is an international movement, active on all continents, communicating across borders from advanced post-industrial nations to some of the poorest developing countries and back again. What all oral historians share is a commitment to best practice in conducting interviews, transcribing narratives and engaging with respondents. No doubt they also share that excitement of embarking on a series of interviews for a new project, a real enjoyment from communicating with people about the past, and for many their engagement is also motivated by a commitment to social or political change. While some of the more arcane or philosophical interpretive trends might not engage attention across the entire spectrum of practitioners, there is a sense that both fact-finders and theory-baggers may be happily accommodated within the oral history community.

What are we interpreting?

Oral history exists in four forms: the original oral interview, the recorded version of the interview, the written transcript and the interpretation of the interview material. These are distinct from one another with the recording, transcript and interpretation mediated and edited versions of the real-time interview. Thus, the historian hears and reads different versions of the narrative using each to create another – the interpretation – in a chain of versions. At each link of the chain a number of practical issues arise which have implications for the interpretation to be undertaken.

There are, of course, some important preparatory decisions to be made by the researcher prior to conducting interviews which will invariably have an impact on the kinds of material gathered and in turn will influence the interpretive approaches to be adopted. We are not considering all these elements here. There are some excellent guides to project design which include advice on recruitment of interviewees, the format of the interview and equipment issues, some of which are listed in the guide to further reading at the end of the book.

The interview

Oddly, it is the interview itself that often receives the least attention in oral history theory. Oakley memorably said that: 'Interviewing is rather like marriage: everybody knows what it is, an awful lot of people do it, and yet behind each closed front door there is a world of secrets.'[26] While oral historians are often at pains to detail the number of interviews conducted, the nature of those interviews (whether formal or informal, with a questionnaire or not and so on) much of what actually takes place in the interview goes unreported. A lot happens between the parties before the interview occurs when there are hidden interactions which are not transferred adequately or at all to the transcript, yet few historians write candidly about interview experiences. The interview is the communicative relationship at the heart of our practice, fundamentally different from most encounters a historian will have with a historical source. One can hardly think of anything more different to the conventional experience of sitting in an archive consulting primary-source documents than collaborating in creating one's source with a living person. We all know that hitting it off on a personal level with an interviewee can make all the difference and that, conversely, poor interpersonal empathy can kill an interview dead. And we know from the application of interview technique in a range of contexts around the world that the interview dynamics that we think we understand in the developed West may not apply in other cultural contexts.[27] So the interview itself is not just a means to an end; it is a communicative event. And, as such, it needs to be given theoretical reflection.

In recent years, the interview relationship has been pushed back into the limelight as oral historians have accepted that oral history is a collaborative endeavour, the result of a relationship between interviewer and interviewee. There are two people involved in an interview, which means two worlds, or subjectivities, are colliding. The collision may take many different characters – deep rapport, polite regard, stand-offish defensiveness or deep incomprehension and alienation. This conceptual shift has moved attention to the subjectivities at play in the interview setting (simply put, the identities adopted by the parties) – taking into consideration class, gender, age, ethnicity and other variables which may affect the relationship – and a consideration of how these impact upon the story told by the respondent.[28] Portelli has described the interview as a 'deep exchange' that occurs on a number of levels.[29] It is not usually a question-and-answer session but give and take, collaborative and often cooperative, involving information-sharing and autobiographical reminiscence, facts and feelings. Given the degree of complexity contained within the interview setting we are surely committed to reflecting on the process that produces our oral history sources.

Daniel James is one of the few historians who has written candidly about his own sometimes difficult experiences as an interviewer in the context of an Argentine labouring community. He notes how his confidence in his skill as an oral historian was challenged by a respondent who was not prepared to engage solely on the historian's terms. James admits that he was 'out of his depth', that he was impatient and intolerant of the man's beliefs, that the physical conditions of the interview scenario – a freezing day in a cold, gloomy house – were not conducive to the kind of interview James had imagined, and throughout the encounter he had 'a sense of intruding on an intimate drama' between the man and his wife.[30] James concludes: 'I felt like a voyeur and found the sensation deeply disturbing. He, of course, noticed my reserve, and the interview wound down.'[31] In hindsight, James rationalised the encounter. He decided that in part it was an uncomfortable experience because he could not empathise with the man's Argentinian politics – 'a brand of religiously intense right-wing Peronism'; but perhaps more significant was his recognition that an academic interview agenda was not appropriate.[32] The 'propensity for aggressive intervention' in James's search for 'historical information' scuppered the relationship.[33]

Of course, we are probably more likely to think about the interview dynamics when a respondent fails to conform to what we are expecting than when the encounter potters along nicely. But both scenarios throw up pertinent issues. The interview in which the parties get along well, share stories, partake in refreshments and part on good terms tends to attract little comment but at the very least we should observe that the respondents in these events are conforming to what is expected, they have some knowledge of the role they are required to play and in some cases they will do their very best to provide the researcher with what it is they think they want. A 'successful' interview – one that perhaps produces a nice coherent and fluent narrative containing a balance between information and reflection – is likely to be the product of shared values between the parties, a good rapport and the willingness of the interviewer to permit the respondent to shape the narrative, avoiding unnecessary interjections. An 'unsuccessful' interview – one that fails to produce a coherent narrative, in which the respondent offers short or factual answers to questions without elaboration or reflection – may have its roots in a poor interview relationship, lack of empathy or rapport, and an absence of understanding or comprehension on both sides. Of course, these are rather value-laden definitions of success and its opposite, but many would agree that the interview relationship (alongside good preparation) is the key to eliciting a narrative response. In fact, every interview lends itself to analysis, and all of the interpretive approaches described in this book at some level have the interview relationship as their base line.

The recording and the transcript

Whilst oral historians are now attuned to the issues implicit in the interview relationship and have written sensitively about the complexities of the interview dynamic, most in-depth analytical work is conducted using the recorded version of the interview and the written transcript. Transcription from tape or digital file to written document is time-consuming and laborious but pays dividends to the researcher. A good recording – one that reproduces the sound clearly with an absence of background noise – facilitates ease of transcription. Given that, for practical reasons, most researchers are likely to conduct their interpretive analysis using oral history transcripts (though often in association with the recording), the accuracy and authenticity of the transcript, the degree of closeness to the original recording, is of some importance. In oral history's early days, powerful arguments were made in favour of maintaining the integrity of the spoken word in the process of translating speech into text. Raphael Samuel in an essay entitled 'The Perils of the Transcript' made an impassioned plea for precise transcription, for the 'role of the collector of the spoken word ... is that of archivist, as well as historian'.[34] Ignoring the rhythms and imperfections of the spoken word, tidying up, decluttering, removing verbal tics, rendering dialect silent and the imposition of the researcher's interpretation of a respondent's words, was akin in his view to vandalism.

These concerns were reflections of a particular moment in oral history practice, starting in the early 1970s when the retention of authenticity and the attempt to render the spoken word as faithfully as one could, was regarded as an essential skill of the oral historian and influenced a generation of practitioners. The motivation underpinning this was a laudable commitment to hearing the voices of the dispossessed, of not silencing those whose voices had been silenced in the past, a commitment to democracy in the interview and research process, and the obligation to be a good researcher. And practitioners today are usually taught to aim to reproduce the narrator's speech as closely as possible because 'faithful reproduction takes us one step closer to actual data, any deviation becomes an error'.[35]

An accurate and complete transcript does permit you to see the interview in its entirety: its shape, its rhythm, its fluency or conversely its disjointed nature. Moreover, a transcript which allows the reader to 'hear' the narrator, one which manages to reflect the narrator's rhythms of speech, dialect and linguistic idiosyncrasies, can be priceless though this is difficult to achieve. My own experience of transcribing interviews with people who have strong accents and who use dialect words suggests that a non-native speaker is unlikely to be able to accurately and consistently translate speech into text. My interview with Agnes Leask from the Shetland islands in the far north of Scotland is a case in point. Although she spoke in a strong Shetland accent my transcript reads as standard-pronunciation English with the exception of a few dialect words. Here is a short extract from that transcript; Agnes is talking about her father:

> by that time he already had two crofts, he looked after the old man on the adjoining croft and he'd left it to him, and of course in those days, same as the present day, you had to have an income outwith your croft. The croft was your home and your way of life, your own food for your table, if you were lucky a few beasts to sell in the autumn to pay the rent and that sort of thing.[36]

But a transcription by a native Shetlander of an earlier interview with the same woman is able to capture to a much greater extent the sound and rhythm of her speech. On being asked to describe her grandparents' croft (a small landholding), Agnes replied:

> Hit wis a crof' probably aboot maybe twal' or fourteen acres, hit wis a braa good crof', da Twatt crofts wis braa good quality, but dey wirna excessively big. But it wis a crof' at wis big enoch ta hae like milkin kye fur da hoose an rair young beasts fur sale an dat sorta thing, plus der ain corn fur mael an suchlike as dat. But of course a wife wi a lok o

young bairns couldna wark it tad a same extent as if dey'd baith been warkin.[37]

A transcript of this woman's speech that had been smoothed out and stan-dardised might even translate the dialect words like kye and bairns into their standard English equivalent – cows and children. Chapter 7 offers some examples of transcription methods that aim to translate not just the words said but the paralinguistic elements of the interview, the gestures, the tone and volume of voice and so on. Most practitioners will also say that the experi-ence of transcribing one's own interviews is invaluable; it brings the interview back to life, and it identifies aspects of the interview that went unnoticed at the time because you were concentrating so intensely, checking the recorder or taking notes.

But it is more realistic to accept that there can only be a semblance of similarity – a verisimilitude – between the narrative as told and the narrative as written down; something happens in the process of speech being translated to text. 'The oral interview is a multilayered communicative event', comments David Dunaway, 'which a transcript only palely reflects.'[38] The interview is a unique, active event, reflective of a specific culture and of a particular time and space. By contrast, the transcript is static and in comparison with the interview, flat. As a result, Dunaway concludes, 'when we transcribe, we as much re-create as translate'.[39] We write down the words said as accurately as possible, even including the hesitations, repetitions and vocal mannerisms, but the words are surface utterances embedded in a thick culture which it is vir-tually impossible to represent or recreate on the page. Without rejecting the need for accurate transcription, especially if one wants to undertake an ana-lysis of linguistic and paralinguistic elements, one should not equate obsessive *accuracy* with the ability of the transcript to convey the *meaning* of the speaker. After all, most historians heavily edit their oral history material for publication, and the embedding of sound recordings in published books and articles still seems some way off, so that readers are still reliant on the tran-scribed words.

So, we rely on the written text, along with our commentary, to convey the speaker's intent. Returning to the example of *Akenfield*, there is a sense in which Blythe's tidied-up yet elegant prose manages to convey meaning at least as well as a faithfully reproduced transcription with all its ragged edges. As an example, here we have a memorable and to my mind evocative extract from the reminiscences of farm-worker Leonard Thompson, a man described by Blythe as 'a little brown bull of a man with hard blue eyes and limbs so stretched by the toil that they seem incapable of relaxing into retirement'.[40] Thompson was speaking about the conflict between farmers and their labourers in the years before the First World War:

These employers were famous for their meanness. They took all they could from the men and boys who worked their land. They bought their life's strength for as little as they could. They wore us out without a thought because, with the big families, there was a continuous supply of labour. Fourteen young men left the village in 1909–11 to join the army. There wasn't a recruiting drive, they just escaped. And some people just changed their sky, as they say, and I was one of them.[41]

Oral historians still differ on this form of recounting interviewees' stories. But would the transcription of Thompson's words faithfully rendered in Suffolk dialect, containing all the normal verbal tics, convey his meaning any better?

There is a balance to be struck in the process of transferring the spoken word to the written document. Conforming to one of the guides to transcription that are widely available and aiming for accuracy and integrity obviates any grievous errors. However, it is rare that any one transcript will please all possible users (remembering that many archived transcripts will be referred to by users without the recording). The requirements of the linguist or the folklorist may well be different from those of the historian. The historian must try to be true to the respondent but most would aim for a transcript that reproduced the words said and the way in which they were said without an added layer of linguistic notation.

The final stage

Whatever kind of historians we are, we all go through the process of selection and interpretation that pulls the interview apart for analysis and edited quotation. Christine Borland explains:

> Oral personal narratives occur naturally within a conversational context, in which various people take turns to talk, and thus are rooted most immediately in a web of expressive social activity. *We* [the oral historians] identify chunks of artful talk within this flow of conversation, give them physical existence (most often through writing), and embed them in a new context of expressive or at least communicative activity (usually the scholarly article aimed towards an audience of professional peers). Thus we construct a second level narrative based upon, but at the same time, reshaping the first.[42]

So, by the time we reach the interpretive stage we are already some way distant from the original interview. Most researchers and community historians who conduct oral history are not content to let their interviews remain uninterpreted and unedited, whether for the purposes of reconstructive history or for analytical interpretive work. The majority of historians still select choice extracts from their interviews, removing the words from their context. Some editing is inevitable for public consumption. For example, Daniel James, whose work with an Argentinian meatpacking community was mentioned before, extensively reproduces the testimony of the subject of his book, Doña María, but the narrative is translated and, as he admits, also shortened, condensed and reconfigured.[43]

We can identify three models of oral history usage at this final interpretative stage. The first is what I will term the reminiscence and community model. This encompasses the tradition of undertaking oral history interviews for the sole purpose of recovering voices and placing them on the historical record. Such projects may regard the collection of material as the ultimate aim but usually produce transcripts and maybe publish extracts or full records of interviews. With this model of practice the theoretical input is likely to be minimal and the emphasis is upon uncovering information and recording voices before the knowledge they hold is lost.[44] The second model is the evidential. This encompasses the application of oral history for evidence gathering, the use of oral testimony as data, providing information to support an argument and illustrative material for publication. In this model the oral history text is likely to appear dismembered from its context, as short, pithy extracts, chosen for their typicality or their ability to say something in a memorable way. Roberts' work on women referred to above falls into this category as does Thompson, Wailey and Lummis's collective study of British fishing communities, and my own early oral history research largely falls into this category.[45] The third model is theoretical and may be sub-divided into two approaches. The purely theoretical approach uses the oral history material as a source on which to apply a particular analytical model. Relatively few historians have conducted this kind of analysis but oral history interview material has often been deployed in this way by scholars in other disciplines. As an expert on oral literature and performance, Ruth Finnegan has analysed the personal testimonies of English residents of a new town drawing on insights from narrative analysis and cultural and linguistic anthropology.[46] The stories told by the interviewees contain much material of use to the urban historian, but Finnegan's approach is to treat the narratives as storied accounts which contain narrative conventions and which draw on wider cultural discourses. An intermediary and much more widespread approach amongst historians is that which combines theoretical or interpretive insight with the evidential. There are many excellent examples of this, notably Penny Summerfield's research on women's narratives of the Second World War, Alistair Thomson's work with Australian veterans of the First World War and Daniel James' aforementioned study of the Argentinian labouring classes.[47] All these approaches to the use of oral history jostle side by side, coexisting within a field which happily accommodates this diverse bunch of people who do their history by talking to people.

We can see already that there is a diversity of approach and output from oral history research. The elements of interview, recording, transcript and interpretation each have significant variations. For the academic oral historian there is a need to lay out and reflect upon the theoretical dimensions of how the work is done.

Why do we need theory?

It is the *practice* rather than the content that marks out oral history as distinctive within historical research. The oral historian creates the resource of the interview and transcript; that it is actively elicited by the researcher is virtually unique in the profession. Elsewhere, historians rely on pre-existing historical sources; oral historians make their sources. Moreover, oral historians make this source in contact – usually a one-to-one meeting – with the memory-giver. The recognition that the oral history interview is unlike any other historical source – that it is dialogic or relational, discursive and creative – demands that we employ theories from other disciplines in order to interpret its significance to the narrator and within culture. Key to this approach is the acknowledgement that the interview is 'a conversational narrative' or a 'communicative event' that has taken place in real time between real people.[48] Oral history sources are also narrative sources, so historians must use theories devised for the interpretation of literary and folklore texts, and those derived from linguistics and psychology in order to gain insight into the meaning as opposed to the content of the interview.

An oral history interview then is an entry point from the present into the culture of the past. In order to gain access to that culture we must take notice of and interpret not just the words said but also the language employed, the ways of telling and the structures of explanation. In addition to attending to the language used, we must be aware of the social structure of the interview – that is the relationship between the interviewer and interviewee. And, embracing all of this is the cultural context within which each participant in the interview and the encounter itself is situated. All of these considerations impact upon how memory is recalled and converted into language. The oral history interview is therefore a complex historical document that contains many layers of meaning and is itself embedded within wider social forces. Theoretical insights can help us decode this document, to enable us to link the individual narrative to the general experience, the personal experience to the public, the past to the present. As historians we are interested in the personal anecdote, the individual version of past events, but ultimately we are aware that all personal narratives are embedded within something much bigger – what we might call culture, or wider social forces or the public-political world or the discursive field.[49]

The following chapters aim to outline for the oral historian some of the most useful interpretive models and theoretical frameworks that can be applied to make sense of oral history narratives. While some of these are familiar to social and cultural historians, others are drawn more directly from other disciplinary fields such as anthropology, psychology, sociology, linguistics and performance studies, but have specific applicability to oral narrative and memory documents. Historians utilising and analysing oral history sources need to be flexible and curious, willing to step outside history's disciplinary boundaries to make the most of their sources which are for sure the most complex and challenging in the primary-source treasure chest. Historians are not generally theorists but are happy to draw on theoretical insights if they prove useful in decoding documents. Oral historians have been more theoretically promiscuous than most in the historical profession – terms such as 'intersubjectivity', 'narrative', 'discourse' and 'self' are now commonplace in oral history publications – but these are often applied with little sense of being informed by specific theoretical positions. Concepts and frameworks drawn from cognate areas such as storytelling and oral tradition, folklore research, literary theory and the study of memory are also commonly utilised. In addition, as a reflection of the maturity of oral history as a discipline, oral historians have developed their own interpretive frameworks grounded in practice: concepts such as the cultural circuit, composure theory and shared authority. No chapter is discrete; each is interconnected, illustrating how oral history theory and practice are necessarily promiscuous in their use of approaches and the propensity to interdisciplinarity and experimentation.

Chapter 2 offers a discussion of oral history's distinctive features which give rise to our need for interpretive models drawn from outside history's natural toolbox. Chapter 3 begins with the person – the interviewee – at the centre of our practice, focusing on constructions of the self, identity and consciousness. In Chapter 4 we move on to the interview itself to examine ideas about how the intersubjective relations present in the interview impact upon the outcomes. Chapter 5 focuses upon memory – how it works, how it is accessed, processed and produced in an oral history narrative and how we might interpret memory stories. Chapter 6 looks at the narrative structures used in the creative production of memory stories, whilst Chapter 7 examines the memory story as a performance. In Chapter 8 the book closes with a discussion of the power relationships inherent in the production and publication of memory narratives. Chapters 3–7 broadly adopt the same format: (a) a description of the theory, (b) a discussion of how oral historians have applied the theoretical approach, and (c) some suggestions for how to translate theory into practice. This book offers the researcher a smorgasbord of approaches, not all of which will be relevant to every oral history project. All I am suggesting is that historians who work with oral history consider the utility of some of these theoretical models in order to gain insight into the complex process of creating an oral history and in the process advance the field of study.

2 The peculiarities of oral history

Introduction: oral history as a distinctive field

Oral history is much more than just another means of uncovering facts about the past. It is a creative, interactive methodology that forces us to get to grips with many layers of meaning and interpretation contained within people's memories. It is the combination of oral history as an interactive process (the doing), and the engagement of the historian with the meanings that people ascribe to the past (the interpretation), that marks it out as a peculiar historical practice. Oral history is not like written sources. As the anthropologist Renato Rosaldo says, it is mistaken to treat spoken testimonies like written documents, because 'as soon as we do we inevitably begin to conceive of oral tradition as "undistorted narrative transmitted through a conduit"'.[1] Oral history is unlike any other historical document or primary source consulted by a historian, and therefore it requires analytical techniques that are peculiarly suited to interpreting its many layers.

In 1979, Alessandro Portelli set out the case for oral history as a distinctive genre or category of historical practice.[2] In an influential article and subsequently in a collection of analytical pieces which applied his methodological insights, Portelli challenged oral history's critics and, more importantly, provided oral historians with a theoretical and methodological foundation for their work. To quote Portelli, oral history is the 'genre of discourse which orality and writing have developed jointly in order to speak to each other about the past'.[3] In this definition then, it is what the historian does, the dialogue with the narrator, the active shaping of the discourse between them and then the translation and presentation of that material, that constitutes oral history as a genre, that is a distinct category or type of practice and source. It is the practice of oral history – the doing of it – rather than the content derived from it that marks out this method of historical research as different.

Oral history involves communicating with living, breathing human beings. No other history method does this. This may seem so obvious that it is not worth saying, but we should always remember that at the heart of our practice are real people: the researcher who is asking the questions and the respondent doing his or her best to answer them. And it is this that is the key to oral history's uniqueness. All the features that distinguish oral history stem from this one element. It is precisely the very complexities that arise from using people as our sources that give rise to some specific issues of analysis and interpretation. So what is peculiar? First, a human respondent cannot be analysed in the same way as a written document, a material artefact or a visual image. While we may ask similar questions about subject position (who produced the source?), the circumstances around its production (why was it produced?) and the intended audience (who was it intended for?), thereafter the historian who chooses to utilise oral history sources finds herself on different terrain to her counterpart reliant on written or printed documents, be they government records, charters, photographs or artefacts. And this is essentially because oral history is a *dialogic* process; it is a conversation in real time between the interviewer and the narrator, and then between the narrator and what we might call external discourses or culture. As a result of these conversations – both the one that is verbalised and the one that is conducted in the narrator's consciousness (essentially the process by which the narrator silently engages with the researcher's questions and decides how to answer) the historian encounters a series of elements which require attention if one is to conduct a meaningful interpretation of the interview.

Portelli identifies six elements that make oral history sources 'intrinsically different' from other historical sources. These are: orality, narrative, subjectivity, credibility, objectivity and authorship.[4] To this list many theorists might add performativity, mutability and collaboration. In what follows I will loosely follow Portelli's schema.

Orality

Oral history deals with the spoken word. Thus it has the character of orality. It can so often be forgotten or put to the back of one's mind owing to the dominance of the transcription and the ease of working with it rather than the recording. Scholars of oral tradition – storytelling, folktales and such like – have always paid close attention to orality, the shape and rhythm of the speech act, because these are taken to be capable of revealing important attributes of the story, the contents, the practice of telling and the culture which produces it. Oral historians have often failed to take the orality of the recorded speech seriously, perhaps because traditionally we regarded the oral history interview as a means of only accessing information rather than thinking about the importance of the speech of one who 'was there' in the past or who is passing on the oral tradition of his or her forebears.

Of course, some non-oral sources used by historians, such as the accounts of court cases and legal depositions, actually originated as speeches by witnesses and defendants in trials – material given as evidence that was written down by a court clerk. Normally, however, these were not transcribed as fully verbatim and faithful reproductions of the speech act; the resulting documents provide what might be described as a mediated and often stylised or formulaic version of what was actually said so that much of the orality of the original is lost. As an example, here is some witness evidence from a case of infanticide heard in a Scottish court in 1854. The words are those of a female witness from the rural labouring classes of Shetland, a part of Scotland which had a very distinctive accent and dialect. The surviving document states:

> I went up to her bedroom to see her, she was in bed and apparently very weak. I asked what was the matter with her and she told me she had overwrought herself and caught cold and was very unwell. From what she said of her state as well as from her appearance I had little doubt in my own mind that the report of her having been delivered was correct ... having had a family myself I was satisfied both from what she told me of her state and from her appearance that she had been delivered but whether prematurely or not I had no mean of knowing.[5]

From this extract we can see that the distinctive voice of the witness has likely been emasculated – translated from dialect into standard English, rendered in a legalese (legal language) that has lost much of its link to the speaker's original words, and has lost intonations and style. When there is an attempt by the court clerk to transcribe reported speech more faithfully, as in the next example, the reader does get a better sense of the orality of the original encounter. Here we have a witness in a Dundee court in 1891 reporting on her encounter with her servant who was suspected of being pregnant:

> I said 'Dear me Lizzie what is the matter with you? – you must be in the family way.' She replied at the same time brushing her hands down the front of her person, 'There is nothing the matter with me.' I said 'do not try to deny it, it will not conceal any longer – you look like a woman near her time' and pressed her to tell me her time as I was concerned because of her being in a bedroom alone. She became silent and would not tell me anything then began to say 'what about it' (meaning the sleeping alone), 'Oh let's alone, I am vexed enough, dinna bother's and dinna rage?'[6]

Here we get a better idea of the character of the narrator's speech. Orality comprises the rhythms and cadences, repetitions and intonations, the use of particular speech forms such as anecdote or reported speech, the use of dialect, as well as the volume, tone and speed. Without attention to these features Portelli warns that we risk flattening 'the emotional content of the speech down to the supposed equanimity and objectivity of the written document'.[7] We should not ignore the orality of an oral history source so that it becomes like any other, like one of those legal documents which have been smoothed out. This is why a careful transcription is needed even though this can only provide a good imitation of the original interview.

Narrative

Implicit in the orality of the interview is its narrative nature. This second distinguishing feature refers to the ways in which people make and use stories to interpret the world; in other words narrative is a form which is used to 'translate knowing into telling'.[8] Almost all oral histories, or at least those testimonies elicited in informal, semi- or unstructured interviews as opposed to a formal question-and-answer format will demonstrate narrative features. The story told will be arranged and dramatised in a narrative form with a variety of elements such as reported speech, diversions, commentary, reflection and so on. It may follow certain codes of structure distinctive to the culture from which it and the storyteller come. For example, here is the testimony of Apphia, an Inuit from the north of Canada speaking (originally in the Inuktitut language) in the 1990s:

> I am Apphia Awa. Now I will start. I will start with a description of my ancestors, my family. How is it? Just a minute. I have to think of where to start ... who to start with ... Just a minute now ...
>
> Now my ancestor family, it goes like this. The Arvaarluk family was my adoptive family. Arvaaluk and his wife, Ilapaalik, they were my adoptive parents ... Arvaaluk had a mother named Aqaaq and a father named Attaarjuat ... Now for my actual relatives: Kublu was my real father, and my real mother was Suula. I don't know all of Kublu's ancestors, but I do know who his parents were ... As for Suula, my real mother, her father was Nutarariaq and her mother was Kaukjak ... [9]

Even from the transcribed and translated interview, we can detect here quite readily, the distinctive structure and manner of recounting family history amongst an older generation of Inuit. It shows the orality and narrative qualities distinct to the Inuit people contrasting with a normative Western model which would conventionally begin with a date and place of birth. Certainly written sources may constitute or contain narrative forms in some ways similar to this, so the element of narrative is not completely unique to oral history. Historians are familiar with the narrative styles adopted by those who record events, from medieval chroniclers to twentieth-century journalists. But written records have in most societies been the product of learned people, the educated elites, usually men and often members of the legal or church professions. As such they have a blandness that has erased distinctive ways of speaking by non-elite groups. The oral history narrative, then, has a sharper connection to ways of speaking and remembering within societies. The important point here is that as historians using oral history we must be alert to the essential narrative nature of oral sources and recognising them as such we need to employ the tools of the narrative theorists to unpack our sources. We will look further at narrative in Chapter 6.

Performance

Orality and narrativity take us to a third quality – the recognition that each oral history is a performance and the understanding that the meaning or interpretation of the source lies not merely in the content of what is said but also in the way it is said. As a means of verbal communication, oral history is in part a 'physical' thing; we form facial expressions as we speak, gesticulate, move our head and arms, we modulate our voice, we present ourselves in a way appropriate to the performance required. All narrators adopt a performance style, some consciously, others not. A performance style will often consist of a combination of narrative form and a particular speech form; hence a clergyperson's pulpit sermon would be a recognisable perform- ance style, as would a politician's speech, or a comedian's stage act, or a storyteller surrounded by a group of children. In the same way, the oral his- tory narrator will adopt a style appropriate to the interview situation. During the interview many will moderate an accent or refrain from speaking in dialect. We might also observe how our respondent dresses and acts as she or he speaks. It follows that the performance element of the interview should be evaluated alongside the content – often the two are inseparable for most interviewees are aware that they are expected to perform and will rise to the occasion. From this, the oral historian can often make telling observations – about the moral code of a 'host' or 'hostess' in the culture concerned, for example, which may demand a clean home and plentiful tea and biscuits for the interviewer.

Subjectivity

Students of history are taught that all sources are subjective, meaning that they are produced from a particular standpoint and identifying that stand- point aids one's interpretation of the sources. Subjectivity then, at least in this sense, is not unique to oral history, but subjectivity – defined as the quality of defining or interpreting something through the medium of one's mind – is what oral history is. The oral historian is not just looking for 'facts' for her or his work but is looking to detect the emotional responses, the political views and the very subjectivity of human existence. We go looking for the personal experience, sometimes as an antidote to generalised accounts of events or to versions of the past produced by those with power. Subjectivity – accessing it, even celebrating it – is the bread and butter of oral history. We ask not merely 'what happened?' but we ask next 'and how did you feel about it?' We encourage our interviewees to tell us about the past *from their own point of view* and to reflect on 'what do you think about it now?' The result is often that oral history provides a conduit to the meaning of an event to individuals, peoples or entire nations. To cite an oft-quoted phrase of Portelli, 'oral sour- ces tell us not just what people did, but what they wanted to do, what they believed they were doing, and what they now think they did'.[10] It is that process of active self-reflection on the part of the narrator that distinguishes the oral history interview, and thus the source produced, from virtually all other sources consulted by historians.

Memory

If oral sources are subjective then it follows that they are also memory documents. Indeed, many other historical documents are also produced from memory to a greater or lesser extent: minutes of government meetings, legal records, journalistic reportage, published memoirs and diaries. Before the advent of sound recording, people made notes either during or after an event. However, these documents are consulted in their written form and too often the historian is apt to forget that memory and its frailties underpin them. In this way, every documentary source will contain a fallibility as to accuracy and bias. For oral historians this should never be a problem, but an opportunity. Memory, with all its imperfections, mutability and transience is at the heart of our practice and analysis. We want to know why people remember or forget things, the warping and mistakes they make, and ask 'why?' It is this use to which oral historians put memory that sets this type of historical research apart.

From this has long arisen the complaint of critics that oral history exposes the fallibility of memory, the ability of memory to change over time, to be 'infected' with outside influences. But for oral historians it is the very process of how this 'infection' has occurred that is interesting. The way a respondent 'borrows' ideas, motifs, sayings and whole 'memories' about the past from their family, community or wider culture reveals much about the collective memory of neighbourhoods, groups and nations. This has generated an entire subfield of oral history studies – that which focuses on collective memory. No other part of the history profession takes this interest in how communities – from the family up to the nation – remember themselves, digging up their past to elaborate the evolution of their identity.

Although we do still rely on our respondents to mine their memories for facts about past events and experiences, particularly in instances where the information is unavailable elsewhere, where oral history really departs from other memory sources – the memoir or autobiography for example – is in the recognition that memory is an active process. The oral history interview is an event whereby, through the relationship between the interviewer and the respondent, a memory narrative is actively created in the moment, in response to a whole series of external references that are brought to bear in the interview: the interviewer's questions, the respondent's familiarity with media representations of the past, personal prompts and cues such as photographs and family memorabilia. We go on in Chapter 5 to look more closely at the working of memory and how it excites the oral historian.

Mutability

Finally, the distinctiveness of oral history lies in its *mutability,* its resistance to being pinned down. Before it has been transcribed, the oral history interview is inconstant, it has a capacity to undergo change. No interview with the same person will ever be repeated the same. Words will change, stories will change, and performance and narrative structure will change, especially if the interviewer is replaced by another. For instance, there is widespread acceptance that the sex and age of the interviewer has a major impact on the testimony from a respondent. This is part of a much wider process known as intersubjectivity – the interaction between the two subjects present at the interview. Moreover, an oral history interview with one individual, especially if it is relatively unstructured and not focused on a single event, may have no natural end point. Likewise, a project to investigate an identifiable event or experience may have no natural boundaries in terms of numbers of people interviewed. This is why Portelli describes oral history as having the 'unfinished nature of a work in progress'.[11] The mutability is only stopped when the recorded speech is turned into words on a page and at that point the oral history source comes closer than at any time to being like any other conventional primary source. For this reason, the oral historian must beware the power of the transcript to transform the source from its natural mutability into unnatural fixity.

Collaboration

The understated element so far in this discussion has been the place of the historian. In what other research context does the historian have such an active role in the creation of the source? It is the historian after all who initiates the oral history encounter, who identifies respondents, who sets the agenda. It is the historian who asks the questions and shapes the interview. And it is the historian who controls the final product, generally transcribing the oral text and then deploying the material as evidence in a product aimed at public consumption. Oral history is the only sphere of historical research where the researcher, with the cooperation of the interviewees, creates his or her own sources. This is a privileged position to occupy, and one is honour-bound to acknowledge one's presence in the source as well as one's power over its creation and how it is used. This leads to many oral historians writing about themselves in their writing-up of an oral history project.

This means that oral history is a joint enterprise, a collaborative effort between respondents and researchers. Once a historian has dabbled in oral history he or she is drawn into the story; neutrality, much less objectivity, is hard to sustain. Hence Portelli's question, 'who speaks?' There can be no pretence that our subjects speak for themselves because they evidently do not, or at least not as pure, unadulterated voices, yet oral history is one of the few ways by which those who have traditionally been silenced in History may be heard. But the historian's presence as 'ventriloquist' or 'stage director' should not be forgotten.[12] The oral history source then is multi-vocal, it contains many voices and more than one point of view. It begins with the orality of the narrator, and that is always our central focus, but it goes through several transformations before it becomes public.

All of these distinctive elements of oral history are summed up by Portelli in a classic description. Oral history, he writes, is:

> a 'text' in the making, which includes its own drafts, preparatory materials and discarded attempts. There will be gradual approaches in search of a theme, not unlike musical glissando; conversational repairs and after-the-fact corrections, for the sake of either accuracy or of pragmatic effectiveness; incremental repetitions for the sake of completeness or accuracy, or of dramatic effect. This personal effort at composition in performance is supported by the use of socialised linguistic matter (clichés, formulas, folklore, frozen anecdotes, commonplaces) and by the example of genres derived from writing (the novel, autobiography, history books) or mass media.[13]

Oral history then, is a mutable genre, meaning it starts out as one thing but may become something else. The form mutates but at the same time several versions of the original coexist – the recording, the transcription and the interpretation – and each informs the others. Within each of these forms different elements are highlighted. In the aural version it is the verbal performance of the narrator that takes centre stage. In the written or transcribed version we tend to focus on the content. In the public version we focus on interpretation. In effect, what starts out as a personal exchange, a private conversation, becomes a public statement or a text which is open to various interpretations and even may be transformed into another genre altogether such as a scholarly article or a film or theatre performance.[14]

Types of personal testimony

Oral history is not only distinct from other historical sources but also from other forms of personal testimony. Oral tradition, storytelling as well as autobiography, diaries, memoirs and other forms of life review all have much in common with oral history. But it is important to identify oral history's distinctiveness from these.

Oral tradition

Of course oral history has many points of connection with oral tradition, that is messages or stories transmitted orally from one generation to another. However, as anthropologist and historian of Africa Jan Vansina makes clear, oral history is methodologically distinct from oral tradition in many ways. To start with, oral tradition is defined as 'oral messages based on previous oral messages, at least a generation old'.[15] Oral tradition then is not contemporary; it has a historical genealogy and may be used as a historical source, particularly in non-literate cultures, but often it is hard to say when the story originated because of its instability over time owing to the chain of transmission.[16] Oral history, on the other hand, is the 'remembering of events and experiences within the lifetime of the narrator' which can normally be situated within a recognisable timescale.[17] We assume that the events and experiences recalled in an oral history interview have been experienced by the narrator unless explicitly stated otherwise.

There is clearly overlap between oral tradition and oral history. Some oral histories consist in part of the relating of stories passed down orally which tell of events not experienced by the narrator. And oral tradition, as Vansina acknowledges, may constitute historical evidence, especially if the tale told is based on verifiable observation.[18] In fact, there has been much debate about the status of oral tradition as historical evidence, particularly in native communities where written documents are partial or absent. Although this understanding of oral history has progressed since Vansina was writing, his key points are still valid. Oral tradition possesses a dynamic nature; it is continually passed on and in that process is transmuted. Each rendering of the oral performance will be influenced by the circumstances in which the telling occurs. Oral history is a narrative about an experienced past told at any one time. The narrative told by an individual may alter in repeated tellings but it is generally not passed on in oral form over generations (though elements within it might be, such as family stories, versions of notable events and so on). What unites oral tradition with oral history is their orality, their performative nature, their subjectivity and their character as interpretive accounts, versions of the past. Broadly speaking, although oral tradition is regarded as a process and oral history a method, they are both cultural ways of transmitting knowledge, meaning and experience.[19]

Autobiography

The task of distinguishing oral history from autobiography is a little more clear-cut. Most oral history is autobiographical in the sense that a person is recounting his or her version of events from the point of view of the reflective self. And many, if not most, oral history narratives will contain much that is autobiographical, details of a life deemed relevant to the story being told. Narrators generally tell their stories in the first person (using the personal pronoun 'I') or from the personal point of view. Likewise, the autobiography is the positioning of a life within a broader conception of the past, a linking of the private with the public, the personal with the political. But the critical aspect that distinguishes an oral history interview – even one that takes a life-story approach – from autobiography is the involvement of the interviewer. 'Although an oral autobiographical narrative may look on the surface very much like any other autobiographical *text,* it constitutes a very different autobiographical *act'*, writes Portelli, 'because the basis of authority is different.'[20] The intervention of the interviewer shifts that authority away from the narrator creating in Michael Frisch's words a 'shared authority'.[21] So, the story to be told may exist independently of the interviewer but the way it is expressed is influenced by the interviewer's intervention. Though there may be influence from editors or publishers, in a conventional written auto-biography the initiative stays with the autobiographer from the first decision to narrate a life to what to include and exclude, how to shape the story and so on. Unlike storytelling or even middle-class autobiography, where the speaker/writer takes the floor with a legitimacy derived from social status or tradition, the narrator in an oral history interview gains the legitimacy to speak from the interviewer. Thus the process and the product is different. Oral history can produce a reimagination of the past that is being shared in a joint moment between narrator and interviewer. Power often shifts throughout the process of the interview and post-interview activities: the interviewee might assert power at certain points – in the post-interview checking and approval of the transcript for instance – but is never solely responsible for the outcome.

Oral history is also distinguishable from autobiography on account of its inclusivity and its political instrumentality.[22] Many autobiographies are of the rich and famous, published because of the subject's celebrity and following. By contrast, oral history has a well-deserved reputation for giving a voice to the voiceless, for empowering the weak. For Joanna Bornat it is oral history's ability to record the stories of those who are rarely heard and its agenda of social and political change that marks out this practice from autobiography, which tends to be the mouthpiece of those with power, fame or privilege. Oral history, Bornat argues, diminishes inequalities of power and can be empowering beyond the frame of the research project whereas autobiography is bounded by a text – that is the text is the end point, offering no further opportunities for change.

Conventions in oral history

Oral history then, has its own form, its own shared conventions by which it is recognised as a distinctive practice. But it also contains or produces a variety of what might be called subgenres – recognisable forms of speech, of narrative formation, and of performance – that is, ways of translating knowing about the past into an expressive narrative. Most of this book is concerned with the theoretical approaches employed to understand and interpret these subgenres so that we can gain a deeper or richer insight into the narrator's meaning.

Most interviews adopt a variety of forms reflecting the changing nature of the conversation. A formal question-and-answer format might mutate into a more informal dialogue or conversational mode as the participants become more comfortable with one another. Respondents might, at points, assume the role of a narrator of a monologue; they might use anecdotes, description, repetition, reported speech, commentary and so on. We know that some of these modes of speech are cultural, that is, in some cultures narrators will more readily adopt a particular communicative form. Storytelling, for instance, has been observed as a common communicative device in societies where orality is privileged over the written text; thus some oral history interviews can lead to long, almost uninterrupted narrations that sound like, and in the transcript look like, old-fashioned folk tales. For another example, some modes of speech appear to be gendered. Women are more likely than men to cite reported speech.[23] Here is eighty-three-year-old Lily Levitt from the east of England describing an argument with her employer on the occasion of her leaving her service as a live-in maid:

> I remember when I left to go to London she didn't like me leaving and she was quite angry because I was leaving. She said 'You're very anaemic,' which I was at the time, 'you'll have lots of stairs to climb. You'll be ill. You're better by half to stop here with me.' I said 'No, I want to go. I'm going.' 'Oh, well', she said, 'I liked your brother Sydney and I liked your father, but I never did like you.' And I said 'And I don't like you.'[24]

This is a classic woman's style of speaking, much less common amongst men, though the differences may have been lessening in the past fifty years. These are just two ways in which the oral history interview can reveal various cultural conventions.

In addition to linguistic and narrative genres identifiable within the oral history interview we may also be able to distinguish certain thematic genres or motifs that are used to shape the meaning of a story. Portelli identifies the war narrative as a common means by which men make sense of their personal life as it relates to History, or at least public history. He found that women, on the other hand, more commonly used the caring motif to talk about their lives and particularly the way they engaged in the public sphere at a time when women were relatively disempowered in society.[25] These may not be universal rules but may be culturally specific. The war narrative is less likely to appear so commonly in stories related by men of the generation too young to remember the last all-embracing war, the Second World War. And perhaps the caring narrative would have less salience today for women who have a more active role in the public sphere. However, just as those who have analysed traditional folk tales have identified a series of universal motifs (recurring themes or elements that make the tales work for the listener or reader – such as the motif of the wicked witch, the speaking animal or the magic number three), it may be possible to do similar work for oral history narratives in particular cultural and historical contexts: the weak overcoming the strong, the disempowered fighting back against authority, the bad man turned good, the monster who turns into a prince, the happy ending.

Research imperatives

Finally we need to reflect on the fact that historians also work within identifiable genres and employ particular methods at all stages of the research and writing process. Historians are trained to work according to certain professional criteria, we possess a set of skills, sometimes described as the 'historian's craft' (which includes ways of assembling and sampling data, reading sources, validating sources against one another, avoiding subjective judgements and so on), and it is hard to jettison these in the pursuit of a story.[26] The historian starts out with an agenda and conducts interviews in order to obtain information that will contribute to answering a set of research questions.[27] Few historians would feel comfortable with the kind of methodology exemplified by Henry Glassie's classic text, *Passing the Time in Ballymenone*, a work of folklore, ethnology and history in a rural Northern Irish community in which the author admits; 'I knew nothing about the community and I had no hypothesis.'[28] He describes his method as a process of interaction and collaboration. Glassie writes that by asking questions 'I would be able to find the community's wise speakers, and while scanning broadly to test their generalisations, I would let them guide me. They know'.[29] Yet the work of the oral historian is often more akin to Glassie's approach than that of her colleagues reliant on documentary sources.

In conducting oral histories one is always aware of a project's open-ended nature in that few interviews stick to the script the researcher has set and new avenues for research are constantly being introduced by the respondent. But historians find it hard to break out from their disciplinary straitjacket. We may assert that meaning is more important than facts, but what oral historian has not asked the question, 'and when precisely was that?' or 'what year did that happen?' Daniel James notes that he frequently interrupted his respondent Doña María to confirm or pin down dates and other 'facts', an honest admission by a historian conscious of what he calls professional ideology.[30] And in adopting this frame for an interview (even unconsciously) we may push a respondent into a form of narration that fits our own agenda or, conversely, in Ron Grele's words, force 'memory to its limits, destroying its very narrative capacity'.[31] In fact, it has been suggested that it is almost impossible for the historian to really represent the point of view of the narrator, the insider's perspective, because their interests are so often in opposition: the historian often inserts the oral history evidence into a pre-existing historical framework whereas the narrator has provided a version of the past as it was experienced in all its complexity, usually containing much that appears tangential to the topic under discussion.[32] So, in doing oral history, the historian sometimes has to restrain the impulse to be a historian at all times; she or he has to push at the disciplinary envelope, employ methods of practice and analysis which might feel strange or antithetical to conventional ways of doing historical research, to move away from the approach that sees oral history merely as a means of answering our pre-prepared research questions.

The public documents we produce, from the transcriptions of oral interviews to our scholarly articles and books and even the publications of community and voluntary organisations, all conform to a set of generic practices and forms into which we bend and shape and sometimes force our oral sources. Since the forms in which academic historians disseminate research are generally written and published in printed or online format, the orality of our sources is lost; online recordings are generally edited and truncated; and even the most precise transcription, which endeavours to reflect the narrator's rhythms and patterns of speech, dialect and intonation, is no substitute for the original oral version. Constraints on the length and form of the scholarly text usually prevents the reproduction of a complete interview transcript. Most commonly the oral history source is embedded into a text as selected extracts, either used as illustrative material or what is described as 'textual verifications of an historical interpretation'.[33]

Increasingly, and excitingly, there are exceptions to this rather unsatisfactory representation of our oral sources. Portelli's moving study of the massacre by Nazis of 335 prisoners in Rome during the Second World War privileges the narrators and their stories over the historian's interpretation. Unusually for a history text, Portelli lists the names of the narrators at the start of the book (rather than hidden at the back amongst the appendices), and each chapter begins with a lengthy story from one of the narrators so that it is the oral history that leads the reader rather than the historian.[34] The extracts are not used merely as window dressing or as particularly good or pithy articulations of a point made by the historian; rather, the oral history narratives convey the different meanings of the massacre and its aftermath from the point of view of those who offered their testimony. Those working outside the rather restrictive conventions of the academy have more successfully privileged the words of their respondents. Works such as Antjie Krog's *Country of My Skull*, a personal account by a South African journalist of the work of that country's Truth and Reconciliation Commission that presided in the years after racial apartheid, places the harrowing words of the witnesses centre stage.[35] Many community oral history projects have taken advantage of the digital revolution, including recordings of oral history extracts on hardware packaged with publications or have decided to showcase their work on the Web where length and form restrictions are less applicable.[36]

The oral history genre remains varied in terms of ways of publishing the material. The practice of reproducing respondent's stories at length and with little additional interpretive material, as in Blythe's *Akenfield*, or Mary Chamberlain's *Fenwomen*, has been continued in works such as John Bodnar's *Workers' World*, a study of a Pennsylvania industrial community, or Eric Marcus' *Making History*, a collection of oral narratives from the American gay and lesbian community. An alternative approach is to focus on the life of one individual as James does in *Doña María's Story* and likewise Sally Cole, a historical anthropologist, whose *Women of the Praia*, a study of the lives of Portuguese women in the past and the present is foregrounded by the oral testimony of one woman, Alvina. Her story, that of a Portuguese fisherwoman in the first six decades of the twentieth century, is presented by Cole as a monologue, uninterrupted by the questions and interventions of the interviewer and unadulterated by the slips, verbal tics and speech imperfections one would normally hear (or see) in such a testimony. This short extract from Alvina's testimony demonstrates Cole's approach:

> I always wanted to work on the sea, and when I was fourteen and old enough I persuaded my father to take me into Vilo do Conde to the Capitania for my license (*cédula*). For the test I had to swim across the Rio Ave, but I didn't know how to swim, so my father gave the man from the Capitania a coin and I got my license. After that I fished with my father and my brother, and when the weather was too bad for fishing I worked with my mother and sisters for the lavradores in the fields (*no campo*). And that was my life day in and day out until my marriage.[37]

Cole writes that life stories are 'pieced together' from several interviews conducted over time and in the course of writing the stories she repeatedly checked with her respondents that she had conveyed their narratives accurately. Nonetheless, the author's intention was to 'provide women the opportunity to present themselves and their lives as they would want them presented'.[38]

Taking things a step further, anthropologists Julie Cruikshank and Nancy Wachowich have engaged in collaborative work with their narrators, acknowledging the fact that life stories, once told, are not the possession of the researcher.[39] Finally, Luisa Passerini creates an altogether new genre in her *Autobiography of a Generation*, interweaving oral history, interpretation, autobiography and psychoanalysis in her study of the generation of 1968 in Italy.[40] Few authors, however (and Passerini is an exception), are happy with placing themselves as interviewers in the published text. Interview questions are rarely reproduced, the to and fro of a conversation is infrequently alluded to. We write about the interview relationship but are loath to be honest about our own role (asking leading questions, sticking to our interview agenda and so on).

Oral history practice has begun to break down some of the genre boundaries surrounding scholarly writing, encouraging historians to engage more with a wider readership and to push at the envelope of traditional academic outputs by foregrounding the voices of those who inform the research. And oral history has tested the limits of conventional historical writing by privileging personal experience, allowing for subjectivity, celebrating memory's inconsistencies and forcing the historian to be reflexive about research practice.

Conclusions

After more than fifty years of methodological and interpretive experimentation, oral history has begun to assume the character of a discipline, in part because of its commitment to sound interview practice and also because it has developed some distinctive practices and conventions in the realm of interpretation. But it is a discipline with undisciplined tendencies, continually drawing upon other disciplinary approaches, and in flux as it defines acceptable practices and modes of theorising. It is at the same time profoundly interdisciplinary, a promiscuous practice that, jackdaw-like, picks up the shiny, attractive theories which have originated elsewhere and applies them to its own field of study. Oral history is a peculiar practice in many ways: in terms of its distinctiveness as a methodology, its marrying of practice in the field with interpretive analysis, and in terms of the ways in which it is used and presented to the wider public.

3 Self

Introduction

The oral historian knows that when a respondent tells a story about an event or an experience he or she is directly or indirectly telling us something about him or herself. In an interview that tackles the whole life course or life history of the individual, the respondent is given the opportunity to tell a story that reveals their present sense of self. This is a view of their self as the culmination of a life. The life-story interview invites the narrator to dig deep, to reflect on the inner self, to reconcile any conflicts and then to reconstruct the self as a coherent whole in the form of a single narrative. In an interaction with the interviewer, the interview becomes a process in which the respondent actively fashions an identity. And even in an interview where the declared aim is merely to gather information it is rare for the respondent not to reveal something of themselves.

The revelation of the self, understood as the autonomous and self-contained individual who possesses a rich and complex inner life or consciousness, has become one of the key aims of oral historians. The use of personal or subjective documents – from autobiography and memoirs to oral history – across the social-science and humanities disciplines was traditionally a means of accessing empirical information and as a window into culture. But in the past thirty years or so the use of life narratives of all kinds in research and in popular culture has constituted a methodological and interpretive turn. This is constituted by a celebration of the subjective and an understanding that life stories are complex and revealing narrative performances which can offer an insight into both identity formation and the relationship between that and larger historical forces. Indeed, it has been said that people in the western developed world inhabit a confessional culture in which the public divulgence of aspects of the self hitherto regarded as private are normalised via public consumption of celebrity interviews, personal accounts of triumph and tragedy in the popular press and intense media focus on the personal lives of anyone in the public eye. At the popular level, the success of American President Barack Obama's two-volume autobiography is evidence of this turn to the personal in popular culture, the notion that an understanding of what made the person who he or she is can open a window onto the cultural forces that shape our lives.[1] The study of the self therefore is seen not only as a means of accessing subjectivity but as a way of studying culture and the relationship between the two.

The focus on the life story as an approach to investigating the relationship between personal experience and culture emerged from anthropology. That discipline began to challenge neutrality and objectivity within its practice and to embrace what has been called anthropological biography.[2] The eliciting of a life story in order to offer a less scientific and more literary interpretation of a culture also provided information on aspects of that culture or perspectives on it rarely encountered via traditional techniques.[3] Marjorie Shostak's biography of Nisa, a woman from the !Kung San hunters and gatherers of the African Kalahari desert, is a prime example of this biographical turn. Shostak reflects that she chose this approach as a means of getting closer to a people whose language, way of life and understanding of themselves was otherwise extremely difficult to access.[4] Within history, in contrast with some other disciplines, autobiography and other kinds of life-writing have always been accepted as legitimate sources, and the writing of historical biography has existed as a respected sub-discipline. However, the use of a life story for another purpose, to offer an alternative perspective on past events was traditionally regarded as unreliable, mainly because the account was subjective. Even the collection of American slave narratives in the 1930s did not attract serious attention from historians until almost half a century later because they were regarded as untrustworthy and unverifiable as historical sources.

In recent decades, the significance of the self has become more prominent in historical writing. Marxist historians in the 1980s saw the self as a site of resistance to structures of domination.[5] At the same time, the rise of feminist, gay and lesbian, black and subaltern histories has challenged the 'white, male and middle-class' perspective of so much historical narrative, often from a personal perspective and likewise stressing agency, the capacity to make personal choices which in turn affect events. Historians of women in particular have been to the fore in putting the personal into the historical, often taking their own personal experience as a starting point as in the case of Carolyn Steedman whose (auto)biographical study of her own engagement with the life of her mother offers a challenging perspective on our historical assumptions about maternalism, class and childhood.[6] Others focused on personal testimony and life-writing as the way to access expressions of the self on the part of historical actors.

Decades of oral history practice have taught us that interrogation of an individual's life history does much more than offer us empirical evidence about past events. The telling of a life story is a complex narrative performance which requires attention to the use of language, the deployment of narrative structure, the articulation of memory, the context within which the life is narrated; in other words, all the devices by which a person represents the self in oral fashion. Having blazed the trail for the use of life-story narratives within the historical profession, oral historians found that these sources, while certainly offering data, had to be studied as documents of interiority, as expressions of consciousness. Moreover, the life history as told in an oral history interview is not just an opportunity for the respondent to articulate a pre-existing or ready-made sense of self to which the interviewer then proceeds to gain access. Rather, the interview itself is a means by which subjectivity or the sense of self is constructed and reconstructed through the active process of telling of memory stories. These days, oral historians privilege interiority; we try to encourage our respondents to produce coherent narrative selves in interview though often we have to acknowledge they find this very difficult to do.

This chapter considers how the conduct of oral history both elicits the expression of a self and facilitates the shaping of a sense of self in the narrator via the telling of the life story. It summarises some of the theories about the self, looks at how the self is narrated via the life story and considers some of the ways in which these theoretical positions on self and self-narration may be translated into oral history practice.

Theory

Theories of the self

The notion of the individualised self, a self that is unique, distinguishable from others (though related to others) is often seen as a modern Western concept. It is important to recognise this because many would argue that the perception of the existence of the individualised self is a necessary precondition for producing a life narrative. According to the feminist philosopher Jane Flax: 'Essential to all Enlightenment beliefs is the existence of something called the "self"; a stable, reliable, integrative entity that has access to our inner states and outer reality.'[7] Furthermore, the life narrative that contains this expression of self is also a relatively modern, Western form, namely a linear, coherent story that positions the solitary hero at the centre of the account. But the concept of the self as it is theorised in Western thought has not necessarily been universal across time and across cultures. The individualism and autonomy we associate with the modern self has been seen as a product of European Enlightenment thought with its emphasis on rationality as the basis of the self-determining individual.[8] Indeed, anthropologists have long alerted us to the fact that the so-called 'invention of the self' is a construct of Western modernity and thus unfamiliar in other cultures. For instance, the anthropologist Clifford Geertz writes:

> the western conception of the person as a bounded, unique, more or less integrated motivational and cognitive universe, a dynamic centre of awareness, emotion, judgement and action, organised into a distinctive

whole and set contrastively against other such wholes and against a social
and natural background is ... a rather peculiar idea within the context of
the world's cultures.[9]

As it evolved in the eighteenth, nineteenth and early twentieth centuries in
Europe, there was a view that the self was an innate entity which the individual inherited by dint of their gender, race and religious heritage. This was the
theory of essentialism, the notion that the self is determined by enduring and
innate qualities – for example, the assumptions that all women are naturally
maternal, that Christianity is superior to other religions, or that all white
people are superior to those of other races. Essentialism is now widely disregarded and considered unacceptable; it fosters sexism, racism and bigotry.
None of us have an essence – an unchanging, pure and stable sense of self.
Instead of being born with an essence that determines our identity, it is now
widely viewed that we construct our identity, our sense of self, of who we are,
within and in relation to our social and cultural environment. The self is
mediated through a series of discourses; for instance, women may regard
themselves as possessing maternal qualities because they have absorbed
dominant messages that ascribe universal maternal feelings to women. This
involves an interaction between the individual's bodily and material experiences on the one hand and the individual's experience of culture and the discourses which we negotiate everyday. In the context of this book we are
primarily interested in how the self is a cultural construction, leading to the
linguistic expression of the self that is the product of narration – the stories
we tell about ourselves. Telling stories about the self is part of the process of
self-formation.

Telling stories has given rise to the notion of the confessional self.
For centuries in European culture, confession was once something associated
with private revelations by the sinning Christian to an absolving Roman
Catholic priest; it was a private act. With the Reformation, repentance
became for some Christians more of a public act. But in more recent secular
culture, confessionalism has become a way by which the individual partici-
pates in a public culture of self-divulgence. This is very familiar within Western societies, expressed via the broadcast and print media and within the
pages of autobiographies, backed up by the widespread use of counselling,
therapists and self-revelation. Celebrities write autobiographies before
they have reached the age of thirty; the celebrity interview is a media staple;
and television is dominated by 'reality shows' in which participants confess
to each other, or to 'Big Brother' in a confessional booth. This practice
has spilled over into our relationship with others on internet networking sites
where the level of divulging private details has risen enormously since 2000.
The consequence is that there is declining inhibition about life history today.
It has been argued that one of the features of modernity is 'self-narration'
whereby one's identity is expressed in the telling of a story about the self.
It might also be said that popular history, as presented in the broadcast and

print media, is now commonly mediated through the personal life story; genealogy television shows, historical depictions of wars and other events, and even television news coverage of recent events, give privilege to a few handpicked personal accounts that 'personalise' the big event, reducing it to a human scale, but crucially based on the personal observation of the ordinary person rather than the chief or the expert. The implication is that our understanding of history is increasingly an understanding of our selves.[10]

It was not always so. Before the nineteenth century in Europe, as in other parts of the world, self-narration has been more likely to elicit stories where people positioned themselves within a group or a community rather than as autonomous individuals, that is, the stories they told about themselves did not place themselves as the subject or hero at the centre of the story. This observation also applies to cultures where, in the words of anthropologist Gusdorf, the individual 'does not feel himself to exist outside of others, and still less against others, but very much *with* others in an interdependent existence'.[11] Gusdorf further notes, 'autobiography is not possible in a cultural landscape where consciousness of the self does not, properly speaking, exist'.[12] So, for example, the anthropological linguist Renato Rosaldo found when conducting research amongst the Ilongot people in the Philippines that narratives about the self – that is, private, interior and intimate stories – were not part of this people's narrative repertoire; instead accounts were focused upon public actions. He writes of his narrative subject, Tukbaw:

> I do not believe that members of his culture were accustomed to telling their life stories in any form, and certainly not in a way intimate, revealing and confessional. Narratives, of course, were familiar; Tukbaw often told the tale of a hunt, of a raid, of a fishing trip. What was not familiar was that he himself should be the subject of a narrative.[13]

Likewise, Hertha Dawn Wong's research on Native American autobiography suggests that in this culture the self is envisaged as part of rather than apart from the community, what she calls a 'communal I'.[14] Recent scholarship argues that we should re-evaluate the autobiographical texts – including oral and written life-story narratives – of non-Western traditions as well as challenging some of the assumptions implicit in the notion of a European autobiographical tradition.[15] We must be aware that first, non-Western cultures have developed ways of speaking about the self which may differ from what have come to be regarded as the norm in the West. This recognition clearly has an impact on the ways in which researchers go about gathering life stories and analysing them in non-Western contexts. And, second, clearly not everyone, even in modern Westernised societies, is able to produce a narrative of the self that conforms to the androcentric, white, heterosexual dominant form, that is, an account that positions the subject as the author of their own destiny.

Self-narration

One of the ways we construct the sense of a self is through self-narration, telling stories about ourselves. According to the socio-linguist Charlotte Linde:

> In order to exist in the social world with a comfortable sense of being a good, socially proper, and stable person, an individual needs to have a coherent, acceptable, and constantly revised life story ... Life stories express our sense of self: who we are and how we got that way. They are also one very important means by which we communicate this sense of self and negotiate it with others.[16]

Linde goes on to identify three characteristics of the self that are maintained by language, by speaking about the self: continuity of the self through time, relation of the self to others, and reflexivity of the self.[17] All three are identifiable features of self narration in autobiography and life history although the first is the most salient to the oral historian.

Continuity of the self through time

The oral historian who conducts a life history interview certainly finds it desirable that the individual is able to construct a narrative characterised by temporal continuity, that is, establishing relationships between past and present and links between events in a coherent chronology rather than a series of snapshots bearing no relation to one another. Most interviewees are comfortable in telling chronologically organised stories that proceed from childhood to adulthood, traversing the usual milestones. If a person is unable to create a sense of historical continuity in a life story, linking events and experiences to each other and to events in the social world, this indicates an undeveloped sense of self or even the existence of a personality disorder. One expression of a failure to achieve temporal continuity is in R. D. Laing's notion of the divided self or, in other words, the self that is unable to achieve a sense of order and continuity.[18]

Relation of the self to others

This second characteristic of the self – the ability to distinguish the self from others – is important as it establishes for the narrator a unique identity. This means that the narrator talks about him or herself in relation to other people: simple comparisons, contrasts and placing of the self in relation to relatives, friends and so on. This feature of linguistic self-narration has been identified as distinctively Western and in the past tended to be more applicable to white males; other cultural traditions, women and minorities, it is argued, were more likely to identify themselves relationally *with* others as opposed to shaping a sense of self distinguishable *from* others. However, women who have lived through the era of women's emancipation are arguably just as likely as men to be able to establish for themselves a distinct or separate sense of self. Here, one of the author's respondents who was interviewed about her life in Britain in the 1950s and 1960s explicitly distinguishes herself from her mother and her mother's generation in an exchange about her tomboy appearance of which her mother disapproved. The judgement Deborah makes about her mother's standards separates her own sense of self from that of her mother and her mother's generation:

> yes, so that was a big disappointment to her, a huge disappointment to her. But I mean er, as I grew up and she saw that you know I could actually groom myself like she, because she was always well groomed. My mother was a person who, before my father came home in the evening, she would go upstairs and change and put make-up on for the dinner, for the evening's dinner, you know. And she would wear make-up during the day and she couldn't understand why some other women in the village didn't. Extraordinary standards.[19]

Reflexivity of the self

The third element also has much relevance in the oral history context. This is the act of the individual being aware of talking about their self and reflecting on themselves. Linde writes 'the very act of narrating creates the occasion for self regard and editing'.[20] In oral narratives we often expect our respondents not simply to tell but to reflect on what they are saying about past events and experiences in the light of their present self. Given that we recognise that all oral history is a telling of the past through multiple lenses including that of the present, in Linde's words creating a 'distinction between the narrator (the person doing the telling) and the protagonist (the person at the centre of the story) of the narrative', reflexivity, or reflection on the self that is being actively created in the interview, is to be expected.[21] In this extract, Deborah reflects on her attitude towards religion and her expected confirmation in the Church of England in her teenage years. The key sections which indicate the active self-reflection in the course of the narrative are highlighted.

> I was probably about 14, but there was no question em you know, I said I absolutely said I had no belief and I felt it was wrong for me to be confirmed but **again it was part of the, part of the village thing wasn't it**, you know … my parents had standing, it was an expectation, **well I mean I had started rebelling by then** so em. I absolutely loathed going for the mothering Sunday service because you – **I was quite a shy little girl I think at the time** – you had to sort of get up and put your hand up and promise to do things … [22]

In other words, reflexivity in telling the life story means that I (the storyteller or narrator) tells stories about the Me (the character in the story).[23]

The life story

The linguistic form which most markedly contains the features of self-narration outlined above is the life story. Oral historians often use the terms 'life history' and 'life story' interchangeably, but the theoretical literature is careful to distinguish between the life story and the life history. A life *history* is a chronologically told narrative of an individual's past. The life history will typically contain recognisable life stages and events such as childhood, education, marriage and so on. Although it is more than a static recounting of facts, there is often an assumption in life-history research that any individual will have a notion of their fixed life history, at least in terms of the facts deemed worthy of inclusion. Chanfrault-Duchet explains how:

> Facts and events selected as relevant are organised within a path, marked out by rites of passage: birth, school, first communion, first love, examinations, first job, marriage, birth of children and so on. The construction of the life course scheme refers, in the interaction with the audience, to a shared knowledge: the models of life experience taken for granted in a socio-historical context.[24]

Thus we construct our life histories in ways in which we think others will understand and recognise. This model has been used since the end of the eighteenth century – it supposes a social and political context that 'allows individual social promotion and personal development'.[25] When I ask my students in a class exercise to write a short life history, the majority invariably produce an account organised in chronological fashion, each beginning with 'I was born on such a date' and including notable turning points, transition stages and educational achievements. This is how we believe our society wants to judge us; we are trained to think this way about our self. And hence it is often assumed that the telling of a life history is a kind of truth-telling; that fabrication and imagination has little place in the life history.

A life *story,* on the other hand, may be described as a narrative device used by an individual to make sense of a life or experiences in the past. According to Bruner, 'a life is not "how it was" but how it is interpreted and reinterpreted, told and retold'.[26] For Portelli, there is a further distinction, between the *life* story (a chronological and largely descriptive account of a life containing events that happened) and the life *story* (a creative narrative which is based upon the narrator's experience).[27] Life-story research is interested in the ways people achieve coherence – both in the sense of telling a coherent story, one that hangs together, from an array of unrelated and often contradictory experiences, and in the sense of telling a story that conforms to a shape that meets the listener's expectations. It is assumed that all individuals possess a life story in the sense of 'the things you need to know about me to know me', but this is an interpretive, creative and changing entity rather than a fixed description of a life based on the facts. It is how we choose to represent events and experiences from our life in order to communicate our sense of self, who we are, to others. Charlotte Linde is the most influential theorist of the life story, thus it makes sense to cite here her definition:

> A life story consists of all the stories and associated discourse units, such as explanations and chronicles, and the connections between them, told by an individual during the course of his/her lifetime that satisfy the following two criteria: 1. The stories and associated discourse units contained in the life story have as their primary evaluation a point about the speaker, not a general point about the way the world is. 2. The stories and associated discourse units have extended reportability; that is, they are tellable and are told and retold over the course of a long period of time.[28]

A life story, then, is a creative and fluid thing which may contain the facts of a life history but which has another purpose. Its meaning is to say something about the narrator. It tells the listener what kind of a person the narrator wants to be seen as, and this is done through the telling of the story (the way it is constructed) rather than via the events or facts included. The life story is at once something bigger and something more interior than the life history, related to consciousness, self and the way that self is told or presented. It is also rarely static or unchanging. A life story is something we continually revise. For instance, a person who experienced a particularly bruising divorce might include it in his or her life story not merely because it was a landmark life *event* but because the *experience* was salient in that person's own understanding and interpretation of his or her life, it affected the person's sense of who she or he was, and had an impact on they way life was lived subsequently. According to Linde, this event's place in the life story is there not only because it makes a moral point about the speaker (for example, a person may include their divorce in their life story because they think it portrays them in a positive light) but also because it can be repeatedly told within a much larger repertoire of stories to create a coherent whole (the divorce also enables that person to talk about their relationship with their children, a subsequent change of career path and so on). The life event – in this case a divorce – therefore has evaluative and reportable characteristics. The life story, again citing Linde:

> is not simply a collection of stories, explanations and so on; instead it involves all the relations among them. Thus, when any new story is added to the repertoire of the life story, it must be related in some way to the themes of the other stories included in the life story ... This means ... that the stories included in the life story constantly undergo revision, to express our current understanding of what our lives mean.[29]

For Linde then, the constant revisioning and retelling of a life story is a means by which we achieve a sense of a stable and composed self; it is the way in which we align our interior self with the exterior world. Oral historians will immediately recognise this formulation as a version of the theory of composure; the way in which the individual creates a comfortable sense of self by aligning the life story with publicly available discourses. (This will be discussed in more detail in Chapter 4.)

The concept of coherence proposed by Linde relates particularly to the property of the text, the life-story narrative. By this she means that first each part of the text or the story must relate to each other and to the story/text as a whole (that is, it cannot exist as a series of unconnected anecdotes); and second that the story must conform to a recognisable text of its type (though this might vary according to cultural context). The life-story narrative, just like the fairy tale or tragedy, must have a recognisable structure. We know what it should look like not only because of its internal components (in the case of the fairy tale this might include the phrase 'Once upon a time', the good-versus-evil dichotomy, the moral message and so on) but also because it looks like other texts of the same genre ('Little Red Riding Hood' or 'Hansel and Gretel', for instance).

In the case of the life story, coherence is generally achieved by the adherence to principles of causality and continuity – that is it has a chronological template and one event or experience links with others.[30] But such an account also achieves coherence if it includes what Linde terms 'coherence systems' and some might term 'discourses'.[31] These are systems of thinking – she names Freudian psychology, astrology and feminism amongst the coherence systems used by her own interviewees – which may be used to give an account coherence or made understandable to an audience. People will make use of different coherence systems in different contexts. Thus, in a study of religious discourse and representations of the self, Ronald Walker, interviewed in the 1970s, told a life story which was given coherence by frequent, explicit and implicit references to the belief (or coherence) system of early twentieth-century evangelicalism. Two extracts from his life story illustrate this point:

> Did your parents bring you up to consider certain things important in life?
>
> Yes, in the narrow non-conformist tradition. Lying was the unforgivable sin, so I'm afraid I've been unforgiven a few times. Turning the other cheek was regarded as a good thing. They would have been pleased if I'd shown any interest in the Methodist ministry which, of course, I didn't.
>
> I was taken by the scruff of my neck very early in life and told to 'sign here', where I pledged total abstinence [from alcohol] for the rest of my life, and I satisfied my conscience when I grew up that that was got under duress and I'm afraid I'm not a teetotaller and I'm not ashamed of the

fact that I was made to sign something that I did not quite understand at the time.[32]

The attraction of Linde's work is her tendency to illustrate sometimes rather abstract or complex ideas about narration and language with very common-place examples with which we can all identify. The data upon which she draws comes from a series of oral interviews with white, middle-class Americans about their choice of profession, a topic chosen as appropriate for demonstrating the processes of life-story-telling because, as Linde states, choice of profession 'is a necessary part of self-presentation'.[33] 'And what do you do?' is a very common communication strategy amongst the middle classes in the industrialised West, a means of opening up a conversation and assumed to reveal all sorts of markers of status and identity. In replying, the respondent is required to say something about him or herself, and the listener will begin to make assumptions based on the answer. To illustrate this point, my own answer to the question 'what do you do?' may vary from 'university pro-fessor', to 'historian' or 'I teach history' depending upon who is asking and the context in which it is asked. All of these answers may throw up sets of different assumptions on the part of the questioner. The reply 'university professor' may prompt the listener to assume a university education (correct), a middle-class upbringing (incorrect) and certain lifestyle or cultural preferences (for example a preference for classical over rock music – incorrect again). But my choice of the label 'university professor' for the job that I do indicates that I might be content for the listener to make those assumptions about me.

Alternative accounts of the self

The problem with typologies such as those presented above is that they may not have universal application. We have already encountered the criticism that the kind of self narration that is dependant on the notion of the individu-alised and autonomous self may be less pertinent to some groups or cultures. In respect of the first generation of Afro-American slave narratives produced in the nineteenth century, William L. Andrews notes how such autobio-graphical accounts had to demonstrate two things in order to solicit the empathy and to counter the scepticism of the white reader: first, that the slave was 'a man and a brother' to the readers of the narratives, and second, that he was a reliable narrator.[34] Yet ex-slave narrators experienced difficulty in conforming to some of the most basic conventions of the autobiography, such as a statement at the beginning of the autobiography stating date and place of birth, family lineage and so on, and hence their reliability could easily be doubted. Take the case of Andy J. Anderson from Texas, interviewed as part of a project by the Works Progress Administration in 1937:

> My name am Andy J. Anderson an' I's bo'n on Marster Jack Haley's plantation in Williamson County, Texas. Marster Haley owned my folks

an' 'bout 12 udder fam'lies ob cullud folks. How come I's took de name ob Anderson, 'stead ob Haley? It am dis away, my pappy was owned by Marster Anderson who sold him to Marster Haley, so he goes by de name ob Anderson. Dey use to call me Haley but aftah Surrendah, I'se change de name to Anderson to have it de same as my pappy's.[35]

Anderson (and his interviewer) were aware of the autobiographical convention of providing personal landmarks, but the early mention of his master rather than his parents and the explanation for his name separates the way in which he was able to tell his life story from the conventional autobiographical form.

Women, it has been argued, are less likely to be able to produce self-narrations that privilege the independent self because a woman is always aware that she belongs to a group that has been defined by the dominant male – or patriarchal – culture. A woman cannot forget her sex and think of herself solely as an individual as a man is able to do. According to Susan Friedman: 'A white man has the luxury of forgetting his skin colour and sex. He can think of himself as an individual. Women and minorities, reminded at every turn in the great cultural hall of mirrors of their sex or colour, have no such luxury.'[36] Moreover, it is argued that the dominant or more acceptable ways of talking about the self are much more appropriate to men than women. Women are less able to talk about themselves using the familiar measures of success – material or work-related – rather, women's sense of self is more likely established in relation to other people. Mary Gergen analysed a series of autobiographies written by well-known men and women in the public eye, from tennis star Martina Navratilova to the American businessman Lee Iacocca. She concluded that the 'manstories' adopt linear, progressive narratives leading to goal achievement, they are individualist and, in Gergens's words, 'seem to celebrate the song of the self'.[37] By contrast, even amongst her sample of self-motivated and very successful women she found their 'womanstories' deviated from the unilinear narrative. Often in order to focus on aspects of personal life, they stressed their emotional interdependency and indeed crafted more complex and fuller stories than their male counterparts.

Feminist theorising has provided alternative ways of uncovering the authentic female self.[38] The socialist feminist historian Sheila Rowbotham argues that women can overcome their silencing by the dominant male individualist narrative mode and come to express their sense of self by recognising that women *as a group* have a common historical experience. On this foundation, women as a group and as individuals can develop alternative ways of seeing themselves. In *Woman's Consciousness, Man's World* she writes that in order for an oppressed group 'to discover its own identity as distinct from that of the oppressor, it has to become visible to itself'.[39] The result, argues Rowbotham, is a shared *and* unique identity.

One can easily imagine how this might apply in the practice of oral history. Summerfield's analysis of women's narratives of their lives in Britain during the Second World War shows how some women's sense of belonging to a group of women workers and servicewomen who had made a positive and significant contribution to the war effort was a liberating experience in terms of how they narrated their stories. The servicewomen in particular were able to draw on publicly available discourses of heroism and self-development to narrate life stories characterised by self-confidence.[40] This, then, was a group of women which was 'visible to itself', in part aided by the public discourse on the heroic service to the war effort by women in the services, and thus these individuals were able to construct coherent selves in the interviews whilst remaining conscious of their shared identity as wartime servicewomen. In a very different context, Blanca Vasquez Erazo interviewed Puerto Rican women who migrated to the USA after the Second World War. She demonstrated how the stories these women tell of themselves as resourceful, ingenious and determined to survive in spite of discrimination and hardship are part of a shared story of Puerto Rican success, challenging traditional views of women from this community as passive and downtrodden. In telling their individual life stories these women created a collective history that provides a positive framework for the self-image of the women of this community.[41]

Sociologist Liz Stanley's approach is to argue that the act of writing a self, literally writing a diary or an autobiography (but also presumably narrating an oral history), is a means by which women 'gain possession of a sense of self' which had been absent or silenced. For Stanley it is the reading, writing and speaking practices that provide women with the tools to resist silencing; identity thus can be constituted through the text. However, the ways in which women produce these accounts are shaped by 'shared ideas, conventions about a cultural form'; hence they are 'not descriptions of actual lives but interpretations within the convention'.[42] In other words, the individual can only produce a version of the self in a form that will be recognised by others. This does not mean that women cannot produce narratives of the self, but it does imply that these narratives are shaped by the dominant understandings of what these narratives should look like. So it is in oral history as well. The respondent talks in formats that he or she finds in culture and uses them in the interview because he or she feels the interviewer will understand those formats. This is reflected sometimes by the respondent saying, 'is this the kind of thing you want?'

The self, as we have already seen, is something produced in a creative and dialogic fashion. If we do away with the idea that we all possess an essential self we accept that our sense of self is produced via a series of relations with other people and ideas and through activities such as speaking and writing. This intersubjective self will be looked at closely in Chapter 4. The self is also storied, that is, we can only produce a version of our self in narrative forms, be these written or verbal, one of which might be the oral history narrative. And finally we have the concept of the 'remembered self'; that is, the self is at least partially constructed by the act of remembering.[43] In Jerome Bruner's words: 'Self is a perpetually rewritten story. What we remember from the past is what is necessary to keep that story satisfactorily well formed.'[44] All of these aspects of self-narration will be amplified in later chapters of this book.

Application

How has this theoretical thinking on self and the life story been applied in oral history? Our first reaction might be to doubt that oral history can ever be trusted or at least relied upon to provide unambiguous answers. We have established that the self is always and continually socially constructed in a series of relationships – with the interviewer, with the social world and with other versions of the self. We have also established that the life-story narrative is a linguistic creation that serves to bring about coherence and composure to make sense of a life. It is hard, then, not to disagree with Philippe Lejeune who remarked that: 'Telling the truth about the self, constituting the self as a complete subject – it is a fantasy.'[45]

Women's historian Denise Riley certainly became disillusioned with the ability of oral history to access the self. In her research on motherhood during and after the Second World War she abandoned her quest to discover women's experience via oral history because, as she put it: 'The trouble with the attempt to lay bare the red heart of truth beneath the discolourations and encrustations of thirty-odd years on, is that it assumes a clear space out of which voices can speak.'[46] For Riley it was impossible to really reveal women's authentic desires or selves via the oral history interview conducted years later because their responses were confused by a miasma of discourses and experiences of the intervening period. Riley felt her research was compromised because the self her interviewees presented was fluid, constantly changing by time period, overlain with altered discourses and reflections. Nothing stayed the same in a person's view of her or himself.

Three issues arise from Riley's observation: the question of historical authenticity or truth, the question of experience and the question of individual agency. All are pertinent to the oral historian's practice.

Historical authenticity

We have established that the life story is distinguishable from the life history. As a vehicle for transmitting a narrative of the self, the life story is a creative endeavour which, although not fictional, may possess an arm's-length relationship with historical truth. Frank's formulation to demarcate the life story from the life history is helpful here: life-story research 'emphasises the truth of the telling versus the telling of the truth'.[47] Oral historians have long accepted and embraced this understanding but at the same time we hope that our respondents adhere to what is called 'the referential pact'. This means that the respondent will at least commit to telling the truth *as they see it*. According to Daniel James, 'the referential pact associated with the oral history text is likely to be, as with autobiography, premised on notions of fidelity to meaning rather than to criteria of strict accuracy associated with information.'[48] What this means in practice is beautifully articulated by ethnologist Henry Glassie with reference to the narrative practices of Northern Irish historians in Ballymenone:

> When they string facts into narratives, they will create something other than the factual past, if only by dint of omission, and the dynamics of presentation, but they do not do so to fool people but to help them by driving at a truth larger than that trapped in the factual scraps ... their joy is finding, holding, manipulating truth.[49]

Surely this is precisely what many of our respondents do: in order to impart meaning they create narratives that may hinge on the 'factual scraps' but which nevertheless contain something more significant than historical information. Daniel James recounts the process by which he came to this understanding in a series of interviews with a militant Peronist in the meatpacking town of Berisso in Argentina. In a series of uncomfortable encounters James realised that his respondent was telling him a series of narratives about his political life which, although not untrue, were shaped in order to say particular things about the community and its politics in the Peronist and post-Peronist years. And this mode of telling clashed with James's agenda, which was to 'track the beast of historical objectivity' by means of skilful questioning and interview technique.[50] James eventually understood that 'what [his respondent] wanted to say certainly had to do with the larger-scale social history data I was bent on acquiring, but it was framed within a personal key and had to do with his place in that broader history, *his sense of himself, the meaning of his life* [my emphasis]'.[51]

Many of us will identify with James's dilemma. As historians, we are used to anchoring our interpretation in historical facts or context such as dates of events, names of participants, chronology of incidents and so on. Even those of us with the most postmodernist tendencies still hanker after something concrete and almost expect our narrators to key their memories into a recognisable historical context, simply because we tend to work within rather traditional historical periodisations. But this expectation may clash with the ability of the narrator to construct a self through a life story with which he or she is comfortable; the narrator may wish to anchor their life in family or community rather than national histories.

Moreover, an account may contain silences, absences or even factual inaccuracies. Silences and omissions were evident in Luisa Passerini's interviews with Italian workers in respect of the years encompassing the Fascist government. The silences were of two kinds: life stories told with no references to Fascism and those told which feature a gap between the Fascist victory and the outbreak of the Second World War. By contrast, life-story narratives had much to say about the period of the resistance, the war and the liberation.[52] One can conclude that the interviewees could only construct a coherent sense of self in which memories of the Fascist era were suppressed and thus their spontaneous life stories are silent on this period because a life story has as its purpose a making sense of a life, shaping a coherence from contradictory and often uncomfortable experiences. Stories of conformity or even passive acquiescence to Fascism, for instance, may not fit comfortably with workers' present sense of self which drew on their identity as workers and as members of the labour movement.

Experience and agency

In theories of the self, there is a tension between two approaches: the freedom of the individual in action and words and the reliance of the individual upon culture for discourses, models and language. It is the tension between the power of culture and the power of individual agency. Is the self free or enslaved? This is a tension felt by the oral historian; how far is the respondent in his or her narration to be seen as the slave of discourses in culture or as a free moral agent? This is a tension that needs to be negotiated if not completely resolved in any oral history study.

Denise Riley had a worry about the inability to facilitate the authentic voice in an oral history interview. This has by and large been addressed by those practitioners who maintain a commitment to hearing voices while at the same time acknowledging that the versions of selves produced in life stories can only be expressed using recognisable forms and drawing upon relevant discourses. Summerfield, for instance, suggests that we as oral historians inhabit a space where we study 'the relationship between cultural constructions and consciousness'.[53] And there is a relationship. We must assume that respondents are able to actively engage with discourses, rejecting some, accepting others. For instance, some of the British men who recalled their experiences in the British home defence force, the Home Guard, during the Second World War, demonstrated how their sense of self at the time was influenced by dominant constructions of military manhood and how membership of the Home Guard gave them access to that identity via comradeship, male bonding and the wearing of uniform. However, at the same time, some respondents expressed their scepticism of the 'all in it together' unity, rejecting the notion that class differences were no longer important. These divergent discourses were not necessarily mutually exclusive.[54]

This approach accepts that narratives of the self can say something personal and meaningful about identity but at the same time draw on public discourses. There is another approach, though, which questions the inevitability of not being able to separate the self from discursive constructions. Michael Roper suggests that all the emphasis on the power of public narratives in shaping how people talk about the self risks ignoring the importance of the unconscious in the articulation of experience. We should not downplay the psychological motivations for individuals telling a story or telling it in a particular way. In the case of war memories, Roper argues that concepts from psychoanalysis can help a person deal with the emotional consequences of a particular experience.[55] For Roper, memory is structured psychically as well as socially. He regrets the fact that 'subjective experience is placed at the edge of historical analysis. The intense emotions that might be aroused by experiences such as war get treated as a matter of linguistic codes'.[56] This approach might help oral historians who want to acknowledge the very real human relationships and physical and psychological experiences that influence the ways in which people talk about themselves. Sometimes the cultural approach just is not enough.

In practice, the oral historian can often hear how a respondent manages to create 'narrative coherence' between discrepant versions of his or her life story not just with reference to previous versions of the life story but also in relation to cultural assumptions about self. This is where theories of the self and theories of the life story coincide as it is precisely by means of telling and retelling the life story that, according to Linde, we (that is those of us conforming to the Western tradition) compose our sense of self. The process is continuous and perpetually revised as we strive to achieve coherence in relation to a changing social world (represented by shifting public discourses and interpretations of the past and material changes in our lives). Ronald Walker, who we met earlier, born in 1902, brought up in a middle-class, religious household in Yorkshire and interviewed in the 1970s, demonstrated very clearly the way he reconciled what appear to be parts of his life story at variance – his life with his parents which was dominated by the tenets and practices of the Methodist religion and his sense of self at the time of the interview:

> I think my parents – thinking of my parents I think they were very sincere in their beliefs. I don't care to discuss whether their beliefs were right or wrong, but they were very sincere about it. All their lives they prayed together. Every night my father read a portion of the Bible to my mother, late at night, and on his deathbed he sent for us all – typical of the time, apart from my brother who died beforehand – he knew he was dying and most embarrassingly he confessed himself a great sinner before he died. He had a feeling this was the sort of thing to get off his chest. His children, my generation, I'm afraid we were falling away from this sort of thing. We went to chapel because we had to. I remember we didn't HAVE to, we went there to please our parents, but I don't think any of my sisters or myself had, at that time, any – we were losing our childish convictions and hadn't got any others, at that time. Hadn't replaced them with anything else.[57]

Ronald Walker moves effortlessly to and fro, from the Edwardian middle-class world in which he grew up and which was personified by his father, to the late-twentieth-century world in which he was constructing his life story. His sense of self has been revised over his lifetime, and the self he presents in this interview is one which makes sense in the secularised world of the 1970s yet which is also able to make sense of the incongruity of his parents' world.[58]

What Ronald Walker was doing is what all of our interviewees do when telling their life story: they select particular memories, arrange them in a particular way and decide how much and what meaning or significance to give to particular episodes.

Practice

Not all interview formats facilitate the telling of a life story, and not all respondents fulfil our expectations to present a coherent self. Just as a vague request to a respondent to 'tell me your life story' is unlikely to achieve a reflective, coherent narration of the self, neither is a rigid question-and-answer model. Unlike the production of an autobiography which is generally self-motivated and designed to tell a particular version of a life with which the author is comfortable (emphasising achievement, for example, or a struggle to overcome the odds) and is the result of many hours of thought, research and self-reflection, the life story, as we have seen, is a form of self-revelation that is constantly being revised. In Portelli's words, 'the oral discourse "runs through our fingers" so to speak, and must be "solidified", "frozen" if we are to hold it'.[59] It follows that a single interview may not be sufficient; repeated interviews may offer the interviewee more space to craft a life story from fragments of memory and experience and will at the same time allow the researcher to facilitate a deeper and more reflective narrative. But however many encounters we have, we must remember that a respondent will rarely present to us a unitary, composed self. The story told to the researcher is just one of many possible versions, shaped by the relationships engendered by the personal encounter with the interviewer and with discourses present in the social world that inform a person's evaluation of what is important and what to conceal.

Not all interviewees are able or willing to narrate an autobiographical self in the interview context. There are a number of reasons for this. Some simply do not conceive of the interview situation as an appropriate forum for self-revelation. They may regard the telling of life stories to be a mostly private practice to be carried out within close kin and friendship groups. Such interviewees may respond in a contained way to interview questions, focusing upon facts rather than feelings and rarely offering more obviously revealing or open narrative answers. Given the advanced age of some of our respondents this is not surprising. Individuals of the older generation may be less influenced by modern Western 'confessional culture' and may have more respect for dominant historical narratives. It is not uncommon for people to struggle to recall major political or foreign-policy events and dates and to attempt to describe notable public occasions, especially if they are being interviewed for a history research project. The context of an oral history interview may predispose a respondent to feel that he or she has to provide factual information to inform the historical agenda. One of my interviewees who responded to my appeal for British women whose formative years traversed the period between the morally conservative 1950s and the onset of 'women's liberation' in the 1970s provided me with much factual information about her nursing career which included lengthy periods spent overseas, but she was reticent on providing much insight into her subjective experience.[60] Such responses may disappoint the researcher who, having read all the theory, is expecting a self-reflective life-story narrative. But we can still gain insights from seemingly unpromising material into that person's sense of self and the way they position themselves within the broader narrative.

Other respondents may more consciously formulate a sense of self in the oral history interview itself. In 1997 I interviewed Frances about her childhood in foster care a short time after she had made some personal discoveries about her birth family.[61] Frances had been placed in care at the age of four months with a couple in a small village in the north of Scotland who already had three children of their own. She was treated the same as her sisters: 'I was just like any other child.' Until the age of seven Frances had no idea she was a fostered child but the taunts of schoolfriends after a falling out prompted her to look for her birth certificate in a box under her parents' bed. All was revealed or, as Frances described it: 'I found out that I didn't belong.' The news perhaps confirmed a niggling suspicion since Frances had always used two surnames: the name on her birth certificate and the name of her foster family which 'was always in brackets after on everything official'. For Frances, notwithstanding her secure and happy childhood, identity was something to be negotiated ever since the day she discovered her true status. The discovery that she was a foster child was a real and a symbolic turning point in her life story and in the negotiation of her identity.

When Frances had children of her own she admitted to some curiosity about her birth family, commenting, 'I'd think, I wonder where that one takes, my family ... the looks ... to hold your baby and say "Oh that's uncle's this and that"', but it was not until she suffered an illness and was asked questions about her past history that Frances decided to discover her roots. It was then she discovered that the family story she had always been told was untrue. 'My foster mother told me, this is what she was told and I know they were told nothing else because that story was told over and over again, "she was only 16 and her mother wouldn't have her".' Frances discovered much more than just her mother's identity. In fact, Frances found out that her mother was a single Jewish woman from the working-class Gorbals area of Glasgow and her father was an unemployed Protestant. Frances was taken into care just ten days after the birth. Her mother had been disowned by her family, and some years later, having not been well for some time, she was admitted to a psychiatric institution. Frances's mother died in 1976 before she could meet her.

The consequences of Frances's discovery of her Jewish identity were profound, and she was still digesting these when I interviewed her. Raised by a strict Presbyterian family, Frances had no inkling of her 'real' cultural and religious origins. Although Frances acknowledged that she had benefited from being placed in foster care, nevertheless she reflected:

> I tried to understand as much as I could, I also read lots and lots of books on Judaism so I think I'm more understanding about it now ... when I found out I was Jewish I thought now I should've had a chance to follow my culture, that's maybe my only regret after ... being amongst Jewish people and thinking, you should know this, because reading up, you'll never be a Jew.

Frances was initially elated at discovering her roots, finding physical resemblances between herself and a photograph of her mother, and at meeting some distant relatives. However, at the time of our interview she was in a state of limbo, unable to become part of her birth family, partly on account of her relatives' apparent embarrassment at her existence, and partly because she was unable to discover any more about her mother or her father. At the same time, Frances expressed ambivalence about the system that placed her in care. While acknowledging that she gained in many ways, she was left with the feeling that 'maybe baby Jews didn't mean much to [the authorities]'.

For Frances, the sense of a coherent self had been destroyed three times in her life: first, when she discovered she was not her parents' biological child; again, when she found out about her birth parents and particularly her mother's religious identity; and third, when she realised that her attempts to get closer to her birth family and her religious inheritance could not be achieved. The sense of closure that many people in similar circumstances believe they will achieve once they have discovered their birth family often results instead in a sense of personal crisis or discomposure as the person they thought they were is dismantled. It can be a difficult process to rebuild the self following such revelations.[62]

Some people then have difficulty in narrating a coherent sense of self. Reminiscence work with older people, particularly those who are socially isolated or in care homes, has been employed to help individuals regain a sense of self which may have been damaged by social dislocation, isolation from family and friends and loss of independence. Joanna Bornat, in a survey of the early days of reminiscence therapy describes how one of the objectives was to 'restore a sense of personal value' in older people. It has also been discovered that the eliciting of life histories can encourage people to articulate their individual needs for the future, thereby helping to inform care plans and the delivery of services.[63] The implication here is that knowing who we are, possessing a sense of self-worth and being able to express that publicly is an essential element in our social well-being.

Conclusions

Theories of the self and understandings of how individuals construct a sense of self by means of the life story have been liberating for oral historians as they open up an analytical terrain that permits the integration of biography with history, the individual story with the general interpretation. We now know that when a respondent tells a story about an event or an experience they are likely telling us something about themselves and about how they position themselves in the social world. It is for us to work out how that story fits into a larger schema for, as Portelli reminds us, 'history has no content without their stories'.[64] The life story is the best way we have of accessing the self, but we must always be aware that there is no natural or unchanging life story: it is created and recreated through the telling. The researcher then has a key role in helping to create the narrative self produced in an interview. In the next chapter this relationship will be put under the spotlight.

4 Subjectivity and intersubjectivity

Introduction

The oral history interview is a conversation between a researcher and a narrator. Usually the narrator is responding to questions posed by the interviewer, and hence the story told is a product of communication between two individuals, both of whom bring something of themselves to the process. Oral history theory is now founded on this idea of there being two subjectivities at an interview, interacting to produce an effect called intersubjectivity which is apparent in the narrator's words. This chapter explores the theories surrounding this idea.

Subjectivity refers to the constituents of an individual's sense of self, his or her identity informed and shaped by experience, perception, language and culture – in other words an individual's emotional baggage (as opposed to objectivity which implies a neutral or disinterested standpoint).[1] In the oral history context we are especially interested in how the interviewee constructs an identity – or subject position – for him or herself by drawing upon available cultural constructions in public discourse. Intersubjectivity in the context of oral history refers to the relationship between the interviewee and the interviewer or, in other words, the interpersonal dynamics of the interview situation and the process by which the participants cooperate to create a shared narrative. The interviewer by word, deed and gesture in the interview solicits a narrative from the narrator; a different interviewer would solicit different words, perhaps even a very different story or version of it.

So there are two elements here which are entwined in a three-way conversation (the interviewee with him/herself, with the interviewer and with culture) consisting of, first, the process by which the subject, the interviewee, constructs a version of the self drawing upon discursive formulations or recognisable public identities available to him or her, and second the subjectivities present in the oral history interview that facilitate the construction of a memory story. In Penny Summerfield's words, 'it is thus necessary to encompass within oral history analysis and interpretation, not only the voice that speaks for itself, but also the voices that speak to it'.[2] The interviewer as well as the narrator is present in the creation of the oral history story; there can be no pretence at neutrality or objectivity.

Acceptance of this has, since the 1980s, turned oral history further away from its social-scientific roots. It runs counter to the traditional but now somewhat outmoded social-scientific approach to research which pretended that the researcher was a neutral presence at the interview. Oral history practitioners now positively recognise the value of subjectivity in the production of memory stories, acknowledging that the process of eliciting memories is a dialogic (or interactive two-way) process, the outcome of a relationship between two people, and drawing upon a wide range of discursive formulations and positions. There is no such thing as an unmediated narrative – a pure or transparent oral representation of past experience. Just as the interviewer forms an impression of the interviewee, so the interviewee may well have an idea of the audience to whom he or she is speaking which may influence what is said and how it is said, and also some sense of the conventions governing the way an oral history interview is conducted. Memory stories are manufactured in an interview environment pulsating with influences – ranging from the words and inflections, moods and the agenda of the interviewer, to the interaction between interviewer and narrator. The narrator's responses – the language used, the emotions expressed, the tone adopted – will be influenced by the immediate interview context. On top of that, there will be outside influences – including the filtering process over the intervening years between the experience and the interview, whereby layers of discourse shape the ways we recall and retell experience and the events of the hours and days prior to interview which may influence views on the resonance of the past with the present. And it is precisely this complex process that makes the analysis of memory stories so interesting for the historian.

In what follows, the theoretical concepts of subjectivity and intersubjectivity will be clarified, then we will consider some of the issues concerning the application of these concepts in oral history analysis focusing on the ideas of composure and the cultural circuit, and finally we will consider what the researcher needs to do in order to incorporate theories of intersubjectivity into his or her interpretation.

Theory

Subjectivity

The concept of subjectivity itself is not simple to grasp because of the number of competing interpretations available. Simply put, definitions of subjectivity have shifted from structuralist interpretations to those that give greater emphasis to individual agency. In essence, what we are trying to understand is the relationship between the states of mind of real people who act in the real world and the cultural formations that 'express, shape and constitute those states of mind'.[3] Structuralist understandings of subjectivity see consciousness as shaped by the social – that is, by the structures evident in society such as social class, race and gender. For philosopher Pierre Bourdieu, for instance, the individual internalises the structures of the external world (such as class or family), and these internalised structures form what he calls a habitus, a way of thinking, a disposition that conforms to the boundaries of the structure.[4] The individual person (the subject) thus has little agency as his or her actions are determined by the habitus which is in turn informed by external structures. Some theorists, such as Anthony Giddens, dislike this emphasis on the impotence of the subject and place more emphasis on individual agency, arguing that people are 'knowing subjects' and thus have the capacity to engage with the structures and to respond to them in diverse ways. In this way, there is dispute as to the freedom of the subject.[5]

More recent definitions of subjectivity have emphasised its contingency, its fluidity. For the feminist Terese de Lauretis, subjectivity is never fixed. Rather, it is 'interpreted or reconstructed by each of us within the horizon of meanings and knowledges available in the culture at given historical moments'.[6] This final definition is useful for oral historians who must be aware that their respondents draw upon a range of ideas and meanings in order to construct the subject in the particular context of the interview but that this subject is not a static entity. It may shift and alter over time, dependent upon a range of independent variables, only one of which is the interview context. This point also applies to the researcher whose subjectivity may change – for instance in interviews with different people or even in follow-up interviews with the same person.

The starting point in exploring subjectivity is awareness by the historian of his or her own subject position. To do that, the historian must observe his or her absence of neutrality. This involves being reflexive about oneself as a researcher: being actively aware of and reflecting upon one's own presence in the research process. Anthropologist Victor Turner remarked that we should 'have an objective relation to our own subjectivity'.[7] Turner was commenting on the turn to reflexivity within the disciplines of ethnology and anthropology, largely in the context of the methodology known as participant observation, and it was from here that the loudest critiques of objectivity emanated. By the 1980s reflexivity was generally accepted as necessary and beneficial to the research process in a number of disciplines, though historians were probably the most impervious to criticism of the objective approach to research. Oral historians, on the other hand, were already beginning to shift their emphasis from the collection of information to the analysis of memory narratives and thus were faced with the analytical challenges of narrative texts produced in circumstances unfamiliar to many in the historical profession. It was oral historians who grasped at the new theories and conceptual frameworks developed in other disciplinary contexts: literature, linguistics and psychoanalysis as well as anthropology. Subjectivity became, in the 1990s, a positive element of oral history research. As oral historians sought to gain insight into other people's personal experiences they encouraged self-reflection on the researcher's own identity. The recognition that subjective identities were not only present in the research setting but that they also influenced the outcomes also had a liberating effect on the ways in which historians began to interpret memory stories.

More recently though, historians' approaches to subjectivity have been informed by poststructuralist theories. They have been influenced by Roland Barthes to regard structures as everyday ideological constraints that need to be honestly exposed (in the interviewer's questions and assumptions for instance); so, social class is not an 'objective' structure but a subjective one, created by society in viewing itself and theorised by scholars. They have also been influenced by Michel Foucault to see the power that those structures have on everyday discourse about 'official' ideas of idealised behaviour. Foucault especially brought attention to discourses on 'correct' sexual behaviour, on the way that women's bodies were controlled in the nineteenth and twentieth centuries not through laws so much as by puritanical ideas on their clothing, sexual knowledge and moral behaviour, rigidly enforced both by their peers and, most importantly, by themselves. In this way, Foucault argued that the historian must recognise the internalisation of discourse: we should detect the structures we impose on ourselves. Historians have also been influenced by Jacques Derrida to regard the act of interpreting speech and everyday life, in the past as in the present, as an act of reading texts (just as a literature student does), and by Jacques Lacan to see these texts as rooted in the mind.[8] These and other ideas from modern philosophers influenced historians to conceptualise the self as decentred – as having no fixed centre or core, as having no stable or unitary identity; what the individual presents to the world, and to themselves, changes hour to hour. As a result, oral historians began to conceptualise the self as the outcome of a dialogic process as an individual's consciousness or subjectivity engages with existing discourses in society.

The self – as we saw in the previous chapter – has become increasingly regarded by more theoretically aware oral historians as having a subjectivity that is fluid. It is expressed in any form of life story, be it an oral history interview or a written autobiography, and is shaped and refracted by the constructions and language available. According to feminist sociologist Liz Stanley, the selves invoked in autobiographies 'are actually invocations of a cultural representation of what selves should be: these are shared ideas, conventions, about a cultural form: not descriptions of actual lives but interpretations within the convention'.[9] In other words, I can only imagine and express myself as a woman today within the conventions and constructions of womanhood available to me. The post-structuralist historian Joan Scott took this position to its ultimate conclusion, arguing that no one personal testimony can ever produce an objective truth independent of discourse because experience may only be recalled through the prisms of discourse. For Scott we can only narrate our 'experience' of the past by using existing discourses and linguistic formulations.[10]

For some within the historical profession, the linguistic turn, the application of post-structuralist theory, appeared to threaten their ability to say anything meaningful about lived experience or social reality because, following Scott and others, subjectivity and experience became merely a linguistic event. Others expressed concern that subjectivity had been reduced to a rather cold, disembodied state, disconnected from the emotional or the psychological. Lyndal Roper, for example, in her analysis of early modern witchcraft, reminds us that gender is not just understandable as a discursive construction but rather that sexual difference 'has its own physiological and psychological reality'.[11] And in his research into masculinity in the First World War, Michael Roper similarly urges us to put the emotion back into subjectivity rather than treating it as a 'matter of linguistic codes'.[12]

These ideas have provided the oral historian with a series of useful conceptual frameworks with which to understand the subjective construction of memory narratives. Once oral historians acknowledge that they as researchers are part of the research process (an unfamiliar feeling for historians more used to archival research with inanimate written documents), it is a simple step to thinking about the ways in which their own subjectivity impacted on the stories they were told (which we turn to next). The historian cannot play such an active and creative role in the production of a primary source and then conveniently ignore his or her own presence in the process at the analysis stage. Neutrality is not an option because we are part of the story. One of the positive outcomes of this turn to subjectivity was the ability to counter charges against oral history's unreliability. Memory stories are not repositories of an objective truth about the past; they are creative narratives shaped in part by the personal relationship that facilitates the telling.

Intersubjectivity

We have established that the interview is a process that involves the dynamic interaction of subjectivities. We accept that both parties are playing roles by drawing upon their pasts and their own context to project particular 'selves' or identities. Intersubjectivity describes the interaction – the collision, if you will – between the two subjectivities of interviewer and interviewee. More than that, it describes the way in which the subjectivity of each is shaped by the encounter with the other. It has become understood in the oral history community that the interviewer actively constructs a subjectivity for him or herself and respondents actively devise 'appropriate performances' in response.

Symbolic interaction theory developed by anthropologists and sociologists helps to understand the process of the formation of subjectivities and their interaction in a social context. In the 1930s George Herbert Mead explored how the 'self' was created or constructed by interactions with others. 'The self ... arises in the process of social experience and activity, that is, develops in the given individual as a result of his [sic] relations to that process as a whole and to other individuals within that process.'[13] In other words, 'we only know ourselves through a series of interactive moments with others', and we may invent different selves for each moment or interaction.[14] In 1959, sociologist Erving Goffman's approach in *The Presentation of Self in Everyday Life* focused on the intricacies of everyday interpersonal interaction and argued that people act differently in different contexts and that they adopt particular roles in face-to-face interactions depending upon the specific circumstances of that context. Individuals, in Goffman's interpretation, play a part on a stage; indeed, he writes of individuals dramatising themselves. 'While in the presence of others, the individual typically infuses his activity with signs which dramatically highlight and portray confirmatory facts that might otherwise remain unapparent or obscure.'[15] Thus he or she is able to choose the props to aid the performance, to present a self in public, the purpose of which is to maintain a coherence to the performance which may be adjusted to any social setting.

Performance is an important concept with a number of applications which will be discussed more extensively in Chapter 7. In this chapter we are interested in gender theorist Judith Butler's argument that gender is a performative act. By this she means that a person has an identity as a man or a woman that is unstable and which is not drawn from a core identity dictated by the fact that they are biologically a man or a woman. There is no one 'true' form of maleness or femaleness, but great variation both within culture but more especially between different historical periods and countries: being a woman in 1900 was very different to being a woman in 2000. Instead, Butler said, men and women *perform* their gendered identity in everyday acts of dress, gesture, deportment and speech which are largely unconscious and draw upon the culture and discourses of the time.[16] Butler's theory is applicable to identity more generally. The consequence of all of these theories is that the self is unstable, performative and draws heavily upon culture.

Subjectivity and intersubjectivity are present in every interview. The oral history document created in the interview is the result of a three-way dialogue: the respondent with him or herself, between the interviewer and the respondent and between the respondent and cultural discourses of the present and the past. This means that individual memory stories are shaped (not determined) by the intersubjective relationships present in the interview and that what we as researchers hear are narrative constructions of memories of experiences actively created for an audience. The story that is told is thus a partial one, or at least a version of the past created within a specific context and for a specific purpose. Two further theoretical concepts developed by oral historians arise from these understandings about the process by which people's stories are elicited. The first is the idea of the cultural circuit which refers to the process by which personal memories of events and public representations of events inform one another. The second is the concept of composure. This refers to the striving on the part of the interviewee for a version of the self that sits comfortably within the social world, an account that achieves coherence or 'subjective composure'. In the next section we will consider how oral historians have employed these theoretical models in order to understand the meaning of their respondents' stories in the context in which they have been produced.

Application

Intersubjective encounters in the interview

Even before the interview encounter has taken place the researcher has likely displayed traits of his or her subjective self to the potential respondent that will contribute to how that respondent perceives the interviewer and how he or she constructs and performs their story. Whether one comes from an academic background or a community context, one is displaying aspects of oneself that will be 'read' and interpreted by the respondent according to the respondent's own subjective position. For example, a letter to a prospective interviewee on university-crested notepaper will be read in different ways, either as sign of credibility, of official legitimacy or perhaps signifying to some respondents an academic gulf between themselves and the interviewer. On meeting, one's gender, race, accent, name, appearance and age as well as status and beliefs may all impact on the relationship between narrator and interviewer in ways that are difficult to quantify and which may vary in importance as the interview commences. Some of the signs we give off about ourselves are conscious and deliberate (how we dress for example). Others are unconscious and out of our control. In the interview itself some quite concrete signs are read by either side: dress, accent, demeanour and body language provide signals which are interpreted by both parties. Respondents may also communicate their attitude towards the interviewer and the interview process by the preparations they have made (or not). Most interviewers have been met by respondents who have made some arrangements (often by preparing food and drink); more importantly, they may have in Summerfield's words 'prepared their memory frame' by setting out old family photographs, personal memorabilia or made lists of things to say.[17] A self has been prepared to be put on show and recorded.

Despite all best preparations, interviewers for their part cannot control the way in which they will be perceived by respondents. Historian Magda Michielsons, for example, was discomforted by her experience interviewing Bulgarian women about their lives before and after the political changes of the 1980s and 1990s. She discovered that her respondents invariably 'constructed' her as a Western liberal feminist who represented what they wanted and could not, by definition, have; she represented the unattainable status of a successful, educated, wealthy woman. And thus Michielsons observes,

> the common ground for their feminism and mine was extremely difficult to find. It got lost somewhere on the road between Sofia and Plovdiv. As a Westerner I simply could not have a problem in their opinion. Because I

couldn't have a problem, I couldn't have a story … my idea of a dialogic interview technique faded away completely.[18]

And in a similar way, Daphne Patai writes movingly of her ethical concerns about the way in which her interviews with poor Brazilian women cast her in a variety of positions (the white foreigner who had come to provide assistance, a solver of problems, an intermediary) none of which she consciously chose.[19]

Interviewers will make assumptions about their respondents too. Often our first face-to-face encounter with our respondent is the occasion for the interview, perhaps following a more impersonal correspondence by letter, email or telephone. We are interviewing the person because we deduce that they can tell us things we want to know. Like it or not, this is a professional relationship, and it is governed by a set of written and unwritten rules and procedures. Human nature invariably cuts across these boundaries. Even the most professional and empathetic of interviewers will sometimes encounter a hostile respondent or will be unable to reach mutual agreement. In the context of interviewing members of a hate group or any other individuals who hold views widely deemed unacceptable or offensive, striving for empathy is not a practicable strategy. Katherine Blee's research with women members of the Ku Klux Klan is a stark reminder that sometimes the idea of the interview as a 'engaged and sympathetic interaction' is not attainable.[20] However, Blee – a white American – was not prepared for the way in which her interviewees' racial stereotyping meant that they assumed she would agree with their views. In addition, many of her interviewees presented themselves as thoughtful, family-centred people with whom it was surprisingly easy to develop a rapport, especially since Blee admits to her 'unwillingness to violate the tenuous empathy that propelled the interviews along'.[21] Elizabeth Harvey, who interviewed German women about their complicity in the occupation policies of the Nazis, did confront one of her interviewees with a report she had written at the time and pressed another on her views.[22] Here we have the tension between the need to achieve a good interview and the desire to challenge the views expressed.

Conversely, what may appear to be an unpromising encounter may develop into a productive one on account of the respondent and interviewer just hitting it off on a personal level. Most of us probably believe that we will obtain a more valuable interview if we establish a good relationship with our respondent, and this must be because we know that good interpersonal relations often result in greater openness, even confidences being shared. We know this because this is how, in Western culture, we establish meaningful and productive relationships in all sorts of situations. Miriam Zukas discusses the implications of the interview as quasi-friendship in her study of interviews she conducted with women on the topic of friendship. She notes that some of her respondents regarded the interview as similar to a conversation between friends and told her they had 'confided things they would normally only say to a very close friend'.[23] Zukas admits her ambiguous feelings about this state of affairs. On the one hand her respondents' openness made her uneasy – unlike in a friendship, the exchange of information was not reciprocal; on the other, this was precisely the situation she had been hoping to create, in part trading upon the knowledge that interviews between women 'capitalise on their natural communication encouragement work'.[24]

The intersubjective dynamics within the interview situation should always be acknowledged honestly. We must be mindful that the resulting primary source, the interview, is shaped by perceptions on both sides. Indeed, this is starkly illustrated by Blee in the study of the Klan referred to above. And when we listen to the recording or read the transcript it is helpful to be aware of the intersubjective relations that underpinned its production. It is reasonable to argue that the outcome of a conversation between a young female interviewer and an older male respondent would differ, both in style and possibly content, from the same interviewee's encounter with an older male interviewer. In her research into modern Scottish masculinities, Hilary Young argues precisely that her subject identity, as a young, educated, liberated woman, affected the ways in which her older male respondents constructed their own historical masculinities.[25] She acknowledged that, in the eyes of her respondents, she represented 'someone who approved of changed gender roles' and in conversation some of her respondents were willing to compose memories of masculine roles which aligned with more modern conceptions of gender roles, in other words they acknowledged through their answers to her questions about gender roles, that they were aware of the discourse of the 'new man'.[26] Others perceived her – or what she represented to them – as a threat. One former trade-union activist adopted a domineering stance in the interview as he held her (that is, women) to account for the threat to the traditional jobs of his male colleagues. After an opening gambit of 'So you've come to hear how Glasgow's men are big sissies nowadays', this respondent's subsequent narrative emphasised the decline of Glasgow men's hard man or macho image, suggesting that it had been undermined by women with the appropriate female skills for the new jobs and the freedom they enjoyed as a result of the contraceptive pill.[27] Young acknowledges that interviews conducted by a male may well have produced different memory narratives, but that the testimony she elicited revealed an important facet of male identity in an era of changing gender relations amidst the decline of Britain's traditional industrial economy.

So far we have been assuming that the interview is conducted one to one – and the majority are. But there are clearly different kinds of intersubjective dynamics at play when interviewing a couple or a group of people. Researchers rarely set up group interviews for the practical reason that transcribing more than one voice is extremely difficult; it can also pose ethical problems regarding revealing personal stories. Although couple or group interviews can be extremely rewarding, as a means of sparking off shared memories for instance, alternative or countermemories may be silenced by the

power of the group narrative.[28] Moreover, researchers who have been confronted unexpectedly with another person in the room – usually a partner –
have made some interesting observations. First, the presence of both partners
can lead to less openness and more guarded answers. Second, where the
topics under discussion have a gendered aspect (parenting for instance, or
home life), individuals tend to fall into the gender roles society has assigned
them. Sarah Cunningham-Burley's interviews with couples for research into
grandparenting demonstrated that grandmothers spoke more, whereas
grandfathers tended to be reticent unless a topic of their own choice was discussed and, in contrast with grandmothers, had difficulty answering what the
researcher thought were salient questions. The author concludes that both
parties to the interview were, to some extent, reacting to common-sense gendered assumptions about male and female grandparenting roles and that the
interviewer's questions likewise drew upon these assumptions.[29]

The key point here is to acknowledge the intersubjective relationships that
are present within the interview situation and to think about how they influence the outcome. It starts with the interviewer being reflexive upon what
impact the self she projects to the interviewee has had on the resulting testimony. Historians, unlike anthropologists, are used to adopting the role of the
outsider to a culture, a time, an event. We rarely conduct participant observation – becoming part of a community or joining cultural events to see what
they are like. In that sense, we are less used to being part of the story. One of
the reasons we undertake oral history interviews is to reach 'another place' –
the past – through the memories of someone who was there. In this situation,
distance between the parties, whether it be in terms of age or gender or
experience, may be advantageous in the sense that a respondent may be more
willing to explain and to describe in detail to a stranger than to a peer. Portelli describes the oral history interview as a 'confrontation of partialities' in
which no encounter will ever produce the representation of an undivided or
whole self.[30] If we keep that in mind, then we can move forward to a more
sympathetic and nuanced understanding of the narratives told.

Oral historians have embraced the issues surrounding subjectivity in the
interview as part of the wholesale shift from information-gathering to a
facilitation of the telling of memory stories. Indeed, subjectivity has not only
become something that must be acknowledged in the interview but it has
become part of a bigger agenda, that of liberating voices and validating
experiences and understanding how people construct retrospective versions of
their lives.

Subjectivity and discourse

A focus on subjectivity requires that we not only be aware of the fact that our
respondent is constructing a subjective version of the past in a dialogue with
the interviewer but that in doing so he or she is drawing upon discourses from
wider culture. This means that we are constantly reappraising our life stories,

telling different versions to different audiences. In order to do this we draw upon notions of how the self is presented in a particular culture and utilise a range of available identities or subject positions to do this (such as the rebellious daughter, the good wife, the hard worker and so on). This engagement is complex. There will be some discourses that will be adopted by the interviewee, but others will be rejected. He or she will have negotiated their way through these views in society, and in the interview this will be reflected in the ways in which the events of the person's life are selected, described and judged.

Constructing and presenting one's self to an audience – be it a group of friends or an oral history interview – is often assumed to be the product of internal desire for self-expression and associated with a modern Western culture of high consumption and liberated cultural opportunities. But, in fact, constructing a subjective account of a life has been part of everyday life for much longer. Lyndal Roper notes the way a German woman Regina Bartholeme in Augsburg in 1685 constructed a singular view of herself as the Devil's lover, information she volunteered in a series of elaborate accounts to an Inquisition court and which resulted in her execution.[31] For many in society, autobiography grew as part of the modern world of record-keeping, as parish or municipal councils collected information about people applying for poor relief or who needed character references for employment (testimonials), or to construct an image of a reliable and truthful witness as they gave evidence in a court of law. By the middle of the nineteenth century, modern bureaucracies collected biographical details to create records checks for the future. Autobiographical performances became embedded in everyday routines.[32] And in the modern Western world of the twenty-first century we are accomplished at producing different versions of our life for different purposes. The curriculum vitae, a chronological statement of one's life containing recognised educational and career achievements, will be created in response to the organisational need to judge and discriminate between one person and another. In contrast, the personal profile posted on a social-networking website is a form of autobiography that privileges a different form of self-expression; but it is just as much a version of a life as the CV, and both are the product of an intersubjective dialogue between the self and the cultural discourses that offer us various models for self-representation. So, while our social-networking page might include personal details such as our likes and dislikes and contain photographs depicting ourselves in a variety of locations, such information would be inappropriate on a résumé for a job application. Both represent the same person, but that person has represented him or herself very differently in each format.

It is precisely the relationship between subjectivity and discourse that engages the oral historian, who understands that memory and the creation of memory stories can only be undertaken by calling upon certain sets of ideas, interpretations and representations which are meaningful to the narrator, which help make sense of an often disparate and disconnected set of memories and experiences. They are the glue that stick the memories together in a way that makes sense to the narrator and that often allow the narrator to position him or herself as the subject of the narrative, whether as a hero, an agent, a victim or in some other role. In the 1990s, I carried out a series of interviews with people who had experienced their childhood apart from their birth family. I encountered a number of ways in which individuals positioned their often uncomfortable memory stories within wider discourses on family and belonging that enabled them to come to terms with their past. Robert is a good example of someone who constructed a narrative that drew on familiar discourses of family life to explain to himself, and to me, his sense of not belonging to a family and thus not really knowing who he was. Robert was removed from his city of birth, Glasgow, at the age of three and sent to live with a foster family several hundred miles away. The absence of a father's name on his birth certificate later made him suspicious of the story he had been told at the time: that his parents had died in a car crash. Robert remembered his childhood as a happy time; he was made to feel part of the family ('we referred to each other as brothers and sisters ... it was the only family I ever knew you see'), and he was keen to emphasise that he was given a better life than many children who lived with their natural parents:

> We was better looked after than the bloody kids with their mother and father I can tell you that, we really were. I used to stand on a rostrum and tell them that you know and yet you was underdog you know in the playground and that you see, you were a Glasgow orphan ... In fact you couldn't be bloody jealous right enough because you were better off than they were.[33]

The frictions that existed in blood families were not part of Robert's experience: 'I'd no traumas to go through.' But he was acutely conscious of his status as a foster child. 'More than once I was told, now you behave yourself or you'll be away.' His narrative is peppered with references to another 'orphan' child in the extended family, one unlike him who was legally adopted. She seemingly became the centre of attention, at least that was Robert's interpretation: 'it was unbelievable how they accepted [her] and everything centred around [her] and [her] kids.' And his experience of being singled out by other children and called names and then later in life being unable to find work in the rather insular fishing community in which he was brought up, resulted in what he described as cynicism: 'I'm more cynical and bitter, it makes you kinda more on your guard throughout life which is no bad thing.' Robert's cynicism was presented as a form of protection against the disappointment of not wholly belonging to either a 'real' family or to his foster family. Robert's narrative was constructed within and against a discourse on 'normal' family life with which he had become acculturated. He was keen to portray himself as part of a family but was troubled by his outsider status.

There are different forms the life story might take, and we shall explore some of the narrative modes adopted in Chapter 6. Of more interest to us here is the relationship between the narrative produced by the respondent and the culture that informs it. Oral history narratives are constructed as means by which men and women 'locate themselves imaginatively within their complexly structured social worlds'.[34] Literary critic Reginia Gagnier remarked that 'what is striking about the mind or personality is not its uniqueness or autonomy, but rather its profound dependence upon intersubjectively shared meanings'.[35] In other words, we can only tell and make sense of an experience if we do so in a way that makes sense to others, and therefore we use common or agreed frameworks and discourses to give a shape and meaning to our stories. Robert could only make sense of his experiences as a foster child and could only make his audience understand, by framing his narrative within the discourse on the ideal family.

Another way of looking at this is to approach the construction of the life or memory narrative as shaped by scripts or templates. 'Whether we are aware of it or not', writes Jill Ker Conway in her analysis of autobiography:

> our culture gives us an inner script by which we live our lives. The main acts for the play come from the way our world understands human development; the scenes and key characters come from our families and socialisation, which provide the pattern for investing others with emotional significance; and the dynamics of the script come from what our world defines as success or achievement.[36]

The story that a person tells is just one of many that are possible. The script is not deterministic. Its shape, form and content is determined by the need for the narrator to construct a memory story with which he or she can feel comfortable at that moment. And a comfortable telling is often one in which the story told coheres with larger cultural understandings. This process has been termed 'composure' and was originally coined by historian Graham Dawson to explain how people tell stories about their lives while drawing upon imagined forms embedded in culture. Dawson was examining the ways in which gender identities are formed and expressed, focusing explicitly upon the enduring popularity of the soldier hero for British masculine identity. It is worth quoting Dawson at length:

> The cultural importance of storytelling lies not only in the stories we are told ... but also in those we ourselves tell, or compose. It is a cultural practice deeply embedded in everyday life, a creative activity in which everyone engages. Even the most mundane of narratives is an active composition, created through the formal arrangement of narrative elements into a whole ... At the same time, the telling also creates a perspective for the self within which it endeavours to make sense of the day, so that its troubling, disturbing aspects may be 'managed', worked

through, contained, repressed ... In this second sense then, storytelling also 'composes' a subjective orientation of the self within the social relations of the world, enabling it to be imaginatively entered-into and inhabited. The story that is actually told is always the one preferred amongst other possible versions, and involves a striving, not only for a formally satisfying narrative or a coherent version of events, but also for a version of the self that can be lived with in relative psychic comfort – for, that is, subjective composure.[37]

Dawson is suggesting two different yet related definitions of composure; the first refers to the process of composing a story, the second to an individual's ability to present a coherent story with which he or she feels comfortable. The theory of composure that Dawson spawned thus sums up the intersubjective relations inherent in the oral history interview very well. As Dawson states:

The social recognition offered within any specific public will be intimately related to the cultural values that it holds in common, and exercises a determining influence upon the way a narrative may be told and, therefore, upon the kind of composure that it makes possible. The narrative resource of a culture – its repertoire of shared and recognised forms – therefore functions as a currency of recognised identities.[38]

Dawson developed this theory in the context of analysing the place of the 'soldier hero' in the British cultural imagination. He describes how he developed his subjective sense of himself as a boy in relation to public representations of the adventure hero:

[T]he imaginative identifications that I made in dressing up drew on the available cultural repertoire of stories and heroes like the Lone Ranger ... in dressing up and acting a part I was representing this imagined self to others and assuming the shape in which I wanted to appear in the world. My imaginings were taking on a more fully social form.[39]

It is not surprising that this theory has been enthusiastically adopted and applied by oral historians since it manages to engage with two key elements of oral history-telling: the story told by the respondent and the way he or she draws upon culturally recognised values in order to construct a past self which makes sense to the respondent and to the audience.

However, as Dawson and others have pointed out, respondents do not compose their stories by drawing upon cultural constructs at random. Cultures contain a range of possible identities, some of which will be dominant or hegemonic, ideal or desirable, others will be alternative or subversive. Within our social world, all of the possibilities are circulated in discourses and presented in a variety of written, visual and aural media forms, but although the repertoire of possibilities may be unlimited, the ability to choose amongst them is 'shaped by the powerful hegemonic constraints of an effectively established culture'.[40] The person who survives 'against the odds', like Robert whose story was discussed earlier, is more sympathetic and more likely to achieve composure than he or she who wallows in self-pity. Effectively, this means that some forms are more acceptable to present in public than others. In modern Western culture, for instance, the identity of the hard working provider is a more comfortable and acceptable position for a man to adopt than the cuckolded husband or the emasculated unemployed. Catherine Kohler Riessman analyses the narrative of a divorced and disabled working-class man called 'Burt' who strives to constitute himself in the interview as a 'devoted husband and responsible worker' – core elements of dominant masculinity in his culture – despite evidence indicating that these characteristics are no longer realistic in his case.[41] Similarly, the ex-miners and construction workers interviewed by Johnston and McIvor for a project on the health hazards of heavy industry recalled the macho or 'hard man' attitude that prevailed in their working days in the mid-twentieth century. Men worked without wearing protective clothing or face masks with dangerous materials because it was considered 'unmanly' and 'cissy' to do so. Interviewing these men after they had been crippled by lung diseases brought on by the dangerous working conditions, they continued to regard that 'hard man' identity as something by which they judged themselves. Consequently, they were unwilling to present themselves as victims. 'Well, obviously I'm no fit to work, eh and that', commented one former miner. 'I worked a' my life ... It was a big blow to me to be told that I'd never work again. Eh, your pride's dented, ken?'[42]

Discourses, like those on manliness, move from society to the individual and back into society again. They are constantly being exchanged in society, put into new forms, but usually changing very little in their main character. The 'cultural circuit', Richard Johnson's term which describes the 'production, circulation and consumption of cultural products ... [and] subjective forms', is a helpful way of explaining how subjectivity or expressions of the self are bound up with public representations.[43] The cultural circuit refers to the relationship between private or local discourses and national or public representations. Local or personal stories and experiences are not necessarily affected or determined by national or public forms, but 'general-public forms, which present stories in more abstract and generalised terms ... than the local variants, may come to have an apparent life of their own, independent of any particular, concrete historical conditions ... thus local and particular accounts cannot escape the conceptual and definitional effects of powerful public representations'.[44] Thus, personal accounts of experience are almost invariably absorbed into public accounts, are generalised or homogenised in the process of being subject to powerful pressures of discourses which have attained governmental and institutional support.[45] As a result, all individual accounts relate *in some way* to these dominant models. At the most basic level, many interviewees will mark or frame their personal memories with reference to public events – wars, political turning points and so on – but it is the ways in which such events are represented in culture that impact more profoundly on the ways in which individuals tell their stories.

These theories, of the cultural circuit and of composure, have been most effectively applied to studies of soldiering and gendered identities. Graham Dawson in his analysis of the dominant masculine identity of the soldier hero in British culture, Alistair Thomson in his study of Australian squaddies in the First World War Anzac campaign, and Penny Summerfield in her examination of gendered stories of work and the war effort during the Second World War, have each demonstrated the workings of the cultural circuit and the value of understanding the process of subjective memory production through composure.[46] But these studies also demonstrate that the relationship between the personal memory stories and discourse is dialogic, it exists in a two-way relationship. People do not merely absorb dominant discourses, use them to shape their own life narratives and spout them back at the interviewer. Clearly there are gaps and tensions between individual accounts and dominant or public representations which may emerge in the interview context. These may be difficult to traverse. In such instances, respondents might experience discomposure, a kind of psychic unease at their inability to align subjective experience with discourse. For instance, Summerfield shows how some women interviewed about their wartime roles showed difficulties in reconciling contradictory elements of their experiences. One woman who spoke with confidence and self-assurance about her role as an aircraft technician during the war – an identity which was bolstered by publicly available images of 'patriotic feminism' – faltered when talking about her return to post-war domesticity and her struggles to reconcile work and children.[47]

Thomson's much-cited study of soldiers engaged in the Gallipoli campaign during the First World War highlights the interpretive gap between national memory and personal accounts. In this influential work, Thomson demonstrates the value of the theory of the cultural circuit and how composure theory may provide some insight into the ways in which individuals construct their accounts over time and in relation to changing public norms. In Australia there is a huge legend of the Anzacs, the soldiers who fought in the two world wars in far-off shores in support of the British Empire, and who died in their tens of thousands. In the period since 1945, the Anzacs have risen to be regarded as embodying Australian national character and identity, with much reverential remembrance on television and in the media, and Anzac Day is virtually the national day of Australia. Thomson studied the men nicknamed 'diggers' for their role in the Gallipoli landings in April 1915, examining the complex relationship between the national myth of Australian manhood immortalised in the term and the personal stories of some of the Anzac veterans.[48] The Anzac legend celebrated in film and in print the bravery and egalitarianism of the Australian soldiers and created a myth around which Australia celebrated its 'coming of age' as a nation. Some of Thomson's interviewees incorporated the Anzac legend into their stories, even recounting scenes from the film *Gallipoli* as if they had been there, demonstrating how private memories may be incorporated into public representation and then reincorporated by respondents.

But for one of Thomson's interviewees, Fred Farrall, the Anzac legend bore no relationship to his personal experiences; he was unable to talk about the war because 'he could find no appropriate public affirmation of his experience as a soldier', which was coloured by fear and the nightmare of losing his best friends in the fighting. Fred experienced discomposure in his initial interviews with Thomson in both senses. He was unable to compose a coherent narrative of his experiences because of the huge disjuncture between the national myth and his own subjectivity – Fred did not conform to the 'digger' ideal and came home mentally and physically scarred by his experiences. Neither was he able to achieve composure, a feeling of comfort in the story he could tell, because he was unable to come to terms with his feelings of inadequacy and fear. 'The public celebration of Anzac heroes was a painful reminder of his own perceived inadequacy as a soldier and a man, and Fred was unable to enjoy the solace and affirmation it offered to other returned servicemen.'[49] However, some years later, Fred experienced something of a convergence between his own experiences and the public representation. By the 1980s, in the context of greater public acknowledgement of the horrors of war and the acceptance that the soldier could be a victim, Fred experienced public affirmation of his role and was able to talk more coherently and proudly of his experiences. In this way, the public memory of the Anzacs became something which, eventually, Fred was able to absorb into a new composure of his own past.

No oral historian is content to assume that respondents' narratives are wholly constrained by dominant discourses; indeed, evidence suggests that most respondents are capable of agency or what Ortner calls a 'critical subjectivity' which involves a subject internalising, reflecting upon and then reacting against a set of circumstances or a widely accepted version of the past.[50] At the same time, we are aware of the 'difficulties of developing and sustaining oppositional memories'.[51] Fred Farrall could barely express his view of war when the popular legend allowed for no deviation from the heroic digger myth; but Thomson argues that the operation of the cultural circuit incorporated the alternative viewpoint in a modern reworking of the legend, a 'generalised, almost nostalgic version' which allows the diggers to tell their stories while at the same time 'subtly reworking the conservative sense of the war, national character and Australian history'.[52]

Some have been critical of the tendency to interpret individual memory narratives as always being a product of public discourse.[53] Yet few oral historians adopt such a position. Oral historians who have applied the theories of the cultural circuit and composure to help analyse the intersubjective relationship between memory narratives and public discourses have been interested in elucidating the dialogue we all engage in with culture at the same time as being interested in the specific personal stories told.

Feminist approaches

Probably the most sustained practical and theoretical engagement with issues around subjectivity and intersubjectivity in oral history has been carried out by feminists. Many feminists embraced the potential of oral history for recovering the voices of ordinary women, for liberating women's experiences from the oppression of patriarchal structures and language. 'Women's oral history is a feminist encounter', wrote one of its pioneers Sherna Gluck in 1977:

> It is the creation of a new type of material on women; it is the validation of women's experiences; it is the communication among women of different generations; it is the discovery of our own roots and the development of a continuity that has been denied us in traditional historical accounts.[54]

But early on, the project to recover women's voices was recognised to be more complex than initially imagined. Two main issues were addressed: the potential power imbalance in the interview and the difficulties experienced by women in expressing authentic experience.

Feminist research method has always rejected any pretence at objectivity. It is always motivated by an ideological position that seeks to explain and to understand women's subordination and, through this, to liberate women in the present.[55] Oral history as a methodology was initially regarded by feminist researchers as a means to hear women's authentic voices that had hitherto been silenced in historical accounts. But it was soon understood that the oral history interview was an imperfect method of liberating women's voices and accessing women's subjectivity for a number of reasons.

First, it was argued that women's voices had less legitimacy in a society in which they were structurally oppressed, and that the stories they did tell were often shaped by dominant or patriarchal discourses rather than being expressions of their own feelings or consciousness. Dana Jack observes that we must appreciate that the language women use is informed by their cultural context, 'one that has historically demeaned women's activities'.[56] Early interviews with female settlers in the USA, for example, revealed little about the women's own experiences since they mediated their stories through the activities of their menfolk 'because they believe that history was made by men'.[57] A common response in my own interviews with women are the words, 'I didn't do anything important', or 'I haven't got anything interesting to tell you'. Women have a tendency to downplay their experiences because they often do not conform to what is publicly presented as significant in mainstream history.

Second, it was noted that some groups of women showed great reluctance or difficulty in narrating their lives because they were unused to public-speaking – they were unable to adopt the 'performative mode' expected of them. Anderson and Jack write about the 'muted channel of women's subjectivity' which refers to the way in which women often subjugate their own feelings in an interview while privileging activities.[58] Third, it was felt that women's 'honest' voices were harder to hear because they were silenced or 'muted' when their experience did not coincide with dominant expectations of female behaviour.[59] Kristina Minister wrote of a 'gender-based communication system' within which women typically possess less power than men and whereby women use communication for establishing intimacy and equality in contrast with men who use speech in different ways, primarily to assert authority.[60] Women, it was suggested, found it difficult to 'turn themselves into narrative subjects'.[61] And, finally and more fundamentally, the interview itself was regarded by some as a 'masculine paradigm', a 'depersonalised' encounter governed by objectivity, detachment of the researcher and grounded in the hierarchies of scholarship. In other words, the interview was not conducive to liberating women's voices.[62] Indeed, Anderson and Jack argue that women will often talk about themselves as they think they are perceived by others; they experience difficulty in liberating their own subjective voices from the 'façade of the acceptable female role': 'Women have internalised the categories by which to interpret their experience and activities, categories that "represent a deposit of the desires and disappointments of men".'[63]

Feminist oral historians' aim was to create an interview environment in which women could speak for themselves, permitting the expression of 'honest voices'. The proposed solution was to reduce the perceived power imbalance between interviewer and respondent. This has also been described as facilitating the production of a narrative focused on the inner self as opposed to the social self, freeing up interiority, a women-centred approach that not only gives women space to speak but which acknowledges what they have to say in their own terms rather than drawing upon social models.[64] So, for instance, Judy Yung's work with Chinese-American women aimed to allow this group to tell their stories unshackled from the traditional and constraining cultural models defined by the dominant community within which their lives were commonly understood, models such as the 'exotic China Doll' and the 'erotic Suzy Wong'. Yung, herself a Chinese-American woman, describes how her insider status enabled her to establish rapport with her interviewees and how she adopted the role of the 'attentive listener' in order to elicit their life stories using a life-course approach.[65]

These ambitions are all consistent with the feminist objective to write an alternative history that gives equal weight to women's experiences and women's interpretation of those experiences. The strategies proposed include treating the interview as a conversation or shared experience, adapting linguistic patterns to the performance of the narrator, dressing differently, allowing respondents to interrogate the interviewer and allowing respondents to influence the research questions and ultimately take some responsibility for the project. In Kristina Minister's view, the key to unlocking women's subjectivity was altering what she calls the 'communication frame' rather than trying to change the woman herself. If these steps are taken, argues Minister, 'feminist oral history is intersubjective history'.[66] Geiger summarises the feminist approach:

> In a feminist relationship between oral historians and researcher, existing differences will be recognised and conditions of mutual respect will be sought. Ways of sharing the 'authority' expressed in written renditions of the oral account or exchange will be explicitly discussed, as will the nature of the working relationship itself, and what is to be produced from it. A feminist research relationship will also be characterised by honesty about its limitations.[67]

The problems with these suggestions have been extensively rehearsed.[68] The main objection concerns the improbability of the academic historian casting off that element of her subjective self that creates the inequality. All interviewers possess some authority merely by means of occupying their position within a project, whether it be academic or community based. As Summerfield states, 'the researcher nurtures, assists and validates the narrator's interpretive role, but ultimately the work of interpretation and analysis, and the time and skills necessary to do it, are her own'.[69] There is clearly a balance to be struck in finding a solution to the question posed by Christine Borland of how we might 'present our work in a way that grants the speaking woman interpretive respect without relinquishing our responsibility to provide our own interpretation of her experience'.[70] For Armitage and Gluck, in a retrospective rethinking of their earlier thoughts on feminist oral history, the next step is to try to find a solution to the problem of 'collaborative meaning-making', in order to avoid clashes of understanding and misinterpretation which may arise from the diametric subjective positions of interviewer and narrator.[71] In other words, they are seeking ways of facilitating the productive interplay of subjectivities. This develops further the thinking of Michael Frisch who urged oral historians to see the oral history process as a shared one, though for him the emphasis was on the empowerment of the speaker whereas feminist researchers have argued for much greater reflexivity on the part of the interviewer, not just as an interviewer or academic but as a social being.[72]

Some of these concerns regarding the power imbalance in the interview relationship are no longer so pressing. In modern Western culture at least, the advent of media interest in all areas of private life and the emergence of a 'confessional culture' in which people are willing to speak openly in public on a range of personal matters means that the personal confession is no longer confined to the therapy session. Arguably, women in particular have become acculturated to this public interest in private life through women's and celebrity magazines and the broadcast media. The public consumption of readers' personal problems and everyday struggles and reality television's warts-and-all portrayal of some of the most personal aspects of people's lives means that, as Summerfield observes, 'women come to oral history interviews with experience of a range of confessional occasions from which they are likely to select a model that seems most appropriate'.[73] This means that many respondents will be confident of what is expected of them and may be able to perform in a way that conforms to the expectations of the interviewer, that is, be willing to put themselves as women at the centre of the story, to open up emotionally, to speak frankly and reflectively about their subjective experience as women. Moreover, the growth of women's history and circulation of accounts of women's public role has created a more amenable framework for individual women's stories. But there will always be individuals and groups who struggle to find composure on account of the difficulty of hooking their subjective experiences onto dominant narratives. For instance, older gay men and lesbians whose sexual identity was suppressed for much of their lives may struggle to compose coherent life stories in part because their experiences and the way they have made sense of those experiences may be hard to express in the language and cultural framework of a more liberated society.

The feminist engagement with issues around the intersubjectivities in the interview has had quite far-reaching impact on the practice of oral history more generally. Amongst oral historians, the notion of the interview as an intersubjective encounter is now commonplace and has resulted in some imaginative reflection on the ways in which memory stories are and can be produced. Indeed, the problems raised by feminists are now regarded as applicable more generally in oral history practice. Frisch's call for there to be a 'shared authority' between interviewer and interviewee, an attempt to 'redistribute intellectual authority' in order to diminish the hierarchical relationship inherent in the research process is one such response. We will return to this issue in Chapter 8.

Practice

It is now commonplace for oral history guides to exhort researchers to reflect on their own role in the interview process and to be transparent about the intersubjectivities present in the interview setting. But how is this to be done? It is relatively simple to provide the reader with information on the identities of the interviewers, but it is hard for the reader to know what to do with this information. Informing the reader of my gender, ethnicity and social class is of little use unless the reader is also told of how this impacted on my respondents. It is difficult to integrate a thoroughgoing analysis of the working of intersubjectivity into one's research output.

Anderson and Jack argue that we must 'learn to listen' in order to achieve the methodological shift from 'information gathering, where the focus is on the right questions, to interaction, where the focus is on process, on the dynamic unfolding of the subject's viewpoint' in order to uncover the perspectives that our interviewees bring to the table.[74] This is just the first stage. The second is to be aware of the discursive constructions available to respondents, both at the time of the experience they are recounting and since.

The third is to be aware of the social interactions underway in the interview itself. The combination of these three levels of analysis may permit the researcher to understand how people go about reconstructing their past in an active and creative fashion in the interview.

An example from my own oral history research might serve to illustrate the three stages described above. In 2002 I conducted a small number of interviews with women in the Shetland islands as part of a larger project on the history of women and gender relations in this part of the British Isles. One of my interviewees, Mary Ellen Odie, was recommended to me as an expert on the history of women in Shetland, an enthusiastic amateur historian and lifetime resident. She told me stories drawn from her own memory, from stories told within her family and the community and drawn from the archives. Mary Ellen's subject viewpoint was as a Shetland woman with intimate knowledge of local families and customs but she was also a woman with a reverence for the past and what the past can tell us. Her narrative was constructed within a context of a pervasive discourse within Shetland of the strength, endurance and power of women in the past in a context in which they outnumbered men in the population. And Mary Ellen was aware that I, a professional women's historian, was approaching her as a local expert. We struck up an immediate rapport; we were both excited to be able to spend time conversing about a subject that was important to both of us. This extract from my interview with Mary Ellen goes some way towards illustrating the intersubjective dynamics present. Here we are talking about the 'hungry gap' – the period of time after the last year's grain ran out and before the new grain was harvested:

> But that hungry gap must have been such a frightener. And one thing in relation to women that I certainly know affected the people in North Yell particularly we have Palmers Evans [local doctor] very poignant note at the end of the list of names of people, was the potato famine it happened just the second year after the Irish, and North Yell got a really bad blight. It was then that the ... meal roads of North Yell were introduced seriously after that year. But then the meal roads had to be introduced just before when the hungry gap had really widened in the late thirties, that was a bad bad time. It comes out, I tell you where it comes out quite graphically is in the Napier Commission [Royal Commission on the crofting system] where people describe what it was like to be, to have your last meal and then know that after that it was just the bare essentials. My great granny knew how to cook a starling, do you believe that? ... Her man was drowned and she was really left destitute, 1851. And they caught starlings in a gun? It was just a kind of set-up with a stick and a net, when they went in the poor things it collapsed and they got the starlings. And they cooked limpets and whelks and all that. So that was always sort of a byword when we thought mam was being a bit mean ... and she says I never had to eat whelks like Granny did.[75]

Here Mary Ellen combines personal memory, family memory, local research and documented history all framed within the discourse of the resourceful, hard-working woman and related to me within the context of an interview set up to find out about the history of Shetland women. The intersubjective relations between Mary Ellen and myself against a background of a shared acknowledgement of the importance of women's history almost certainly influenced what she told me, what was included, and the references to historical sources, all bound up within a family and island narrative.

A fine but very different example of the application of such an analytical process is Graham Dawson's painstaking and sophisticated study of the event in 1972 known as Bloody Sunday, when Northern Irish civilians were shot by British soldiers at a civil-rights demonstration, an event that marks a pivotal point in the 'Troubles' in Northern Ireland. Dawson conducts a deep and multilayered analysis of the construction of subjectivities as people endeavoured to remember the traumatic events. Dawson is attentive to the many layers of official and popular interpretation, commemoration and representation of the events over the course of more than thirty years through which people attempt to tell what happened. He writes,

> the possibility of any individual articulating his or her own account of this multi-faceted, subjective relationship to the past depends on a relationship with others, who listen, bring to bear memories of their own, and interpret and reinterpret the meanings that are made: it is necessarily, 'a collective, intersubjective affair'.[76]

Ultimately, Dawson's account is about how considerations of intersubjectivity at all levels – the dialogue between the respondent or witness to the events and circulating stories or myths about the event, and the dialogue between the respondents and Dawson – influence how people remember, how they call up a particularly traumatic experience through the lenses of talk and reportage journalism and history writing.

Conclusions

The oral history interview is a three-way conversation: the interviewee engages in a conversation with his or herself, with the interviewer and with culture. The challenge for the historian is to analyse and decode these conversations, bearing in mind that each influences the other. This is a difficult process, which Ron Grele says we can only achieve if we listen very hard and if we do this we can isolate what he calls 'the problematic', the theoretical and ideological context, which informs the interview.[77]

Issues around subjectivity pervade the entire oral history process, from the conduct of the interview to the analysis and writing up of the research. It is so basic that it impacts upon all the other interpretive models discussed in this book. Power relations are, as we have seen, part and parcel of the interview relationship. Memory is refracted through the subjectivity constructed by the respondent and shaped by the intersubjective relations in the room. An interviewee's performance is conditional upon the subject position he or she adopts for the interview. The style of narrative and the ability to give a narrative account may be contingent upon the ability to achieve composure, to find a place within cultural discourses where one is comfortable enough to tell one's story.

5 Memory

Introduction

The oral historian, broadly speaking, asks people questions to discover four things: what happened, how they felt about it, how they recall it, and what wider public memory they draw upon. At the heart of this lies memory. Memory and the process of remembering are central to oral history. The recollections of memory are our primary evidence just as the medieval manuscript or the cabinet-office minutes are for historians working within other traditions. Because of this, oral historians have drawn upon research from a variety of disciplines in order to try to understand better how memory works in the individual and within the collective or group. Why do we remember some things and not others? Does what we remember alter with age and with gender? How do we order and relate our memories to ourselves and to others? And how reliable is memory as a historical source? All of these questions have been extensively debated by historians, psychologists and sociologists amongst others, resulting in a number of usable theoretical models upon which oral historians have drawn.

This chapter will examine some of the approaches to memory derived from the disciplines of psychology, sociology, cultural anthropology and history and show how they have been utilised by oral historians to better interpret what they have been told by respondents. It is important to note here that memory is intricately bound up with the other themes of this book. The ways in which people remember and the ways in which they relate their memories are influenced by intersubjective relations, are shaped by narrative structures and forms and are expressed in performances. Memory then is at the heart of this book and at the core of oral history practice. It is no longer just the source of oral history but the subject of what we do.

Memory as a source

Memory is not just the recall of past events and experiences in an unproblematic and untainted way. It is rather a process of remembering: the calling up of images, stories, experiences and emotions from our past life, ordering them, placing them within a narrative or story and then telling them in a way that is shaped at least in part by our social and cultural context. In the psychologist Daniel Schacter's words, memory is about the way we 'convert the fragmentary remains of experience into autobiographical narratives that endure over time and constitute the stories of our lives'.[1] Memories are always produced within a wider frame. Memory is not a storehouse where one can search around and find a ready-formed story. 'What is really important is that memory is not a passive depository of facts, but an active process of creation of meanings.'[2] This oft-quoted statement from Portelli sums up the position of most oral historians today. This is just another way of saying that memories are not pure; they are contingent. They are as much about the present as the past. Memory, writes Annette Kuhn, 'is neither pure experience nor pure event. Memory is an account, always discursive, always already textual'.[3] The memory recovered through oral history is not always 100 per cent reliable in objective or measurable terms though it has a truth value for the person remembering. Acknowledging this fact can only be helpful to the oral historian.

Memory (and remembering) for the oral historian is not an abstract concept but a practical and active process of reconstruction whereby traces of the past are placed in conjunction with one another to tell a story. Memory is not just about the individual; it is also about the community, the collective, and the nation. In this regard, memory – both individual and collective – exists in a symbiotic relationship with the public memorialisation of the past, so we must always be aware that memory expressed in an interview exists within a field of memory work that is going on at many levels in our society. In other words, one person's memory operates within a wider context that includes memory produced and maintained by family, community and public representations. Individual memory then, is not seen as a straightforward psychological phenomenon but as a socially shared experience.[4] For instance, when we ask a respondent about the 1960s, we need to be aware that the memories recalled will not only consist of very personal experiences – things that only happened to our interviewee – but that these individual memories are recalled in relation to the memories of family and friends and are informed by a host of public representations of the 1960s. Most of the female interviewees in one of my oral history projects on women's experiences from the 1950s to the 1970s identified the miniskirt as a key marker of change. Certainly all of them wore this fashion item but it would be naive to ignore the fact that the miniskirt is one of the most frequently cited icons of popular culture in public representations of that era. These women were not lying but their memories of that time were framed by a public memory of the era.

When oral historians first began to use memory as a source for historical research in the post-Second World War decades they were in the 'vanguard of a renaissance' in Paul Thompson's words, reigniting an engagement with oral evidence that had thrived before the development of a historical method that privileged the written document.[5] But almost as soon as this renaissance had got underway, the practitioners of oral history were bedevilled by the issue of the reliability or its obverse – the fallibility – of memory. Critics of oral history aimed to pull the rug from under the upstart's feet by striking at the most vulnerable element: they claimed that oral history evidence could not be relied upon because memory was notoriously unreliable. The attempt to validate the experiences of ordinary working people by talking to them about their memories was attacked by some as unverifiable. One reviewer of Ronald Blythe's *Akenfield* commented: 'What all this amounts to is that not enough facts are included for the reader to check Blythe's account of rural life for himself.'[6] 'Facts', it seemed, were incompatible with the supposed fragility of memory.

Critics contrasted the utilisation of memory as the oral historian's primary source with the use of written documents which, since the nineteenth century, had been fetishised as the basis for scholarly historical study. Oral history was positioned way down the hierarchy of sources because it seemingly did not produce 'data' which could be verified and counted. In terms of their reliability, contemporary letters, reports and parliamentary papers were at the top and supposedly more subjective sources such as diaries and autobiographies at the bottom. Many years ago, oral history pioneer Paul Thompson, amongst others, effectively undermined this distinction between so-called reliable and unreliable evidence: all evidence is socially constructed, all is a product of a purpose, and many documents were deliberately shaped to present a particular picture or interpretation of an event or phenomenon.[7] In this sense then, there is little distinction to be made between an oral history interview based on memory and a minute of a meeting, also reconstructed in part based on memory of what was said; in fact, the ordinary participant's memory will likely contain a frankness of observation missing from the contrived 'neutrality' of the minute-taker.

However, in its early days, oral history needed defending from the doubters who said oral history was anecdotal, unverifiable and subjective. The response was, in some cases, to treat oral evidence like any other source. This has been described as the 'textual model' of memory or treating oral evidence like a text or other written document.[8] Some oral historians became obsessed with objectivity in order, as they saw it, to legitimise the subject within the History profession. Others became a bit obsessed about checking or verifying what they had been told by cross-referencing with contemporaneous printed sources. Of course one can check to see if a respondent remembered certain 'facts' such as dates and names correctly, but this is probably about as far as one can and should go, for memory, as Trevor Lummis said, 'is a complex phenomenon which cannot be tested for truth by the application of a set of rules'.[9]

So oral historians generally say that memory cannot be authenticated for its veracity in an objective sense. Indeed, memory is the site of struggle for competing meanings. Portelli has vividly demonstrated this point in his discussion of the ways in which the death in 1949 of a steel worker, Luigi Trastulli, was remembered. The written historical record shows that Trastulli was killed in that year in a confrontation with police during a factory stoppage in Umbria to protest the signing of the NATO treaty by the Italian government. Yet numerous oral testimonies gathered thirty years later from rank-and-file workers date Trastulli's death to the occasion when more than 2,000 workers were fired from the factory in 1953 which was followed by a walk-out and street fights. As Portelli explains, this misremembering of the date cannot be ascribed to numerous individual memory lapses; rather, it can be explained by the narrators shifting the death from a time and place that symbolised defeat and humiliation to a context where it could be explained as part of an event of which the workers could salvage some self-respect. 'The discrepancy between fact and memory', writes Portelli, 'ultimately enhances the value of the oral sources as historical documents. It is not caused by faulty recollections ... but actively and creatively generated by memory and imagination in order to make sense of crucial events and of history in general.'[10] To paraphrase Portelli, memory is about the relationship between material facts and personal subjectivity, and it is precisely that interplay between what we remember, how we remember and why we remember that is of such interest to oral historians.[11]

Some oral historians would not go so far as Portelli in celebrating the telling at the expense of the veracity of the content. Paul Thompson, for instance, worries that since we know that one cannot rely on an individual's memory of an event (as opposed to a memory of private experience) the historian should still attempt to verify what has been said 'and even then you should be sceptical about it'.[12] But maybe we do not always need to be as concerned as Thompson about the instability of memory. Oral historian Alice Hoffman tested the reliability of her husband Howard's memory of combat during the Second World War, using corroborating records to establish the validity of what he was able to recall. She found that although Howard was not able to accurately recall dates and some other detail, he was able to reliably remember and reconstruct his experiences 'and to amplify and extend the existing written record'.[13] The Hoffmans concluded that there are some memories that are permanent, resistant to degeneration, here described as 'archival memory'. These are memories of events deemed significant at the time and which have been consequently rehearsed and consolidated over time, ready for recall.[14] Thus events and experiences deemed significant at the time they were experienced are the most likely to be recalled accurately.

Today there is much more confidence amongst oral historians about the unique nature of their source and much less defensiveness. It is still too common for an oral historian to have to justify the use of memory sources to colleagues unfamiliar with or sceptical of oral history. But when this happens researchers are now able to say that an oral history source based on memory offers up insights into the interplay between the self and society, between past and present and between individual experience and the generalised account; in addition, it will often provide emotional content that a written version of the same story will not. For many research topics in twentieth-century history, the eliciting of oral histories based on personal memory is integral to our understanding and will perhaps become more so as the rise of electronic communication media – email, digital documents, text-messaging and mobile telephones – supersede the traditional written record.

Theory

Like all the theoretical frameworks discussed in this book, memory theory has been developed by a number of disciplines. Ideas from psychology, sociology, cultural anthropology and history have been drawn upon by oral historians, though it is fair to say that more recently the latter have played a role in developing their own theories about memory and remembering as a result of their practice. As practising oral historians we try to facilitate remembering. We are not particularly interested in unconnected fragments of experience; we are interested in the stories that our respondents create from their memories because it is meaning we are after, not just a litany of facts. Oral historians do not often consciously think about how the memory-retrieval process works in neuroscientific terms but it is worth knowing something about how people remember if only to help us unlock and then analyse memory narratives. We know that the memories we hear are not unadulterated recollections, that they are shaped by the context of the telling, amongst other things. The knowledge that there are different kinds of memory systems may help us to understand why some respondents can remember some things very well, such as everyday or habitual routines and events but are less able to recall others such as emotions.

The significance of memory cannot be understated. Memory is key to our identity; without our memory we have no social existence. We depend on our memory in order to conduct our daily lives. Amnesiacs, people who have lost their memories, are apt to say they have lost their life. According to the philosopher and novelist Umberto Eco, our memory of the past is essential to our ability to construct a sense of self; in other words, our identity is grounded in our memory of the past. In Eco's novel, *The Mysterious Flame of Queen Loana*, the central character suffers from partial amnesia. He is unable to remember who he is and his personal past is lost to him, but he has retained his 'textual memory' and can recall verbatim huge chunks of all the literature he has ever read.[15] In order to recover himself, he sets out on a quest to recover his past through texts of novels, comics and magazines. But he ultimately fails; the memory he recovers is not his personal memory but the memory of a generation. The message here is that without personal memory we are unable to satisfactorily construct a viable sense of self. Memory then is about the present as much as the past. It is 'that through which people interpret their lives and redesign the conditions of possibility that account for what they once were, what they have since become, and what they still hope to be'.[16] In other words, our memory is our roadmap: it tells us where we have been and aids us finding where we want to go. Although there have been contradictory views on this point, with some suggesting that an inability to recall the past is not necessarily a bar on constructing a viable self, most oral historians would concur with Eco's position.[17]

Oral historians don't need to know how memory works in a biological or neuroscientific sense.[18] But it is helpful to understand something of the different kinds of memory systems.

1   Semantic memory is the system that deals with factual and conceptual knowledge, a kind of reference book for names, places and facts rather than emotions.
2   Procedural memory is the system that facilitates the learning of skills and habits.
3   Working memory is the system that gets us through everyday life; it is short-term and instrumental, enabling us to remember a telephone number for long enough to make the call for example.
4   Episodic memory is the memory system that enables the recall of particular events or incidents (episodes) as a kind of 'mental time travel' whereby we remember not just the event itself but one's place within it.[19] The broad category of episodic memory is sometimes also called autobiographical memory, and it is the kind of memory most called upon in oral history interviews.
5   Flash-bulb memory (sometimes called vivid memory) is contained within episodic memory and refers to a memory that is captured in vivid detail – having photographic or visual quality. The event itself is often one of great personal significance and sometimes emotion.

Now let us look at how memory works. In a general sense, we only remember something that we have recorded or encoded at the time we experienced it, and what we record will always be partial and dependent upon a variety of factors such as our emotions at the time, our knowledge or interest base. So, for example, if I attend a football match with my football-obsessed friend, while he might remember the series of moves that lead up to the goal, I would be more likely to remember the conversation with the man sitting next to me. Our memories of the match would be quite different even though we had both experienced the same event. This encoding has to occur at a deep level in the brain for a memory to become fixed, and the information has to be associated with other meaningful knowledge in order for it to be remembered.[20] In order to remember the complex and numerous moves leading to the goal, my friend has, for instance, to understand the rules of the game, to identify the players involved and to possess memories of past matches involving this team.

The next stage in the remembering process is to retrieve those encoded fragments of experience. Generally what happens is that we remember something when we are prompted or cued to do so, that is when something jogs us into recollection (although we all experience those incidences when memories pop into our heads apparently unbidden). The best-known illustration of the cueing process appears in Marcel Proust's novel *In Search of Lost Time* when the narrator is prompted to remember when he tastes the little sponge cakes called madeleines. 'Undoubtedly what is thus palpitating in the depths of my being must be the image, the visual memory which, being linked to that taste, is trying to follow it into my conscious mind.'[21] It can be a particular smell that transports us back to a memory of an event or experience in childhood; a photograph likewise can prompt the retrieval of memories of the past, or a visit to a memorial or special place.[22] Annette Kuhn's autobiographical study, *Family Secrets*, offers an illuminating insight into the ways in which certain cues – in this case family photographs – can unlock a series of memory stories.[23] Photographs appear to trigger what is called a 'memory response': a reaction to the image which is emotional (the photo arouses flashbacks perhaps or even the recollection of feelings) and also one of reflective consideration.[24] The viewer uses the photograph as an aide-memoire to recall people, places and experiences. In the same manner, in the oral history interview our questions and sometimes just the topic of the interview act as the cueing mechanism, resulting in the respondent's retrieval of a series of memories which are then remembered and narrated.

Once the event or the experience has been recalled it is then ordered and shaped by the narrator; the bits and pieces of memory are linked together, and sense is made of them using our knowledge of what such an event or experience should look like – whilst at the same time being influenced by the context in which one is retrieving the memory. Schacter sums this up by saying 'when we remember, we complete a pattern with the best match available in memory, we do not shine a spotlight on a stored picture'.[25] Put another way, individual or autobiographical memories are not simply stored away and retrieved just like new but are newly constructed combining the information stored with the immediate situation.[26]

So what are the factors that influence what things we remember and how we remember them? In addition to the cue discussed above, it is clear that the environment in which the respondent finds him or herself when cued to remember will influence how the past is reconstructed. Few would now agree with Freud's position that it is possible to 'excavate the patient's "true" memories from the scattered debris of the past'.[27] Rather, psychoanalysts who conduct memory work with people accept that psychoanalysis creates a 'retrieval environment' that facilitates a reconstruction of the past.[28] Rather than an archaeology of memory, their work fosters re-creations of the past. In this environment the analyst or therapist creates the environment that permits remembering and then offers cues and responds to memories in ways that may unlock deeper or hitherto hidden experiences. Now, a distinction must be drawn between the medical and the historical. Oral historians are not psychoanalysts; we are more selfish in that we are trying to gain insight for ourselves rather than offering a talking cure to a patient. But we do attempt to create an environment in which the respondent feels comfortable, and we may have some stock questions or triggers which we hope will unlock memories in a more or less free conversation about the past. Beyond this, though, we are usually powerless to influence other aspects of the environment (which may include family dynamics, economic situation, and other variables) that may shape a person's remembering. In any event, oral historians are not, and should not aspire to be, therapists or doctors of the mind.

Finally, a point about misremembering (which is not the same as forgetting or lying). Experimental research has demonstrated that it is quite easy to induce subjects to make false reports.[29] And the results of research on eye-witnesses to crimes show likewise that a person may misremember a detail if they have been introduced by someone else to new or alternative information immediately after the event.[30] The implication is that the interviewer should be aware of the power to distort or at least shape the memories that are recalled. Research by those involved in witness testimony demonstrates that people are very susceptible to suggestion.

There are many other reasons that cause a person to misremember or to remember inaccurately. The 'prestige enhancing shift' is one: a person may exaggerate something in the past that presents them in a good or self-important light.[31] Research conducted on people's attitudes towards parti-cular issues in the past, such as abortion, or how they voted in a past election, showed that when people remembered inaccurately the error could be explained by the person's present beliefs; this was because people tend to reflect onto the past the attitudes they hold now.[32] Some interviewees may wish to put across a certain image of themselves which 'the facts' do not fit and thus either deliberately or unconsciously they tell fibs or at least a version of the story with which they feel comfortable. In the words of Julia Ruuttila, the union organiser at the centre of an article by Sandy Polishuk addressing this issue: 'Some of my errors were intentional. I was embarrassed by your questions. And I did not, and still do not, like to dwell on that painful period in my life.'[33]

Misremembering can also occur on a collective as well as a personal level. Amongst Jewish communities in Britain a common story is told about the arrival of first-generation Jews on British shores in the late nineteenth century. On disembarkation, so the story goes, people thought they were in America and were shocked to discover their true destination. 'When they came here they had no idea where they were landing. But they thought it was America, they never even knew, hadn't a clue!' reported a Glaswegian Jew of his parents arrival at the port of Greenock on the Scottish west coast.[34] This story of mistaken destination is widely told even today; it is useful in that it helps Jewish immigrants tell the moral tale that they want to tell – which is about survival and success against the odds in a place they didn't want to be.

The phenomenon known as 'false memory syndrome' is another con-troversial possibility to explain why people misremember. 'False memory syndrome' was a term coined by the False Memory Syndrome Foundation (a lobby group of professionals and accused parents) in 1992 and describes the theory that some adults who recall instances of sexual abuse from their childhood as a result of therapy are mistaken, that is, they are remembering things that did not occur. This theory is much disputed, with mainstream opinion broadly rejecting the existence of such a syndrome while accepting that memory is fallible and some people might be prompted to recall such events under the influence of suggestive therapy techniques.[35] Whilst not denying its possibility, there is currently little plausible reason for the oral historian to consider it as a tool in general historical research, and it should not be accepted as a valid criticism of oral history methodology.

Autobiographical memory

The description of how memory works in the last section applies to what is called autobiographical memory. We will consider later in this chapter the different case of what is called collective or popular memory.

Autobiographical memory has been described by W. F. Brewer as:

> memory for a specific episode from an individual's past. It typically appears to be a 'reliving' of the individual's phenomenal experience during the earlier moment. Thus these memories typically contain information about place, actions, persons, objects, thoughts, and affect ... They are accompanied by a belief that the remembered episode was personally experienced.[36]

So, autobiographical memory is, in simple terms, the events of one's life as they are personally reconstructed in the mind (rather than faithfully recalled). It follows that this reconstruction is dependent on the development of the self, that is, certain things, events, experiences will be remembered and reconstructed in different ways depending on the stage in one's life.[37] And in autobiographical accounts, such as a life history, we use memories in a number of ways: to explain an event to others, to illustrate our personal place in an event, as a guide to subsequent behaviour and as a means of reassurance.

It is autobiographical memory that past critics of oral history found so problematic on grounds of accuracy and its usefulness to historical explanation. This criticism was misplaced. There is little evidence to suggest that people generally misremember events or experiences and certainly not deliberately or consciously so. Even age does not appear to affect the veracity of memory. Overall, people retain memories over long periods of time with no significant memory loss. Rather, the quality, vividness and depth of an individual's memory of a specific event or experience will be dependant upon the encoding that happened at the time and the circumstances in which the remembering is taking place. It seems that people remember what is important to them. Some details might fade but the broad contours of the memory remain throughout life.

Yet, there is conflicting evidence about what people are *most likely* to remember. Some say that habitual or repetitive experiences are more likely to be held in the memory. For Trevor Lummis:

> The conditions of everyday life are firmly held in the memory and hardly distorted at all by later experiences or changes in attitude. Maybe this is the only field where oral history can be regarded as a direct way of tapping the past, although it still requires an interviewer who can open up informants' minds to those areas that they may otherwise take for granted or neglect.[38]

It certainly seems to be the case that when interviewed about the habits and routines of everyday life, even several decades in the past, many people are able to recall in considerable detail the things they carried out on a routine basis: their walk to school for instance, or the processes engaged in at the workplace. For example, Scottish women interviewed in the 1980s about their early work lives recalled at length and in great detail the individual components of the work roles they undertook – sometimes fifty years earlier. This was in spite of the fact that their jobs (as retail assistants and factory workers) had not been regarded as particularly skilled.[39] Mrs P.3, for example, born in 1904, described her job working on the carpet wool machine in a woollen mill:

> The spinning was a single thread, you see, and then it went to, maybe mixed with another two or three bobbins, to make it three ply or four ply, you see. And then that went on to a bigger thingmy. And then it went from there, on that twisting, and it went from there to the reeling, and it put on the reel and they made it into the hanks. This went round about on this big thing like a drum, and it went round about there; made it into hanks of wool. And they were tied up and weighed and then all put so many together. And then it went from there up to the second flat where I used to work. And you put it on a hook thing, and you pulled it out here, and twisted it round about, then put it like that, then. That was in a hank then, you see, made it into a hank of wool, like what you buy. You don't buy them in hanks now but it used to be in these days.[40]

This extract displays a common feature of oral testimony: the detailed recall of repetitious and skilful tasks in which the respondent had taken evident pride. Their identity is clearly closely associated with this memory. So, pride in a job as much as repetition contributes to the ability to remember the exact detail of mundane tasks.

Memory of a single event, and its personal or emotional experience for an individual, is less easy to recall. The memory system does not appear to be able to deal with the recall of emotion particularly well. The events and experiences that caused the emotion are more likely to be remembered; one exception is traumatic experiences which will be dealt with later in this chapter. The more emotion an event arouses in the present, the more likely a person is to recall the central details of the event. For instance, memories of major national or international events such the assassination of US President Kennedy in 1963 or the attack on the World Trade Center in New York in 2001 are generally remembered very accurately – both the event itself (usually as broadcast in the media) and the details of the place where the person heard the news. But it is much harder to recall the emotion that was engendered at the time. We can recall the cause of grief, distress, disgust or extreme pleasure, but the emotion itself is less easily accessed after the passage of time.[41] Negative or upsetting emotional feelings in particular are difficult to express in retrospect and gaps, and stuttered responses may result. Christine, one of my interviewees, tried to tell me how she felt at the age of eight upon arriving at an orphanage upon the death, in very quick succession, of both her parents:

> At eight you really don't – I remember [one of my cousins] coming up the stairs to me in the bedroom in the morning and saying 'you haven't got a mother or a father', I says 'I have got a mother, I haven't got a father', 'oh but there was a policeman at the door just now and told me your mother's died as well' and that's how I was told my mother was dead, isn't it awful? however from then I got back to Burghead because, I don't know how I got there but I remember seeing my Mum in her coffin, two pennies on her eyes so she must have, I just remember that ... As I says I suppose you're unhappy but you just don't, you just don't remember very much about it.[42]

A respondent, in order to retain composure, will find a way to talk about a difficult experience in order to avoid dealing with the emotions the recall might bring forth. In Christine's case we see a combination of matter-of-fact recall of events, a flashbulb memory and an inability to express in words the emotion she felt. In this regard, the will to retain composure moulds the articulation of memory.

So far, the focus has been on what we might call private memory. But the recall of personal experiences does not exist independently of public memory or the recall of more impersonal events. Oral historian Trevor Lummis suggests that most life-history interviews are a combination of personal and public memory. People structure their stories using a personal chronology, using personal and family events to shape their narratives, and only refer to wider public events when these had a significant impact upon them. Hence, interviewees who lived during wartime are often quite voluble on that event because the totality of the wartime experience impacted profoundly on people's personal lives, whereas more mundane public events such as a change of government had much less impact. Yet people do use notable events to cue their personal memories. In this extract, a woman recalled her memories of the First World War in Scotland:

Well, eh, that would be 1918 eh, 1914 to 18. Well, I would be nine years old when it started because I was born in 1905. I remember it, the first Zeppelin. I was at school, the German Zeppelin flew over Cambusbarron. The first plane that flew over, we got, we all got out of school to go and watch it landing down at a farm, a big field in a farm and it was great. It was exciting because the pilot just seemed to be sitting, was just like straps of wood, you know, and he was sitting outside, I can remember that as plain, <. . pause. .> and eh, then on Armistice Day, we, that would be four years after, eh, we all got a holiday at school and had great celebrations, you know.[43]

Her memories of living through the war years as a young girl are 'hooked' onto a public framework, but it is notable that whereas she recalled the airship in some detail her recollection of Armistice Day contains nothing that is personal – despite the fact that no doubt all British schoolchildren were given a holiday and enjoyed the celebrations of the end of the war.

Historian Annette Kuhn argues from the experience of her own 'memory work' that public and private are in fact often intertwined. 'If the memories are one individual's', she writes, 'their associations extend far beyond the personal. They spread into an extended network of meanings that bring together the personal with the familial, the cultural, the economic, the social and the historical.'[44] Moreover, she notes that what she calls 'memory texts' are not owned solely by the one who remembers – they are also shaped by collective acts of remembering.[45] So, for instance, my personal memory of summer seaside holidays as a child will be shaped not just by my own encoded fragments of memory but also by the remembering of other family members, family photographs and by more general public representations of seaside holidays in the UK in the 1960s and 1970s. The thousands of memories of the Second World War posted on the BBC's People's War website provide many examples of individual accounts of the war on the home and fighting fronts but are invariably also shaped by subsequent public representations of wartime: war films, television documentaries, museum displays and publications on the subject. The contribution of one man who was a child in London during the war nicely combines the intensely personal within a framework reminiscent of the more light-hearted filmic representations of the war. Here he recalls the atmosphere following the German invasion of France:

In May 1940 when the Germans broke through, I remember looking with apprehension at a map of France and the destruction of our army. With the debacle of Dunkirk we were prepared by the Government controlled radio with the idea that we might be invaded. All road signs were removed and anybody asking directions was automatically suspect. Tales of spies and German parachutists dressed up in nun's clothes abounded. I with my friends joined in the hunt and followed anyone who looked suspicious. Nuns were not frequently seen in Plumstead but any we met were subjected to being tailed. Although we were often sure we had uncovered nests of spies, we never got up sufficient pluck to report our misgivings to the local coppers.[46]

Here we can sense the mingling of public memory of the war with the individual's personal experiences. Like a landscape painting, we place ourselves as a speck on a much wider canvas.

None of these observations about how people shape their memories when converting them into speech in an interview deflect from the ultimate reliability of the autobiographical account and the historian's interest in it. By and large people do not *make up* stories for the researcher; they tell the past as it appears to them. And this is the source of interest for us. The vulnerability of memory is not a problem for the oral historian; it is an opportunity. It is for the researcher to work out why some memories are recalled and not others and how the memories might be shaped by public discourses and by the interview context.

Memory and ageing

Anecdotal evidence seems to suggest that as we age, our powers of recollection change. Memories of childhood and young adulthood may be recalled with greater sharpness by older respondents, whereas short-term memory – what they did yesterday – seems to dim. Yet research into the relationship between ageing and memory demonstrates that in fact memory functions do not necessarily deteriorate with age as long as the subject remains healthy.

When older adults were asked to report 'flashbulb memories', that is, memories for which the subjects held vivid images, the highest percentage of reported memories clustered in the age range twenty-one to thirty.[47] Indeed, the apparent ability of the elderly to recall their younger days with acuity and at some length may be explained by two factors: first, memories of one's young adult years tend to be the most stable, and, second, older adults have a better ability to narrate the past than younger people. At the same time, research with older adults demonstrated that around 80 per cent of reported memories in response to prompt-word tests were from the recent past. However, the phenomenon of 'life review', a reminiscing about the past, does appear to be more common amongst those in late old age. Indeed, since the 1960s life review or reminiscence has been regarded as a positive part of ageing, whereas it had hitherto been seen as a sign of cognitive deterioration.[48] Given that older people tend to be the stock-in-trade of the oral historian, these observations by neuroscientists and cognitive psychologists are helpful. There is no reason to think that an older person's memory is less acute or reliable than that of a younger person. Whatever our age, we remember what is important to us.[49]

Memory and gender

There is no evidence from memory tests that women and men have different memory functions; all the evidence points to any differences that do exist to be due to differences at the stage of encoding.[50] And women and men probably encode in different ways as a result of gendered socialisation.

Anecdotally, oral historians will sometimes say that women are better talking about family life than men and that they have a better recall for names and dates relating to family events. One of my research students conducting interviews about home life in the 1950s and 1960s has discovered that women's recall of domestic life and home interiors appears to be more detailed and vivid than that of men. This may be because men had other preoccupations such as work and social life and spent less time in the home, hence their memories are less detailed. Alternatively, the male respondents may not feel empowered to talk with authority about the home as a consequence of gender-role stereotypes that made the home 'a woman's place', especially if they are interviewed alongside their partner who looked after the domestic space.[51] In a study that asked husbands and wives to answer a number of questions about the history of their relationship, women demonstrated much more vivid and detailed memories (such as of their first date) than men. Moreover, the men agreed that their wives were much better able to remember details about incidents in their past.[52] This difference is cultural. Women are generally the 'relationship experts' in Western culture; they have been socialised to pay attention to intimate relationships, they are the ones who stay in touch with relatives, and this may also explain why women in many families tend to be the ones who remember key family events such as birthdays and anniversaries. There is also some evidence to indicate that women are better able to talk about their feelings and emotions than men but again this may merely reflect gendered socialisation patterns than any concrete difference in the ways the male and female memory operates in a cognitive sense.[53]

There is a significant amount of evidence to show that there are marked gender differences in the degree to which men and women use reported speech in their narratives suggesting that women are perhaps better at remembering dialogue than men. But in fact while the phenomenon does seem to hold water, there is no evidence to suggest that women's facility for reporting speech is based on their accurate recollection of what was said. That is to say, female preferences for quoting conversations and dialogue as in 'I said and then he said' has nothing to do with the way in which memory works and much more to do with social and cultural differences in the use of language. In short, women 'conceive of communication as a co-operative activity, and men view communication as a competitive activity'.[54] To quote Deborah Tannen, 'dialogue makes story into drama and listeners into an interpreting audience to the drama'.[55] Thus the use of reported speech in narratives is a device more often employed by women than men to create an inclusive interpretive community. It seems to have little to do with memory.

Similarly, research shows that women tend to place themselves as the subject within a web of relationships in their narrations (using 'we' or 'us') whereas men tell a story with themselves at the centre (using 'I' or 'me'). This perhaps tells us more about the ways in which men and women choose to narrate their memories rather than what they remember.[56] Or are there differences in the ways men and women encode their memories of events, with men largely positioning themselves at the centre of worldly events while women position themselves as central to family and domestic events? Marilyn Cohen's oral history interviews with Northern Irish working-class women, and Elizabeth Roberts' with women in the north-west of England, show that women located themselves within a web of relationships with kin, neighbours and the wider community and that their memories highlight mutual dependence and reciprocity.[57] But this gendered form of recollection may be receding in the twenty-first century. As women's roles in economic, political and public life have increased, it is to be expected that male–female differences may be diminishing.

Memory and trauma

Some people have traumatic memories. They may witness deaths in accidents, earthquakes, floods, murders, genocides or wars. And many experience rather more everyday traumatic events such as the death of a loved one, which may also prompt complexities in remembering.

Oral historians have worked with survivors of trauma. These include events with global consequences such as the Holocaust of 1941–5 in which at least 6 million people were systematically murdered by Nazi Germany, and the terrorist attack on the World Trade Centre in New York in 2001 in which more than 3,000 people died. They include traumatic events with more localised effects such as that experienced in New Orleans following Hurricane Katrina in 2005 in which 1,900 died, the Hillsborough disaster in England of 1989 in which ninety-six people died in a spectator crush at a football match broadcast live on television, and the Dunblane massacre in Scotland in 1996 in which sixteen primary-school children and one teacher were shot dead by a lone gunman. This kind of oral history interviewing is not for the faint-hearted because of the sheer intensity of the grief. Certainly, the inexperienced practitioner is not advised to attempt this. The circumstances are fraught, complex and could result in a catastrophic error of judgement that brings additional grief to all those involved. But it is important for us to reflect here upon the special features of trauma oral history in relation to memory.

Oral historians, while conscious of the sensitivity required and the ethical issues which undoubtedly arise when working with people who may have been traumatised by what they have witnessed, argue that first-hand accounts not only present an authentic picture of an event and its human impact but may also help participants reflect on their experiences as a first step on the road to recovery. Stephen Sloan sums up these considerations in the context of

conducting oral history interviews with the survivors in the immediate aftermath of Hurricane Katrina:

> A primary consideration in an interview project so soon after the occur-
> rence is the ubiquitous truth that the experience is raw. Devastation, both
> emotion and physical, is palpable ... People are hurting, confused, and
> unsettled. Composure is often elusive and emotions can be overpowering.
> Residents are in the process of trying to understand what happened while
> beginning the slow course of mending.[58]

Bearing this in mind, there is general agreement that traumatic experiences
are remembered differently from the everyday. But there is disagreement as to
the precise relationship between trauma and memory.[59] In some cases, a particularly emotional event may be recalled with great vividness and accuracy;
in others, the subject may be unable to recall the detail or to provide a
coherent narrative. There are clearly subconscious factors at work here.
Some people repress difficult or painful memories as a protective or survival
mechanism. In the First World War, soldiers refusing to fight any more were
initially regarded as cowards (and some were executed by military tribunal),
but late in the conflict it became seen as a medical condition known as 'shell
shock'. Nowadays, the syndrome is known as post-traumatic stress disorder
(PTSD), a severe and ongoing emotional reaction to an extreme psychological trauma in which one's own, or someone else's, life is threatened. This may
explain why some people are either unable to remember trauma or conversely
recall it in all its appalling detail. Cultural constraints can muffle or silence
the memories of those who experienced traumatic events. For instance, veterans of the Second World War often adopted 'silent coping strategies' when
they returned home and were rarely diagnosed as suffering from any psychological disorder.[60]

   What is clear is that the memory narratives produced by trauma survivors
are different from conventional stories, largely because the respondents have
still to come to terms with what happened to them in the past; recalling our
earlier chapter, they haven't attained, or possibly even sought to attain, composure. Oral history of trauma is often conducted soon after the event, not
decades later, and the experience survivors felt has not yet been fully assimi-
lated and reviewed. This may prevent them from producing a mature or
coherent memory narrative. Their accounts may be verbally disjointed, deeply
emotional and disturbing to narrator and listeners alike. Using the language
of the psychologists, such survivors have not achieved closure. According to
Dori Laub who was himself a Holocaust survivor who worked with other
survivors: 'Trauma survivors live not with memories of the past, but with an
event that could not and did not proceed through to its completion, has no
ending, attained no closure, and therefore, as far as its survivors are concerned, continues into the present and is current in every respect.'[61] Such a
response to trauma is illustrated in interviews with French Jewish survivors of

the Holocaust whose parents had died. They spoke of the fact that at the time they had not been sure of their parents' deaths and had been unable to grieve. Even in old age they still carried 'a hurt so painful, so omnipresent, so all-encompassing, that it seems impossible to talk about it even a lifetime later'.[62] The survivor is trapped, and only some form of therapeutic treatment can facilitate the reconstruction of the traumatic event in an attempt to reach closure. We should take care not to assume that the oral history interview might fulfil this role. The South African Truth and Reconciliation Commission after the fall of apartheid showed that allowing stories to be told, and reliving memories, does not necessarily lead to closure because the big historical problems remain unresolved, and the consequences can be to prolong emotional agony and revitalise antagonisms.[63]

The extent to which memory and the process of remembering may be affected by trauma can be analysed by looking at two elements: veracity or reliability, and the ability to recall emotion. Doubting the reliability of memory of trauma survivors can seem insensitive. Often the events being recalled are distant and difficult to express in words. We should expect such testimony to contain some inaccuracies without compromising the value of the testimony as a whole. And as one scholar notes, 'since testimonies are human documents rather than merely historical ones, the troubled interaction between past and present achieves a gravity that surpasses the concern with accuracy'.[64] There is no evidence that trauma survivors are more likely than anyone else to misremember events. But, as Mark Roseman shows in his sensitive and illuminating analysis of the testimony of Marianne Ellenbogen, a Holocaust survivor, attention to accuracy or discrepancies between a personal account and contemporaneous records can reveal something about that person's attempts to deal with the trauma. In Marianne's case, the discrepancies discovered by Roseman were all related to the moments of intense trauma (in Marianne's case her escape before her family and fiancé were deported from Germany to Poland). In turn this trauma instigated feelings of intense guilt. Roseman suggests that the small discrepancies in her testimony (for instance stating that she spent the last night with her fiancé when it was clear from other sources that she did not) were an attempt to cope with this guilt. Marianne was trying to impose some control on a memory which could not otherwise be borne. 'The details were not so important', writes Roseman. 'What was important was not to be exposed quite so powerlessly and passively to an unbearable past.'[65]

The oral historian might expect such traumatic experiences to be recalled by respondents with great emotion; in fact the attempt to elicit accounts of this kind often trigger emotional responses. Roseman recounts how one of his respondents burst into tears on seeing photographs of his brother who had died at the hands of the Nazis – he had no photographs of his own. Yet there is much evidence to show that many trauma survivors recount their experiences 'matter-of-factly', without much emotion.[66] This detachment is a coping mechanism that distances the narrator from the events. But, as was noted earlier in this chapter, it is difficult, if not impossible, to recall emotion as it was experienced. James says: 'The revivability in memory of the emotions ... is very small. We can remember that we underwent grief or rapture but not just how the grief or rapture felt.'[67] While memory for an emotion-inducing event might be quite accurate in terms of information, memory for the emotion felt at the time is likely to be inaccurate or at least very difficult to articulate. So perhaps we should be wary in an oral history interview of asking a respondent, 'and how did you feel?' The answer we receive may only be a description of the event or at the most a best effort to recall the emotion expressed at the time.

The extensive oral history work conducted with survivors of trauma is testament to the skill and empathy displayed by researchers who are persuaded that it is valuable for survivors to tell their stories. Working with veterans of the Second World War, Hunt and Robbins concluded that 'the veteran is someone who has been traumatised and has developed a narrative about his traumatic experience, someone who needs to talk about the experience in order to deal with the memories ... only through narrative development will they find peace with their memories.'[68] But people relating stories about a traumatic event may find it difficult to tell the story or even to make it coherent to themselves, let alone an interviewer. As Barclay says from his experience of working with Holocaust survivors, 'there are no known narrative structures than can be used as referents from which to reconstruct traumatic experiences like those associated with the daily experience of seeing others selected and exterminated'.[69] The result of being unable to tell the story of one's past (not because one cannot remember but because there are no frameworks to contain and order the memories) is 'the construction of fragmented personal histories, and isolated moments of horrible and unspeakable knowledge'.[70] Chapter 6, which analyses the narrative structures inherent in memory stories, will look at this facet of oral histories in more detail.

Collective memory

The concept of collective memory (sometimes termed social memory) has proved to be of immense importance to oral historians in aiding our understanding of how individual memories are constructed.

The term 'collective memory' was coined by sociologist Maurice Halbwachs in his book *On Collective Memory* published in 1950. He argued that individuals use social frameworks when they remember; that is, 'individual memory is a part or even an aspect of group memory'.[71] He elaborated:

> We can understand each memory as it occurs in individual thought only if we locate each within the thought of the corresponding group. We cannot properly understand their relative strength and the ways in which they combine within individual thought unless we connect the individual to the various groups of which he is simultaneously a member.[72]

In simple terms, Halbwachs was suggesting that an individual's memory is always situated within a collective or group consciousness of an event or experience. Memory might feel personal to us, but it is always influenced by shared memories, whether at a family, community or even national level. Furthermore, for Halbwachs, the function of memory is to unite us socially, which means that commonly agreed upon memories will tend to predominate and alternative ones will receive little recognition and therefore fade.

For Halbwachs and some of his followers, individual memory or consciousness was inseparable from the collective. 'The very language and narrative patterns that we use to express memories, even autobiographical memories, are inseparable from the social standards of plausibility and authenticity they embody.'[73] This means that individual memories are recalled using the language and frameworks deemed acceptable or understandable in society or within the group with which the individual identifies. So, for example, memory stories told by gays and lesbians might be framed within the 'coming out' narrative, women who grew up in the 1960s might tell their stories within the framework of women's emancipation. But as Fentress and Wickham state, this leaves the problem of 'how individual consciousness might relate to those of the collectivities those individuals actually made up', so that we are left with a 'concept of collective consciousness curiously disconnected from the actual thought processes of any particular person'.[74] To be fair, Halbwachs was not asserting that there was no such thing as individual memory or that individual or autobiographical memory could not exist independently of collective memory, but rather that 'the framework of collective memory confines and binds our most intimate remembrances to each other'.[75] It is the relationship between the autobiographical and the collective that has drawn the attention of oral historians used to collecting individual memories or groups of individual memories, but aware that these are framed and shaped by external influences including collective remembrances of the past. The result is that for the oral historian the concept of collective memory makes sense to us, but our experience interviewing respondents on an intimate basis prevents us from seeing how their narratives may merely be an expression of a collective consciousness.

Helpfully there are a number of theoretical middle ways that acknowledge the concept of collective memory and its power to shape or frame personal reminiscences but that also recognise the uniqueness and the authenticity of individual memory – and the struggle between the two. In 1982, the term 'popular memory' was coined by the Popular Memory Group in Britain as a means of identifying the relationship between the personal and the collective. They argued that popular memory involves the production of memory of the past in which everyone is involved and which everyone has an opportunity to reshape. While they recognise that at any point in time some representations of the past have greater power or dominance, they posited that no public representation can ever be 'monolithically installed or everywhere believed in'.[76] Indeed, there are always struggles over representations of the past involving dominant, subordinate and marginalised groups, but there is always a reciprocal relationship between private and public memory. They explained it thus:

> [Popular memory] is a necessarily *relational* study. It has to take in the dominant historical representation in the public field as well as attempts to amplify or generalise subordinated or private experiences. Like all struggles it must have two sides. Private memories cannot, in concrete studies, be readily unscrambled from the effects of dominant historical discourses. It is often these that supply the very terms by which a private history is thought through ... Similarly the public discourses live off the primary recording of events in the course of everyday transactions and take over the practical knowledge of historical agents.[77]

Here then we have a theoretical model that allows for both personal or individual memory and for a recognition of its constitutive effect on popular memory and vice versa. At the same time, though, this theoretical position acknowledges the relations of power that exist in the realm of popular-memory formation. History-making, or the construction of views of the past in any society, is the product of a struggle for dominance of a particular interpretation of an event or period. And when a hegemonic view emerges it generally excludes or mutes alternative or counter interpretations. Those who hold alternative interpretations have difficulty narrating or expressing their memories because they cannot fit them into the dominant narrative, the collective memory. So in the past marginalised groups were often silenced because their memories did not coincide with the dominant or hegemonic version of history. This can apply on an individual basis as Alistair Thomson's work with Fred Farrall demonstrates (discussed in detail in the previous chapter), or on a group basis.[78]

Collective or popular memory is not static. Dominant interpretations of the past shift and alter as formerly marginalised voices are heard and incorporated. This is where oral history can play a part in the struggle over memory. In a recent study of memories of the so-called 'Winter of Discontent' in 1978–9, when Britain was paralysed by industrial action, Tara Martin has shown how subsequent media and political re-readings of the period have helped to shape a collective memory of that time as a 'depository of different events across 1974–85 that collectively signified the bad old days of socialism'.[79] And yet in interviews with those who were labour activists during the years of political and economic turmoil Martin highlights an undercurrent of memories, what she describes as a 'subterranean memory' that contrasts with the meanings commonly ascribed to that era in public discourse. Individual countermemories, especially those of women involved in union activity, portray the period as a time when women especially were able to make advances in what had hitherto been the 'man's world' of the labour movement.

Similarly, the history of the Women's Liberation Movement in Britain in the 1970s is the subject of a struggle between representations: a dominant representation of the women's movement as angry man-hating 'bra-burners' created in large part by the media, a second and generally heroic story told by some of the leading feminist figures in memoirs, and more recently a third type of recollection based on the local and family struggles of rank-and-file feminists.[80] The contest over memory in this case concerns not so much what happened but rather the meaning. For the media today, the Women's Liberation Movement is often and lazily equated still with a particularly 'unattractive' form of radical feminism, a representation that bears little relation to memory in any form. For the former leading activists, memory confirms their version of events which pivots around public meetings, conferences, publications and political and ideological confrontation, sometimes on an international level. Grass-roots sympathisers, on the other hand, hold personal memories of their town or village, which may confront the versions conveyed by the media and former leading lights and which simultaneously convey very personal experiences of intellectual and material engagement with the women's movement. In this way, there is no single 'collective memory' that has risen to dominance; rather, the memory of the women's movement is tending to become more fractured as the ordinary membership are given a voice by new researchers.

Collective memory often transmutes into what is called 'public memory'. This is a term used to refer to the ways in which events or experiences are commemorated or memorialised in public (sometimes under the auspices of the State and sometimes through media presentations), thereby reinforcing a particular version of the past. When this stage has been reached the tension between individual memory and collective memory may become even more acute. In the case of Australia's public commemoration of Anzac Day as a day of public patriotism based upon the celebration of the Australian 'digger', Thomson showed how this public remembrance could at once function in an affirmative way for some veterans but for others like Fred Farrall it created a deep sense of unease.[81] In Britain, the annual ritual of public commemoration of past wars on Remembrance Sunday creates a public image of who is acknowledged as worthy of remembrance. The exclusion, until very recently, of women veterans who worked in the Land Army and the so-called Bevin Boys, men called up to work in the mines in the Second World War, meant that members of these groups had no affirmative framework for their memories of the war years.[82] A similar situation was experienced by Caribbean soldiers who fought for Britain, who were shocked to discover that British people were largely ignorant of this fact.[83] In the case of the Home Guard, Britain's civil defence force in the Second World War, Summerfield and Peniston-Bird show how men's oral testimony of Home Guard experiences was shaped by official public rhetoric which accentuated the notion of the people's war as a time of national unity, when everyone was required to 'do their bit'.[84] But memories were also reflected through the prism of media representations of the Home Guard in the form of the very popular television series *Dad's Army*, which portrayed the Home Guard in a humorous and satirical light. The authors show how, for some respondents, the series 'cramped the possibilities of reminiscence' while for others it provided a framework for recall.[85]

Application

How has memory theory been invoked by oral historians? Most obviously, they have largely moved on from merely accessing people's memories, treating them as a storehouse of facts, in order to reconstruct the past. Rather they are more likely to be interested in *how* the past is remembered. In this enterprise they are shadowing the much bigger 'turn to memory' in historical research, an enterprise which incorporated interest in commemoration, representation, memorialisation and 'bearing witness'.[86] This is what has been described as a cultural history of remembering, a complex interweaving of personal memory with historical memory. Oral historians are at the sharp end of creating and writing this kind of cultural history because they are active in the work of creating memory stories and thereafter making these memories public, what Linda Hamilton describes as 'making memory social'.[87] At the heart of this work is the relationship between personal and social, private and public memory. Intrinsic to almost all oral history interviews is the interplay between individual memory and collective or social memory.

The relationship between individual and collective memory

Theories of collective and popular memory have been immensely useful to oral historians seeking to interpret the ways in which individuals recall the past mainly because as historians, although we are interested in people's personal memories we want to be able to use these to paint a larger canvas. But there have always been concerns about losing sight of the individual. Popular memory theory, as we have seen, proposed one way of dealing with this. The concept of social memory as proposed by Fentress and Wickham is another. For them, there is a process by which individual memory becomes social – 'the *action* of speaking or writing about memories'.[88] The very process of remembering is active, whether it is via the recital of a poem or a folktale or the recall of a shared experience. This is precisely the point made by anthropologist Julie Cruikshank in her studies of the stories told by people in Canada's Yukon. Their narratives are systems of knowledge which are embedded within the social and which sustain it.[89] This can operate at a local or a national level. Reminiscence work amongst the elderly, oral history work with immigrant groups and large-scale national projects such as the BBC's memories of the Second World War website can all serve the same purpose, facilitating a process of remembering that feeds into a big conversation about the past.

The trend amongst oral historians to emphasise cultural context over individual remembering has, however, been subject to criticism. The reference in some of this work to cultural scripts or templates by which individual memory is shaped strikes the critics as problematic, leaving 'little space for the consciously reflective individual, or for the role of experience in changing the ways in which individuals view the world'.[90] The criticism is not so much of the theoretical insights being employed by oral historians but the way in which they have allegedly been utilised in a too dogmatic or determinist manner. Anna Green, for instance, objects to what she regards as the rigid deployment of cultural, social and psychoanalytic theories in a 'culturally determinist' way, thereby reinforcing 'the notion that individuals' memories conform to dominant cultural scripts or unconscious psychic templates, and are recalled within the constraints of "particular publics"'.[91] She goes on to say that it is thus too easy for theorists to downplay the significance of individual remembering and to 'subsume it within the concept of collective memory'.[92] In a more measured response to what he sees as the dominance of a cultural constructionism (in this case in respect of masculinity studies), Michael Roper seeks a more balanced approach to the relationship between biographical experience and cultural scripts which creates a space for the emotional and the subjective in human experience.[93] Certainly, the social world and within that, language, have an impact on the way an individual experiences and expresses his or her subjectivity.

The task for the oral historian is to figure out how the interaction between personal and public occurs. In some instances the memory frame or template which helps shape a memory story is quite a rigid one; in others it is still fluid. Michael Frisch cites the example of eliciting oral histories of the Vietnam War in the USA. In the 1980s, the experience was still relatively raw, and public or media representations offered a variety of positions which meant that the issue of how to place memories within a story frame was quite problematic.[94] The current preoccupation in Western Europe and North America with the 1960s offers a similar example. Not all oral history respondents are able to fit their memories into the stereotypical 1960s story as beloved of the media (sexual liberation, music festivals and political protest). Conversely the story of the Second World War on the home front in Britain has been repeatedly rehearsed in all representational forms from documentary to feature film to novel and internet discussion board so that it is not difficult for an individual to find a way of framing their personal story. The ongoing process of recovering the home-front experience in the public realm in Britain, from officially sanctioned events such as the seventieth-anniversary marking of Operation Pied Piper, the evacuation of children from threatened cities to the countryside, and the very popular television dramatisation of an ordinary woman's experiences based on her Mass Observation diary, have offered up new frames for memory work for those whose wartime experiences have perhaps hitherto been downgraded.[95]

There is a distinction to make here between collective memory and historical memory. Historical memory, following Halbwachs, is a memory (or a representation) of a past that is lost, whereas collective memory is anchored in the social group that actively preserves and reinterprets the past via the consciousness of those who are still alive. The distinction might be illustrated in the context of the Holocaust. A collective memory exists amongst the few survivors who can still remember based on their lived experience. A historical memory of the Holocaust also exists amongst later generations for whom the events are a 'learned historical experience' informed by a variety of narratives conveyed in the printed and visual media.[96] However, in the case of the Northern Ireland conflict between the 1960s and 1998 it is harder to distinguish between collective and historical memory because the conflict is still so present in some people's day-to-day lives. Graham Dawson describes how a generation born after the early years of the Troubles 'lay claim to a personal memory of events that took place before they were born'.[97] In the words of a poem about Bloody Sunday, 'I remember the lies. / And I wasn't even born.'[98] In this context, the shared memory of the Catholic community of Derry has had such a powerful impact on those growing up within it that they have adopted the memories as their own and seek to ensure that these memories (and the victims) are not forgotten.

A distinction should also be drawn between collective memory and official memory. The latter may be defined as a public (and often government approved) interpretation of a particular event or experience often expressed in commemorative acts or representations such as museum displays or popular histories in the form of school textbooks for instance, or television series. Official memory is often a rather simplistic and unambiguous version of the past, often upholding a patriotic position.[99] Commemoration, as historian John Gillis argues, involves the 'coordination of individual and group memories, whose results may appear consensual when they are in fact the product of processes of intense contest, struggle, and in some instances, annihilation'.[100] Pierre Nora's concept of sites of memory (*lieux de memoire*) has also been influential in our understanding of official memory. For this French historian, a site of memory is something – a memorial, a museum, even an archive – which has become a symbolic element in a community's memorial heritage. The impact of the site of memory is, according to Nora, to fix memory in that it represents a selective and static version of the past. Unlike collective memory then, which may frame personal recollection but which is not determinist, official memory has the potential to muffle and even silence individual accounts which do not coincide with the official representation.

The starkest example of the power of official memory is the case of totalitarian regimes which have the power to suppress not just the public articulation of memories that contradict or challenge official accounts of the past but also the ability to remember at all. In Passerini's words, 'there is nothing left to transmit if nobody is there to receive the message'.[101] Orlando Figes' study of private life in the Soviet Union offers an insight into what happens when personal and family memories conflicted with the values of the regime. Figes notes, 'family history was a forbidden zone of memory – something they would never talk or write about'.[102] Before the advent of Glasnost (openness) in 1986, memory in Soviet Russia was dangerous; people were literally afraid to remember – even amongst close family members – at a time when history was rewritten.[103]

However, in more liberal political contexts, official memory exists in a much more fluid relationship with personal memory. In his study of the murder of 335 Italians by German soldiers at the Fosse Ardeatine in Rome in 1944 in retaliation for an attack by partisans that killed thirty-three German policemen, Portelli demonstrates how the *lieu de memoire,* in this case a tomb containing the graves of the murdered men, far from fixing or repressing memory actually evokes conflicting emotions and memories. The memorial has been used in variety of ways by different groups – Communists, religious groups, politicians, the military, school parties – and by the families of the murdered men. Portelli explains how the memorial and the annual commemoration ceremony became a site of tension as the families resented the usurpation of their memories by the State's official rituals.[104] In addition, over time the public symbolic function of the memorial has shifted from being a national symbol of the nation's resistance to fascism to, in the post-Cold War era, a memorial that has been incorporated into the much wider memorialisation of the Holocaust (many of the victims were Jewish). For the younger generation of Italians in the 1990s, the 'memory' of the massacre at the Ardeatine caves had become part of the Holocaust narrative. In the words of one young man, 'Fosse Ardeatine – I don't have much memory. Yes, I did study it in school: the deportation and then the concentration camps, the ovens, *Schindler's List* … '[105] His words demonstrate that the commemoration of the massacre had been subsumed into a Second World War narrative dominated by the Holocaust.

The relationship between individual and collective memory is not a one-way street. Personal memories are not and cannot always be subsumed within a collective narrative. Graham Smith advocates the analysis of individual memory as the product of an active engagement with social processes, in particular the process of talking, reconstructing experiences with others, sharing a language to recollect past experiences. Using the concept of 'transactive memory', defined as 'the combination of individual minds and the communication among them', Smith analysed a series of group interviews or discussions in which this process could be observed.[106] He concludes that while the process of memory-sharing illustrates in some instances the power of cultural discourses within which people fit their individual stories, this is not the only way in which individuals remember. People may also articulate alternative or oppositional accounts. The example is given of Ruby whose wartime experiences in the Auxiliary Territorial Service fitted nicely into public accounts of wartime solidarity and comradeship but whose account of an unhappy marriage was less easy to express within the frame of a cultural script. The two accounts existed side by side within the same 'transactive conversation', with Ruby consenting to the group construction of the war as a time of female emancipation and autonomy while also articulating a personal account of a marriage which was hard to fit into any existing discourse.[107]

As is often the case, the historian who can lead us through this conflicting position is Alessandro Portelli. For him, individual memory and collective memory coexist, with individual memory often the means by which people challenge dominant narratives and collective memories which may have been promoted to support particular ends. Portelli writes:

> If all memory were collective, one witness could serve for an entire culture – but we know that it is not so. Each individual ... derives memories from a variety of groups, and organises them in idiosyncratic fashion. Like all human activities, memory is *social* and may be *shared* ... however ... it only materialises in individual recollections and speech acts. It becomes *collective* memory only when it is abstracted and detached from the individual.[108]

So, individual memory for Portelli is not *dependent* upon collective memory; the two have a relationship. In Portelli's analysis of the memories of another Second World War tragedy for Italians, the 1944 massacre at Civitella Val di Chiana in Tuscany when German occupying soldiers murdered 115 civilian men in retaliation for an attack by partisans, he shows how memory of the massacre is divided. The official or institutional memory commemorates the actions of the Italian Resistance, and the victims are represented as heroic martyrs. The memory of the survivors or the community is personal and focuses on the loss of their brothers, fathers and husbands and, crucially, blamed the partisans rather than the Germans for the massacre thereby setting itself in opposition to official commemoration. But Portelli demonstrates that what really exists is a 'fragmented plurality of different memories' not merely divided between official and communal but internally socially and politically divided.[109]

Practice

How might reflection on memory mould new oral history practice? Principally, the practitioner is no longer concerned with the primacy of infallibility in memory but in its creative functions. Ultimately, what the oral historian is interested in is whether a respondent can remember events and experiences that are significant to him or her, not whether they have a good memory per se. We must be aware though that what is significant to an individual may change over time and thus what is remembered and how it is remembered will also change. To quote Valerie Yow, 'as historians we can work only with the memories that can be translated into words and thereby made conscious'.[110] Furthermore, we can only work with the memories that are told to us, not with those that are withheld, either deliberately or unconsciously.

In the interview situation the oral historian is a facilitator; we ask questions, provide prompts or cues, demonstrate interest and empathy, all in order to encourage a respondent to access their memory and convert their memories into a narrative. Some respondents achieve this with ease, seemingly possessing memory stories that are easily accessible, stories they have told a number of times. Others require help from the interviewer. It is sometimes possible to literally 'see' or hear a person accessing their memory store; when asked a question they are not expecting they will have to search around in their memory to find an answer. This is often flagged by the respondent grappling for the right words, in pausing, making false starts and disjointed sentences. Yet the oral historian now can work constructively with all of this. All of it is meaningful for analysis: the silences, the gaps which signify forgetting (conscious or unconscious), the inability to translate memories into a coherent narrative or a sign that an interviewee does not wish to discuss a particular topic. Evasion is the most common response in the last instance, a polite way for an interviewee to indicate that he or she is uncomfortable answering a question. The researcher cannot always know the reason, but we can observe the existence of evasion and hazard an explanation.

Luisa Passerini's observation of the silence of Italian workers on the topic of the Fascist era – analysed as a self-censorship – alerted oral historians more widely to the vicissitudes of memory: 'Oral sources refuse to answer certain kinds of questions; seemingly loquacious, they finally prove to be reticent or enigmatic, and like the sphinx they force us to reformulate problems and challenge our current habits of thought.'[111] Passerini describes the variety of silences that may be 'heard' in an oral history narrative. They range from personal silences or repressed memories to the silence of a people and a kind of collective or official silence which in turn may have consequences for personal remembrance. The Roma are cited as an example of the silence of a people, a group persecuted by the Nazis but who have responded by not speaking, by not engaging in the kind of 'monumental remembrance' adopted by the Jewish people. The French government's silence on the repression of a demonstration against the Algerian War in 1961 when scores died at the hands of the police is an instance where 'imposed amnesia' effectively silenced the eye-witnesses.[112] The war-widows of Guatemala's 'La Violencia', a period of state-sanctioned war against that country's rural indigenous population between 1978 and 1985 have been silenced by their refusal to accept the government's version of the war, while at the same time they do speak about their experiences in exclusively female safe spaces where they employ language and gestures not understood by outsiders to their culture.[113] Similarly, the British government's silence on the events of Bloody Sunday in Derry in Northern Ireland in 1972 for a long time muted the accounts of the survivors and the victims' families. Graham Dawson argues that it was only when a book was published in 1992 documenting the life stories of those affected that the experiences that had been hidden within families could be brought into the open.[114]

Conclusion

Oral historians are not psychoanalysts or psychotherapists who aim to discover the obstacles to a person's memory and, by analysing these, to effect a
cure. Neither are we trained to understand why a person has repressed particular memories or to react appropriately when uncomfortable memories rise
to the surface. The best we can do is to create an environment in which a
respondent can call up memories in a state of comfort, to provide the cues to
the recall of memories which aid us in our research. Most respondents will do
their very best to remember; they may struggle to recall detail and may have
difficulties with chronology, but they come to the interview prepared to
remember in a helpful way. The interviewer's task is to facilitate their
remembering and then, in our analysis, to consider the various influences that
have shaped their recall. The important point here is that memory is not just
a source; it is a narrator's interpretation of their experience and as such it is
complex, creative and fluid.

6   Narrative

Introduction

The term 'narrative' has become ubiquitous in oral history in recent years. We speak increasingly of narrators instead of interviewees or respondents, and of narratives instead of answers or responses. This chapter aims to clarify what is meant by narrative and narrative analysis as formulated by linguists and literary scholars and then employed by oral historians.

Narrative is one of the ways by which people make sense of experience and communicate it to others.[1] A narrative is an ordered account created out of disordered material or experience. In theorist Hayden White's words: 'So natural is the impulse to narrate, that the form [narrative] is almost inevitable for any report of how things happened, a solution to the problem of how to translate *knowing* into *telling*.'[2] Narrative is fundamental to the ways we recall the experience of our lives, including to ourselves. For Barbara Hardy narrative is all-encompassing: 'We dream in narrative, day-dream in narrative, remember, anticipate, hope, despair, believe, doubt, plan, revise, criticize, construct, gossip, learn, hate and love by narrative. In order really to live, we make up stories about ourselves and others, about the personal as well as the social past and future.'[3] Like everybody else, oral history respondents speak in narratives, and it is important for the researcher to approach testimony alert to the issues.

Narrative analysis identifies and then explains the ways in which people create and use stories to interpret the world. When we experience something in our daily life, we place it in a story. The result is that our past is 'storied', with each memory packaged within a story or narrative.[4] And these stories are part of everyday life. When we communicate with friends and family, when we visit the doctor, when we socialise with work colleagues, on each occasion we tell stories. In turn, these stories get reused. Stories circulate in families acting as the glue that maintains relationships ('do you remember the time when … ?). We use stories to explain ourselves to relative strangers and to keep in contact with friends. We use narrative every day.[5]

So, narrative is not merely the content of the story, but the telling of it. It incorporates not just the sequence of events or facts but emphases, embellishments, cadences, structure, digressions, silences – in short the arrangement and dramatisation of the story. Narrative is something we do without thinking; it is part of everyday affairs, a means of communicating what we know about the world and a way of establishing connections with others. We use narrative to tell a story about ourselves and about others. It follows that the narratives we construct are informed by and embedded in the cultural world in which we live. But sometimes the ways of telling the story are distinctive to the teller and their family and friends; the narrative might not be told using a simple language but might contain embedded meaning and even codes that are understood by the close circle for whom it is significant. It may contain linguistic patterns and allude to certain ideas which require analysis in order to reveal meaning. For the outsider, like an oral historian coming to interview, the way a person tells a story is not necessarily transparent; the narrative may need to be decoded.

Current oral history practice regards the respondent's production of a narrative as a desirable outcome of the interview. In earlier decades, oral historians tended often to seek responses to standardised questions, using questionnaires, and these sometimes elicited abrupt 'yes' or 'no' answers, making the event seem more like an interrogation than about hearing somebody's reflective memories. Here is an example of the limited, non-narrative, rather staccato-style answers provided by Mrs Clara Wilson, one of the respondents in Paul Thompson's Edwardians project. The respondent's answers (in italics) are generally shorter than the questions.

Did your father ever go to a club, or pubs?
  No. He didn't never drink. Nor smoked.
And what about your mother, did she go out?
  No, she never drank.
Did your father, before he was ill, take part in sport or go and watch sport at all?
  No, no sport.
Did they not go out, really, at night then?
  I don't know 'cos I was too young then to notice all that.
But when you were older?
  No they never went out. They had their business and that was that. That was their life, that was their livelihood.
Did they ever belong to any savings clubs?
  I don't know.
You said they had friends, the customers dropping in.
  Yes.
Did they also have friends who weren't customers, who weren't to do with the business?
  No, it was always business people, not many neighbours.
And when the business people came in, did they entertain them at all, give them a cup of tea?

Oh, yes, they used to do that.
What about having tea together and that kind of thing, did they do that?
Oh, yes.
They did. I just wondered what the social life was like.
Well, of course, you have to do that sort of thing in business, don't you.[6]

The problem here is that the interview tended to become a narrative constructed by the questioner or the questionnaire-writer. Nowadays, the preference is for the interviewer to give the greatest possible room to the interviewee to produce a narrative of his or her own. This shift from questionnaire-style oral history to narrative style is a movement in practice which is reflected in the widespread use of the term 'narrator' in addition to, or in place of 'interviewee' or 'respondent'. It reflects how the researcher desires a narrative response in order to be able to conduct narrative analysis on the recording or transcript, a form of interpretation that seeks to dig under the surface of the words spoken.

However, as Portelli has pointed out, there is no distinctive narrative genre (such as a poem or a speech) explicitly designed to convey historical information; though many do, this is not their sole purpose.[7] Therefore, narrators in oral history interviews are likely to create an amalgamation of narrative styles drawing on all sorts of available narrative forms which suit the story they are telling and the meaning they wish to impart. Commonly an interviewee will shift from the storytelling genre to anecdote to use of reported speech; they may tell their story as an epic or a tragedy. They may also position themselves in the story as hero or victim. All of these things are important to the oral historian. The language and linguistic devices used will tell us something about the meaning assigned by the speaker (and perhaps their family, friends and community) to the narrative.

Narrative analysis has not always been part of the armoury of the oral historian. Indeed, historians traditionally would have defined narrative as the chronological unfolding of a sequence of events in the past. But the rise of narrative studies in other disciplines and the widespread recognition amongst historians more generally that the past is constructed by competing narratives – including those written by historians themselves – has pushed this particular methodological approach into the foreground so that now a narrative is seen as a means of symbolically representing the past.[8] The postmodern recognition that there are multiple, competing and non-definitive representations of the past has meant that the individual's account has received greater attention. This trend has been emphasised in the rejection of metanarratives (overarching or totalising explanatory frameworks) which provided the means by which societies and groups understood themselves and which historians used to interpret past societies. Thus, the Eurocentric metanarrative of male superiority was traditionally employed as a generalising framework to explain male dominance and female subordination, whilst the history of European empires produced metanarratives of racial and religious

superiority over non-white and non-Christian peoples. As these metanarratives of superiority have withered since the mid-twentieth century, so alternative narratives have blossomed such as feminist, gendered, multi-cultural
and multi-faith narratives, which have transformed representations of the past
with complex reasons for the historical sexual division of labour, slavery and
empire, and Christian proselytism and evangelisation. Just as no one narrative
accounts for major historical processes, so the oral historian seeks out the
diversity of narratives from respondents. The interviewee is the new narrator.
One of the consequences of this turn to narrative is a focus on not only the
stories told and the information imparted but the mode of telling. This is
because narratives can provide an insight into culture: they are in Riessman's
words 'essential meaning-making structures'.[9] Narration is the creative and
active way we make sense of and communicate what we know in a way that
the narrator expects will engage the listener.

For the oral historian there are several levels of narrative to identify in an
oral history recording or transcript: first, the narrative created by the respondent; second, the narrative models upon which the respondent draws; and
finally the narrative crafted by the historian from the accumulation of oral
histories. In this chapter we will focus primarily on the first and second of
these. We will introduce some of the approaches to narrative analysis and
identify some possible narrative structures which help to shape people's oral
histories. We will then discuss some examples of the utility of narrative
analysis for the oral historian focusing on the uses of narrative strategies in
people's oral accounts.

Theory

What is narrative?

Narrative is a concept employed by theorists across the disciplines. Although
linguistic theorists will speak of narrative as something embedded in every
sign or text – such as a gesture or photograph for instance – in this discussion
I am going to talk about narrative in a narrower sense as it applies to language and communication. Oral history, after all, depends primarily on words
spoken and to a lesser extent on signs or other forms of text, so it is upon
words that I focus.

Narrative is the main means of communication, the way people use language to communicate experience, knowledge and emotions. A narrative is a
story told according to certain cultural conventions and can be found within
almost every mode of communication and within every culture. Narrative at
its most basic level contains characters, a plot and a chronology. It is usually
a communication about a life event and might take the form of any of a
number of genres: a fairytale, a memory story, a speech, an anecdote, a folktale or an everyday speech act. It is, in the words of two theorists, 'the name
for an ensemble of linguistic, psychological, and social structures, transmitted

cultural-historically, constrained by each individual's level of mastery and by his or her mixture of communicative techniques and linguistic skills'.[10] Sometimes a narrative is easy to spot. It may have a recognisable beginning: 'Once upon a time' in the case of the fairytale narrative or perhaps 'You'll never guess what happened to me today' in the instance of a conversational narrative. And the conclusion may likewise be obvious: 'and they all lived happily ever after'. A narrative thus often has recognisable beginnings and endings, and bits in the middle too. But narratives in oral history contexts are usually less clearly marked. They do not always have a beginning, a middle and an end though they do usually have a storyline.

It is important at the outset to distinguish narrative from discourse. The latter refers to a message which may be delivered and circulated by all kinds of modes of communication (the broadcast and print media, government organs, everyday conversation) and which often contains injunctions to act (such as those contained within the discourse on female respectability for instance). A discourse is thus quite complex and multilayered and may be contained within a narrative. In this regard, narrative may be one of the means by which discourse is circulated. But it is not a discourse in and of itself. It might be helpful to think of the narrative as the structure and of the discourse as the message within it. We will return later in this chapter to see how particular narrative styles are used to effectively deliver particular discourses.

Narrative analysis

Narrative analysis is an interdisciplinary field of study. The 'narrative turn' was taken by social scientists in the 1970s as they increasingly rejected positivist methods drawn from the natural sciences which emphasised the importance of isolating 'facts' and began instead to look for ways of understanding how people organise their lives, construct their selves and represent themselves in relation to the wider cultural context by telling stories about themselves. Informed by developments in literary, anthropological and linguistic theory, scholars developed what has been termed 'narratology' – a methodological and theoretically informed mode of study which places storytelling, or the construction of narratives, at the centre of the investigation. They shifted the emphasis from the empirical to the subjective, from the facts to the framework of the telling, and from what was said to how it was said.

Narrative analysis in the hands of linguistic and literary theorists tended to adopt a structuralist approach that analysed the rules and forms of language embedded in the text (which might be oral or written). They employed a practice known as parsing or syntactic analysis, whereby the researcher analysed the text by breaking it down into distinctive components, clauses or segments in order to reveal the basic structure of a narrative including recurrent patterns and narrative techniques. Deploying this method, researchers looked for universal codes and patterns in syntax, seeking to reveal a kind of 'deep structure' of narrative that lay beneath the surface of the story.[11] Taking a short extract from a life-history interview with a Scottish woman born in 1894, we can illustrate in very simple terms how this is done. The letters indicate separate episodes within the narrative, the numbers identify independent clauses. The interviewee was asked if there was a lot of poverty in the village in which she lived as a child.

A	1	Drinking. Drink.
	2	I think I mentioned General Booth.
	3	He came.
	4	I was as near to his car as I am here,
	5	and his fight was against drink,
B	6	because they pawned.
	7	And if they didn't pawn they'd, < . . pause. . > their mothers pawned;
	8	took their clothes
	9	and spent it on drink.
C	10	One little boy that I was very fond of,
	11	in the snow and cold,
	12	his whole shoulder was bare.
	13	Three times I bought him a new woolly cardigan.
D	14	She pawned them every time for drink.
	15	I know
E	16	and I would come up from Felling Station,
	17	up the hill on a winter night,
	18	there would be a cluster of children sitting on the step of a public house,
	19	waiting for a mother to come out,
F	20	and it made, < . . pause. . >
	21	it formed a feeling in you,
	22	which of course, I never saw up in Bridge of Allan,
G	23	but, < . . pause. . > oh there couldn't be,
	24	they couldn't be like that,
	25	'cause they put the clothes into the pawn shop.
	26	Three Golden Balls,
H	27	you know, so they say, it's gone now.[12]

A linguistic analysis of this text would identify a number of features: the frequent use of the connective word 'and'; repetition ('and I would come up', 'up the hill') and a series of narrative episodes marked above by letters. This kind of analysis may strike the oral historian as mechanistic and too heavily indebted to linguistic techniques. It seems rather one-dimensional, paying no attention to the relationship between the narrator and the audience. It focuses our attention on what is happening within the narrative linguistically rather than on the telling of the story within a wider context. Indeed, for one influential narrative theorist, 'narrative is a relation among clauses rather than an interaction among participants'.[13] Few oral historians would be willing to accept this statement uncritically and, in fact, even linguists who apply this kind of analysis to oral narratives are unlikely to adopt such a position, preferring to situate the analysis of syntax within the wider context of the encounter.

Narrative analysis had traditionally been conducted upon major written literary and fictional texts. But beginning with linguists Labov and Waletzky in the 1960s, scholars argued that studies should be made of the narrative technique to be found in oral versions or verbal tellings of personal experiences, thus shifting the emphasis towards everyday and non-fictional narratives.[14] This kind of analysis allowed the form of the oral narrative to be related to its function in everyday life. And it was argued that most oral narratives typically consisted of up to six linking stages or components, namely: abstract, orientation, complication, evaluation, resolution and coda. Thus, a narrator will typically:

- summarise the events to be recounted (abstract);
- outline the context of the story (orientation);
- set up the specific event to be recounted (complication);
- reflect on the events narrated (evaluation);
- tell the outcome (resolution);
- and finally return to the present (coda).[15]

Many of us can immediately recognise these components – some if not all – as commonplace in the oral histories we hear, though it is in fact quite rare to encounter a narrative that conforms completely to the above model. If we look at the oral history extract cited above again, this time represented as free-flowing narrative, we can see that it demonstrates some of the six structural elements we have described.

> Drinking. Drink. So I think I mentioned General Booth. He came. I was as near to his car as I am here, and his fight was against drink, because they pawned. And if they didn't pawn they'd, <. . pause. > their mothers pawned; took their clothes and spent it on drink. One little boy that I was very fond of, in the snow and cold, his whole shoulder was bare. Three times I bought him a new woolly cardigan. She pawned them every time for drink. I know and I would come up from Felling Station, up the hill on a winter night, there would be a cluster of children sitting on the step of a public house, waiting for a mother to come out, and it made, <. . pause. .> it formed a feeling in you, which of course, I never saw up in Bridge of Allan, but, <. . pause. .> oh there couldn't be, they couldn't be like that, 'cause they put the clothes into the pawn shop. Three Golden Balls, you know, so they say, it's gone now.[16]

Although this narrative does not entirely conform to the six stages, we can identify the orientation (the mention of drink and General Booth, founder of the Salvation Army and temperance advocate), complication (the story of children suffering from the consequences of their parents' drinking), evaluation (where the respondent remarks on her feelings about this scenario from her privileged perspective) and the coda (her comment that the pawn shop no longer exists returning the listener to the present). By analysing this woman's narrative for its internal linguistic structures and its form we can see that her telling of the story takes the form of a moral commentary, embedded within the context of Christian evangelicalism (identified by the references to drink and the pawnshop that bookend the story).

So, there are two linguistic approaches – analysis clause-by-clause, and by narrative stages. The importance of this kind of linguistic analysis for those using oral narratives was to encourage the analysis of the 'situated uses of narrative structures' or, in other words, to investigate how the structures of narrative can be analysed within their cultural context and thereby provide insight into the interpretation of meaning.[17] In the 1980s, when many disciplines, from psychology to history, had taken the 'narrative turn', it was recognised that 'the story form, both oral and written, constitutes a fundamental linguistic, psychological, cultural and philosophical framework for our attempts to come to terms with the nature and conditions of our existence'.[18] An immediate problem is that neither of these approaches pays attention to the intention of the teller – that is whether the narrator is simply relating a sequence of events or aiming to tell a good story.[19] A second problem is that there is no contextualisation and no research into the author and the period in which, and of which, she or he is speaking.

This is important. For most oral historians and theorists today, narrative and the circumstances of its formation are intimately connected: text and context go together. Modern narrative theory pays attention to the wider framework in which a text or narrative is produced. Current narrative scholarship adopts a flexible and grounded approach to the text, observing the ways in which narrative is constructed and used by respondents within the specific contexts of a narration such as an oral history interview which, as we have already established, presents a very particular environment for narration.

Another approach to narrative analysis emerged in the 1960s and 1970s when literary specialists and philosophers started to study the structure or shape of written texts – novels, romances and so on. One of the most well known is that of Italian theorist and novelist Umberto Eco who analysed Ian Fleming's James Bond novels and argued that each was structured according to a set of rules; contained within each novel were up to twelve narrative 'moves' or episodes, and each of these contained binary oppositions – for example, Bond and the villain, Bond and the girl, democracy versus totalitarianism and so on.[20] Eco called this a 'narrative machine', a plot structure that familiarised the reader and carried the reader forward. This is not dissimilar to the narrative stages discussed above. It is likely that many other writers of fiction adopt similar patterns or formats. The detective novel, for instance, will generally include a whole range of narrative devices and conventions without which it would not be recognisable as a detective novel: a murder, suspense, the introduction of characters who are only gradually revealed, red herrings, a character detective, a devilish antagonist. Many nineteenth-century novels were epic life stories modelled on John Bunyan's famous religious novel of 1678, *Pilgrim's Progress*. In Charles Dickens's *David Copperfield* or Thackeray's *Vanity Fair*, the author adopted the structure of the melodrama in order to tell stories of the upward moral progress of the central character. Within the melodramatic narrative the hero or heroine negotiates life, often overcoming insuperable obstacles, on the way encountering and dealing with dilemmas that encapsulated moral opposites: good versus evil, hard work versus idleness, and so on.

Historians have identified a whole series of narrative models in written texts which possess identifiable characteristics. The evangelical narrative structure, which typically contained a series of episodes centred on the opposition between a religious young woman and an unbelieving man was parachuted into anything from romance novels to horror fiction.[21] And the twentieth-century Mills & Boon romance stories adhered to a quite rigid formula depending on the social context in which they were published. For example, the 1950s novels tend to be shaped by domestic themes and the 1960s novels are more likely to have independent working women as heroines.[22]

It has often been noted how narrative strategies are culturally and gender specific. Scholars who analyse storytelling narratives have focused particularly on gender differences but within oral history more generally narrative structures or styles have been seen to vary not only with the sex of the narrator but also with ethnicity.[23]

Application

Oral historians have taken up narrative analysis. The methods described above to identify narrative shape and strategies in fictional works may also be applied to oral testimony, not least because we know that people draw upon narrative styles circulating in the social world to construct their own stories. They tend to tell stories in formats they have found in novels, newspapers, television soap-operas and dramas. Narrative structures are borrowed by us all the time; this is called 'intertextuality'. When you find an oral respondent borrowing a particular style, it may be because he or she sees it as appropriate to his or her own story and the context of the oral history interview. The heroic story needs a melodramatic style, a fantastic journey may need a fairytale structure, and so on. So, the oral historian may detect what the narrator *means* by a story from the narrative structure he or she adopts.

There is no disciplinary consensus on how to conduct narrative analysis, but all the approaches work on the basis that people communicate orally and in writing using narrative structures with which they are familiar and with

which their listeners are familiar. Thereafter, oral historians use slightly different methods. Some pay close attention to language and syntax; others give
more attention to the shape or form of narratives. All work best when applied
to a single or a small number of texts. Narrative analysis is not practicable if
applied to large collections of oral history data – the task becomes unmanage-
able. The result is that the oral historian becomes interested in micro-analysis
of small numbers of testimonies, drawing conclusions with much wider rami-
fications.

In 1975, Ron Grele defined oral history as a 'conversational narrative'.[24]
He stated that the analysis of the 'linguistic, grammatical and literary structure' of the interview had the potential to reveal 'hidden levels of discourse'
and thereby revealing what Grele termed the 'problematic' which informs the
interview, in other words, the ideological and theoretical context of the conversational narrative.[25] There are a number of different ways in which oral
historians strive to analyse their oral histories as narratives which might
broadly be divided into two approaches: the linguistic-oriented and that
which has more in common with literary analysis. Historians have traditionally been far less likely to adopt the former analytical technique, in part
because the technical skills required to parse texts are not normally part of
the historian's skill base but also because historians' use of oral history
material was more likely to be for empirical reasons; it was *what* was said that
was important, not *how* a person shaped their story. But the use of oral history methodology by other disciplines has demonstrated that narrative analysis, even that of the close textual kind, may offer the historian new insights
into historical concerns.

Analysis of narrative structure

There is no single approach to the analysis of oral history narratives. Some
researchers prefer to carry out a close textual analysis of linguistic structures
while others pay attention to the forms or shapes the narratives take. However, analysis of the structure and form of the narrative is usually carried out
on the written or transcribed form of the interview. Oral historians have
employed a number of analytical strategies to narrative analysis in order to
access the meaning as opposed to the content of their stories.

One of the clearest examples of how to conduct a narrative analysis of a
series of oral histories is Ruth Finnegan's study of the English new town
Milton Keynes.[26] She demonstrates that in telling their personal narratives,
the narrators deploy a number of well-known conventions or universal ways
of telling a story in order to give their stories coherence. All of the narrators
temporally frame their story (that is they situate them in time) and use temporal staging points – childhood, schooling, first job, marriage and so on – to
mark out different stages of life or to highlight turning points. This way of
framing a life story is to be expected in the Western life-story model as we
saw in Chapter 3, as is the second convention identified, the inclusion of

protagonists in the story, a cast of characters with whom the narrator inter-relates, drawn mainly from family members. Again Finnegan notes that this is to be expected: 'These *are* the standard, yet emotive figures through which tellers expect to present their narratives and marshal their experiences'.[27] Third, the narratives feature the individual actor, the 'I', as the central hero of the story, not just as a character in the action but as a means of conveying individual motivation and reflection on past experience, lending the narrative its coherence. The point here is that the telling of a personal story, as in an oral history interview, is not a random performance but is guided by a series of conventions that give a unity to the narrative and which are recognisable to the listener.

Another approach is taken by Portelli who suggests that an oral history narrative may fall into three main narrative modes, each of which can be categorised according to the point of view adopted, and the social and spatial contexts. The first is the 'institutional' (a third-person account, 'it was the custom or the rule', located nationally or vis-à-vis the State and focused on politics, government and so on); the second is the 'communal' (an account narrated in the first-person plural – 'we did this', located in the community, the locality, the workplace and focused on work-related action, neighbour-hood activity and so on); and the third is the 'personal' (a first-person sin-gular account, 'I did this', located in the home and focused on family and other personal issues). Of course most respondents will skip from one mode to another in the course of an interview, and they may converge in the course of telling a particular story.[28] But in recognising these modes Portelli argues that we can gain a deeper insight into the ways in which respondents repre-sent themselves. If a narrator continually uses the personal mode we may imply that the person is able to position themselves as the hero or heroine of their own life. Conversely, persistent use of the institutional or communal mode suggests a respondent who has less confidence in the significance of their own story.

Marie-Françoise Chanfrault-Duchet has applied the techniques of narrative analysis to the life stories of two women interviewed about their perceptions of the changes in French women's lives since the First World War. Her approach has three stages. First, it is to identify, through close attention to the tran-scribed text, what she calls 'key phrases' used repeatedly by her respondents which indicate the relation they have to society. In the case of Marie the key phrase is 'one was obliged' – used by Marie to express the conflictual rela-tionship she had with society. Once this key phrase has been identified, argues Chanfrault-Duchet, it is possible for the historian 'to map and decipher her life experiences' in defiant terms.[29] The key phrase for Germaine is 'I did not want to … but what could I do', accompanied by a gesture that expressed fate. For Germaine, the key phrase 'conveys the ambiguity of her relation to society, as she searches for a compromise between self and social constraints'.[30]

The second stage of analysis is to identify the narrative models used by her narrators, here borrowing from theorist Hayden White's categories of emplotment (romantic, tragic, comic, satirical, but also adding epic).[31] Marie and Germaine choose to be epic heroes in life stories which resemble a novel that 'expresses the quest for authentic values in a degraded world'.[32] And finally, in the third analytical stage, Chanfrault-Duchet identifies the collective myths that represent the world-views of her respondents and that shape the narration of their life stories. Marie's world-view is informed by class struggle, and in turn this is informed by the collective myth in French history of the Revolution. Germaine's world-view, on the other hand, is characterised by the myth of the 'land of milk and honey', which in turn is borrowed from Judaeo-Christian beliefs. For Chanfrault-Duchet, narrative analysis can take the historian beyond the bare statements or 'preconstructed discourses and surface assertions' of the life-history interview to begin to understand how the narrator constructs his or her life in relation to culture.[33]

For Chanfrault-Duchet, narrative construction is not a conscious act; she describes it as pre-conscious. For her, 'the narrative encompasses not only the temporal and causal organisation of facts and events considered significant, but also the value judgements that make sense of this particular life experience.'[34] So, the most important or revealing information is not contained in the content of the answers given but in the 'narrative organisation' because it is this that tells us how the narrator positions herself within the social order, within culture (and that means not just the relationship between the self and the social sphere but also between the self and the collective representation of women in this case). For her, 'facts and events take their meaning from the narrative structure within which they are embedded'.[35] This approach, she argues, enables the historian to go far beyond what might be achieved if one is merely analysing information imparted or what she describes as the 'surface assertions' collected in a survey model or research. In short, it takes us closer to meaning or what the respondent is revealing through her choice of language and narrative structure.

But other narrative analysts suggest that there is a degree of conscious self-construction in these accounts, or in other words, we use language to constitute a sense of self but also to persuade a listener of the veracity of our version of events. Catherine Riessman is a good exponent of this position in her study of the ways in which one man – 'Burt' – constructs a positive masculine identity in spite of his disability and his divorce in the context of a life-history interview.[36] She does this in three key ways. First she identifies in the transcribed text of the full interview the boundaries of narrative segments, then she parses the segments to identify how the clauses function in relation to the listener (for instance, to orient the listener, to move the action forward and so on). Here is a brief extract from a segment of text in which Burt tells of how his wife had problems with his illness (precipitating the divorce):

01   Well in '75 I was diagnosed
02   you know, at that time I was still able to walk but I had to
03   drag my right leg

04   and as the years went on
05   the leg got worse
06   my right arm started to get weak
07   I'd start losing my balance
08   my coordination was going
09   and un then I – naturally I had to start using a walker
10   and I don't think she liked the idea of
11   having to help me all the time in the morning[37]

Second, Riessman identifies 'thematic and linguistic connections between the narrative segments'.[38] And then finally she identifies the kind of narrative genres chosen by the speaker – for instance the chronological or habitual narrative genre when someone describes 'what happened', or the non-narrative genre where someone might interpolate a story or episode into the telling. Riessman shows how Burt uses a number of narrative strategies to construct a positive sense of self with which he was comfortable while at the same time utilising certain narrative forms in order to draw the listener into the point of view of the teller. These strategies include inserting stories into the interview, dramatising important points in the narrative and incorporating into his account more extended passages which relate his thoughts and feelings – an effective strategy to bring the listener round to his perspective. For instance, in one of these passages, Burt describes his feelings about separation: 'You're used to sleeping with a woman for 25 years and now I am sleeping in my own bed. And there's no-one beside me to keep me warm, let's put it that way. Nights are cold ... Somebody to hold on to, I miss that.'[39]

The result of this close attention to Burt's narrative for Riessman is that we can see how he 'is able to project a strong masculine identity, even in the face of behaviour that violates common sense definitions of masculinity'.[40] In other words, Burt, a man confined to a wheelchair and abandoned by his wife, is able to retain a positive sense of self in the interview by using particular narrative devices, for example by telling the listener that he was a 'devoted husband', by placing the blame for the divorce on his wife's drinking rather than on his illness and by portraying himself as a steady worker. And of interest to the oral historian is that all of these strategies for telling are produced by the narrator by breaking the frame of the research interview, diverting from answering the questions with a straight answer and instead telling stories – narratives – which serve the purpose of presenting the protagonist in a positive way.

These examples of narrative analysis are conducted in the context of fairly conventional oral history interviews and demonstrate how such analysis can get beneath the surface evidence to reveal how narrators make sense of experience. Such examples are quite context-specific – here we have drawn on research on new towns, the First World War and divorce – but narrative analysis has also provided insights into the ways in which members of particular groups narrate their stories.

Gender and ethnicity in narrative

Research in the field of linguistics and communication studies seems to suggest that men and women adopt different narrative styles in everyday conversation.[41] In summary, whereas men's conversation with other men is often characterised by boasting and male topics such as football and cars and acts as a way of confirming their membership of the gender group, women's everyday talk tends to be more cooperative and collaborative though no less important as a form of 'identity work'.[42] Likewise, storytelling research in everyday conversational contexts suggests that the female storyteller adopts different strategies and narrative styles than that of the male. Men, according to Baldwin's research with a family in Pennsylvania, told stories with linear narratives, they dramatised dialogue and action and distinguished this from conversation and, markedly, men tended to tell a story about a specific, remarkable event 'with a point worth tellin''.[43] And the purpose of the male storyteller is to entertain within a hierarchical context; the story he tells is designed to be better, funnier, more remarkable than others.

Women, on the other hand, tend to adopt conversational styles, and their stories focus on the usual or general rather than on the remarkable. Other characteristics of women's storytelling styles include emphasis on collaboration, cooperation and the shared modes of telling they have – all narrative strategies that tend to maintain horizontal relationships amongst a group rather than the more male establishment of hierarchies. In contrast to men, women are more likely to support one another (by means of verbal and non-verbal responses), interrupt in a supportive way (questions, overlapping, making humorous comments which are supportive of the story and the narrator) and adopt politeness strategies in order that all members of the group may share in the telling.[44] Researchers suggest that women's storytelling is a 'means of sociability' whereas men's is a means of 'self-aggrandising'. Women, it is said, undertake 'narrative labour'; they carry within families and kin groups the responsibility for facilitating the telling of stories (organising family events and gatherings for instance), and they maintain what is termed 'the kernel story', a story that is already known within the family group that can be called upon and retold to cement family bonds.[45]

Narrative analysis in oral history has identified some significant differences in the ways in which men and women tell their stories. Women are more likely to include reported speech; this means that they report what other people said, word for word, whilst men tend to talk in what they suggest is their own words. Women speak in non-linear plot-lines – mixed-up chronology with much repetition and back-tracking, the inclusion of considerable circumstantial detail and the use of very long sentences with numerous sub-clauses.[46] Bennett argues that women's use of these features, far from marking them as 'wordy and incompetent narrators', has a clear rationale: such devices provide a structure to their stories, signalling the different narrative stages; they help to pace the story; and they mark climactic moments or events.[47] If we take women's use of descriptive excursions or asides in the midst of a story as an example, Bennett shows how we should not regard this strategy as deviating from the narrative or losing the plot but rather as a device to slow down the story, making the listener wait, and at the same time amplifying or reinforcing what has already been said.[48] In other words, women use classic storytelling devices in order to get their message across.

The implications for oral history is that we should be looking closely at women's and men's narrative techniques. For Langellier and Peterson, the purpose of women's storytelling strategies (what they term spinstorying) is to share meanings and thereby to transmit a culture. Women are more likely than men to tell personal stories and to tell them in a collaborative way using certain narrative devices because:

> they cannot draw upon a shared history at a social level when their history is particularized, deprecated, regulated and silenced. Their focus on mundane, everyday events and the use of supportive strategies does not occur out of politeness alone, but from a realistic assessment of 'transmission possibilities': if care is not taken to discover, share, and connect these stories with other experiences, then they cease to exist.[49]

Is it the case that female respondents are more likely to engage in a conversational narrative with the interviewer and are less likely than a male respondent to place themselves at the centre of the story? Anecdotal evidence suggests that men are more likely to try to tell 'tellable stories', that is to tell stories which are memorable in some way, which have a point, but this is one area deserving more research. It is likely too that the intersubjectivities present within the interview will have an impact on how women and men respond. Kristina Minister has exhorted feminist oral historians to create a 'feminist frame' for the interview in order to facilitate a shared culture of female-to-female communication or dialogue; this, she argues, holds out the hope of liberating women's narrative styles from the straitjacket of the 'male sociocommunication subculture'.[50] Studies of male communication styles in oral history interviews are badly needed.

However, examples of cross-cultural interviewing practices have shown that 'gender is not enough'.[51] Narrative styles or strategies may also vary according to culture or ethnicity. The linear or chronological model described at the start of this chapter is a Western model which may not be applicable to other cultural traditions. Catherine Riessman's analysis of two interviews conducted by an Anglo-American woman (on the subject of experiences of marital separation and divorce) – the first with an Anglo-American woman, the second with a Puerto-Rican woman – demonstrates very clearly how different narrative styles are used by each. In short, while the Anglo-American respondent adopted a chronologically linear narrative, relating her marital history using time as the structure, the Puerto-Rican respondent organised her story 'episodically', that is, she eschewed a chronological narrative for one which was organised around a series of incidents or episodes. Despite the interviewer's empathetic position and her sensitivity to gender, there remained a comprehension gap between the two women on account of the different narrative styles. As the author writes: 'The lack of shared experience between the middle-class, white interviewer and the working-class Puerto-Rican interviewee has created barriers to understanding. In this case, gender congruity is not enough to create shared meanings.'[52]

Linguists have a lot more to say about the syntactical differences employed in different languages which affect not just how something is expressed but what it means to the speaker and the listener.[53] This kind of analysis is unlikely to be especially fruitful for the oral historian unless one is working in more than one's native language. However, analysis of narrative form used by different cultural groups has offered us insights. Research on African storytelling has identified six structural types which differ from the classic or predominantly Western six-stage model we discussed earlier in this chapter.[54] And Julie Cruikshank's work with the peoples of the Yukon is a prime example of how attention to the shape of stories is crucial to understanding their significance.[55]

Narrative and trauma

Narrative is a way of making sense of experience, and this holds true for most people's experiences, even disordered or unhappy ones. Narrators can create an ordered or coherent narrative from a disordered experience or to make sense of such an experience, from the mundane to the extraordinary. Narrative gives 'reality a unity that neither nature nor the past possesses so clearly'.[56] However, there are some experiences that are far more difficult to translate into narrative and may be impossible to be narrativised because they cannot be made sense of and then wrapped up in neat discursive structures like stories.

Many narratives of traumatic experiences are never told because, as Robinson notes, 'such experiences produce shame, anger, often guilt in the victim, and are regarded as secrets rather than as stories to tell'.[57] And when they are told they are often structurally and functionally different from conventional narratives. There is a growing body of research on the narrativisation of traumatic experience though the distinctiveness of such narratives was recognised as early as the First World War.[58] When soldiers returned from combat it was often reported that they would not or could not talk about their experiences with their loved ones. The philosopher Walter Benjamin explained the muted soldiers in these words:

> Was it not noticeable at the end of the war that men returned from the battlefield grown silent – not richer, but poorer in communicable experience? What ten years later was poured out in the flood of war books was anything but experience that goes from mouth to mouth. And there was

nothing remarkable about that. For never has experience been contradicted more thoroughly than strategic experience by tactical warfare, economic experience by inflation, bodily experience by mechanical warfare, moral experience by those in power.[59]

Following the Second World War, this sense that traumatised individuals were unable to construct recognisable narratives was reinforced by witnessing the attempts of survivors of the Nazi-organised Holocaust to put their experiences into words. As one female survivor put it: 'I really felt that people didn't understand it. I felt like people in the United States could not empathise, could not understand. Their questions put me on edge. It was very difficult.'[60] Today this speechlessness may be defined as one symptom of post-traumatic stress disorder (PTSD). It has been found that survivors of collective trauma such as war, natural disasters and state violence and of individual trauma such as sexual abuse often have severe difficulties in translating their experience into coherent narratives because there is no language and no narrative device that can adequately convey the knowledge of and experience of such traumatic events. Barclay notes that 'embodied experiences of atrocities do not yield a set of image schemata that lend themselves to a metaphoric language of extermination'.[61] In other words, there are no reference points which may be used to speak about such experiences, and the consequences of this are fractured and fragmented histories as well as an extreme form of discomposure or self-incoherence which results from the inability to find meanings and explanations for the experiences.

'Speechlessness', writes trauma counsellor and oral historian Dori Laub, 'is a hallmark of collective mass trauma.'[62] The language that is commonly used in public to talk about the Holocaust – genocide, barbarism and so on – is not meaningful for the witnesses. 'There is no language of extermination' were the words of one survivor.[63] In his memoir of the concentration camp at Auschwitz, the Italian novelist Primo Levi summed up this dilemma:

> Just as our hunger is not that feeling of missing a meal, so our way of being cold has need of a new word. We say 'hunger', we say 'tiredness'. 'fear', 'pain', we say 'winter' and they are different things. They are free words created and used by free men who lived in comfort and suffering in their homes. If the [concentration camps] had lasted longer a new, harsh language would have been born; and only this language could express what it means to toil the whole day in the wind, with the temperature below freezing, wearing only a shirt, underpants, cloth jacket and trousers, and in one's body nothing but weakness, hunger and knowledge of the end drawing near.[64]

In his interviews with Holocaust survivors, Mark Klempner noted individuals speaking of 'holes in their memory'.[65] A similar phenomenon has been noted following the attacks on the Twin Towers in New York in 2001. In her oral histories with New Zealand Second World War veterans, Alison Parr observed what have been termed 'trauma signals' within their narratives. These included silences, inability to construct a story, loss of emotional control and observable changes in voice and body language.[66] While recognising the sensitivity required in conducting interviews with these men, Parr also notes that for some people, the opportunity to tell their stories, in effect to be encouraged and facilitated in constructing a narrative of traumatic experiences, can be a therapeutic experience; in other words, it may be a way of achieving what is often called closure. Indeed, oral historians and therapists alike seem to agree that traumatised individuals will only come to terms with their memories by constructing a narrative of those memories. In Laub's words, constructing a narrative can enable the survivor to 're-externalise the event'.[67]

The difficulty of framing traumatic experiences within an understandable or recognisable narrative structure means that listeners face problems in comprehending what they are hearing. The listener may already have in his or her mind a public version of a narrative of an event, and survivors' stories might not coincide with that understanding or they may simply not be able to comprehend the sheer scale and horror of what is being described. Sean Field's discussion of oral history in South Africa with refugees of the Rwandan massacre of 1994 starkly points up this issue. While urging interviewers to undertake 'sustained listening' and 'empathically imagine' oneself into the stories one is being told, he admits that this can be almost impossible when the stories are almost unimaginable containing death, rape, mutilation and other memories of human-rights violations.[68] Survivors then may be effectively silenced not only by their own inability to articulate a coherent narrative but also by listeners' inability to listen without judgement or difficulty in imagining what they are being told. The South African writer and journalist Antjie Krog's reactions to the stories narrated by witnesses to the South African Truth and Reconciliation Commission affirms this problem. Krog was part of the team assigned to report on the Commission's work. Her response, like that of her fellow journalists, is fractured, often uncomprehending, and, like the witnesses, she finds it hard to find the language to express what she has heard. On a question-and-answer session for a radio broadcast Krog recalls:

> I stammer. I freeze. I am without language. I put the receiver down, and think: resign. Now. You are clearly incompetent. The next morning the Truth Commission sends one of its own counsellors to address the journalists. 'You will experience the same symptoms as the victims. You will find yourselves powerless – without help, without words.'[69]

Practice

There are two main ways in which oral historians can apply narrative-analysis techniques. They can analyse the narrative shape of an oral history, and they can analyse the narrative content. Both presuppose that there is a recognisable narrative to work with. What we want is the interviewee who can produce a substantive narrative. So, how can the oral historian facilitate a narrative style in our respondents? How do we encourage our respondents to weave their experiences into the kinds of stories that we believe reveal the ways in which the respondent makes sense of his or her life?

It is important for the oral historian to adopt an open, informal and semi-structured approach to the interview, encouraging creative, discursive and lengthy replies. Susan E. Chase also suggests that narrative fluency may be accomplished by inviting the interviewee to take responsibility for the meaning of what they tell, or in other words allowing them to tell the story they want to tell. For historians this is easier said than done.[70] As we have already noted, many historians will often interrupt the narrative in an attempt to force the narrator to shape the story to historical conventions (for example, by asking for precise dates or eliciting more categorical information) or to try to meet our own research needs (by diverting a respondent back to a particular theme for instance). Chase argues that the interviewer must orient the questions so that they elicit the telling of the interviewee's own experiences rather than the interviewee providing an answer to what was asked or what the interviewee perceives to be the correct answer. She gives the example of a sociologist asking her women interviewees to explain to her what they thought the relationship was between their family socialisation and their resistance to oppression in the workplace. The answers she received were framed by sociological thinking and were thus 'abstract and uninformative'. So instead she asked for life stories, and the result was narrative responses which contained fulsome and complex answers to her research questions.[71] The key here is to ask questions that relate to life experiences – what Chase calls 'a good life story question' – rather than questions that require a particular kind of response. Moreover, the interviewer must continue to reiterate these kinds of questions throughout the interview.

Some concrete examples will illustrate the difference between a narrative and non-narrative response and how the researcher might interpret these. Mrs X1, born in 1897 and interviewed in 1987 for a project on the lives of women in the first half of the twentieth century provides a good example of someone who is unable or unwilling to produce a narrative response to a series of questions following a life-course approach. The pattern of her responses can be seen in this exchange:

Q: And what was your father's job?
  An engine driver.
And did he have any other jobs before or after that?
  Yes, as a young boy he served his apprenticeship as a baker and he joined the railway after that.
And did your mother have a job before she was married?
  She was a dressmaker.

And did she work after she was married?
  No.
Did your parents attend church?
  Yes.
Did they go regularly to church?
  Every Sunday.[72]

Over the course of a lengthy interview covering the respondent's childhood, schooldays and working life, this respondent rarely strays beyond a brief and precise answer to the question put, that is until the interviewer reaches the two world wars. At this point there is a clear shift in narrative style as Mrs X1 tells a number of anecdotes centred on her memories of wartime.

Q. So have you any memories of the Second World War? You mentioned that you did First Aid work?
  First Aid work in the Home Guard, and I remember the night the bomb fell down in Springkerse. Went down to the office in the morning and couldnae get nothing but splinters of glass, it fell just about the railway, you know the railway bridge? Fell just about there and the office was just over the bridge. And then the boss had been called out during the night, he was on police duty and he'd been called out down to his own place. The windows were all broken and there were big stone just at the side of his desk. A few memories of that.
And so can you remember what the story was in relation to that bomb? How did it happen to get dropped? How did the Germans manage to bomb Stirling?
  Well it was a main line and this Ordnance Depot out there, the gas works and there was the soldiers parked in the field next, but they'd have done a lot of damage if they had struck except where they did. They missed the gas works and missed the main line. And in the morning we went up to, <. . pause. .> I was the First Aid, supposed to be in the First Aid post and fainted in the middle of the floor. My mother said, 'That's you!' And my mother's brother was staying with us at the time, he says, 'I'll go down with you' and my mother said, 'No, you will not go down!' 'She's not going'. So Dr. Wilson, he says 'Your place is at home with your mother.'[73]

Suddenly and without notice this woman's response style has altered. It is impossible to know precisely the reasons, but perhaps she had prepared a memory frame for the interview which focused on her place in History. While she may have regarded many of the questions put to her about her personal and family life as lacking in historical importance (and she may also have been unfamiliar with the conventions of the oral history interview), she may well have regarded her war stories as significant within the context of an oral history project. In the extract above we can see that she positions herself as the subject within the story of the bomb, something that is not evident elsewhere in the interview transcript suggesting that within this particular episode she regarded herself as part of History. Another explanation for her relative narrative fluency here is the possibility that she had told this story many times before; it was part of a repertoire of war stories. This is supported by her memories of the First World War when she tells a story that would be familiar to anyone who had a passing knowledge of recruitment and send-off stories:

> Well I remember the soldiers marching down to the station and away in the trains. And then the boys all going up to sign on to get their arm bands and 'The shilling' as they termed it in these days. And there was quite a number of boys that were at the school with me killed in the 14th Argyll's. But my mother had a sister in Australia and she gave quite a few her address to call when they were across.

This narrative account of a war memory, while containing a personal story, seems clearly framed by public and popular accounts of the early days of the First World War, accounts which resonated with her own recollection and gave her the means to find an identity in the recollection of the Great War.

In contrast, other respondents effortlessly adopt narrative fluency. They know what is required of them or else they produce a response that is informed by their cultural context. Researchers, not surprisingly, may regard this type of response as ideal, providing substantial material for a subsequent analysis. But one should be on guard for stock responses, stories that have been told repeatedly. Some people have a repertoire of composed narratives – stories, anecdotes or just practised ways of answering a question they may have been asked before. Some interviewees have become repeat-respondents, the person to whom everyone turns for an interview on a particular topic. In these circumstances, the interviewer may have to work hard to find a chink in the armour, to ask a question that makes the interviewee think about how to formulate an answer. The result can be a more considered response.

I encountered a repeat-respondent when undertaking a project about the history of women in the Shetland islands. One of my interviewees was Agnes Leask, a woman recommended to me as a fount of knowledge about crofting and former President of the Shetland Crofting Foundation. Agnes turned out to be a weaver of narrative, responding to my questions with extremely long, detailed stories about all aspects of her own experiences in a crofting community. Agnes had been interviewed before, and when I compared my transcript with that of a previous interview undertaken some sixteen years previously, I discovered a number of similarities, not just in the information related but also in the stories told. The story of the sick calf is a good example. A calf was a valuable animal in a crofting family, and all manner of cures would be tried to keep it alive. Agnes's account of how the calf was cured is told here in the two interviews, the first in 1986 (conducted by a native Shetlander and transcribed in dialect) and the second in 2002 interviewed and transcribed by myself. It is interesting to compare extracts from the two versions.

Version 1, recorded in 1986

Anyhoo dis calf lay aa dis day, an he stunkit an he grind, an den Maggie cam ower, an dey tocht at well dey wid maybe try da calf wi a grain o opening medicine. So dey wir a bottle o some kinda concoction made up an poured doon wi da calf. But be next morning he wis nae better, an dey wir naithin ta'en effect, an dere were some mair stuff poured doon wi him; I dinna ken – whedder it wis stuff at wis bocht fae a sho or wis it mebbe ony kind o 'erbal remedy. I ken some o hit wis treacle because I ken mind me midder spoonin treacle oot o a jug ... An I thinks, weel bairns, whit ails da folk, at dey canna put da vaam (cat) upo da calf an better hit? An I wis as witless den as whit I am still, an I t'inks, weel, if dey wilna do hit, I'll do hit. So I picks up da cat, an I laachs across da hoose wi da cat in me skirt. I baals da cat on, keeps a haad o her tail so at I shall fetch her a good rive upo da calf. Da cat sank her claas inta da calf. Da calf raised wi a aafil skröl he just sprang I da air wi a skröl ... [74]

Version 2 recorded in 2002

mm, and the cat was called Venck. Now if an animal was sick and you put the Venck upon it, it had this magical powers to cure it, and what you had to do was pick the cat up and throw it on the sick animal ... and the old lady who lived next door she was very clever at medication for animals so she was called over – 'oh yes, give it a good dose of epsom salts' – so it got a good dose of epsom salts ... and by night it was still no better so er she come over herself and 'how was the calf?', oh it's just the same, 'is that medicine not worked?', no no nothing happened, 'oh well did we have castor oil?', oh yes castor oil and surely the best part of a bottle of castor oil was – and she would come back first thing in the morning, so she came back in the morning, and no no nothing had moved, 'oh well give it a good dose of epsom salts' this time and for good measure they put treacle in with it. So this treacle had to be melted and the epsom salts mixed in with the melted treacle, this was all poured down, and she would come back later on to see how it was, so about lunchtime she came back and it was more or even more, it was just blowing up then like anything and her and mum standing discussing it well they doubted, they doubted and that was it and she'd go out and Mum was crying – she wasn't crying making a fuss but tears were running down her cheeks and she was wiping them away and I knew it was over the calf and the cat was in front of the fire. So I thought what is wrong with the [calf] that they don't put the Venck on it? See I'd heard about the cat curing any illness on any animal [inaudible]. ... threw it on the calf and of course I was hoping that – you can imagine yoooooww – the claws out into the calf. The calf sprang to its feet and honestly it was like a little bit of effort was all that was needed to set in motion all these potions that had been tipped down it ... [75]

This was a story much used by the narrator. The sick-calf story contains many elements of a story traditionally performed for an audience: suspense, detail, dialogue, drama and a denouement – in this case a happy ending. It and others like it were used by Agnes to convey her own sense of the past and her place within it. The interview consists of a series of narrative episodes, all of which have a point of saying something significant about life in the Shetland crofting community. The sick-calf story may be interpreted on one level as containing empirical information about the superstitious beliefs and practices of Shetlanders. But if we approach the story as a narratologist we would see that the story serves a purpose; it conveys in rich and vivid detail the meaning of the crofting life, the value of animals and the reliance on community reciprocity. The story was told in the context of a wider discussion about the crofting lifestyle and followed on from comments about the importance of valuing and respecting other people and nature. For this respondent the story told is not just a narrative in an abstract sense but a means of accessing a social world, and the fact that the story had been repeatedly told merely underscores this fact. Moreover, Shetland has a storytelling culture, and Agnes's oral performance clearly drew on it, and in turn she had become for oral historians of the turn of the twentieth and twenty-first centuries one of the foremost upholders of the cultural tradition.[76]

Conclusion

Narrative is the means by which interviewees translate experience into words. Some are skilled storytellers, others struggle to create coherent narratives from disparate memories. Both kinds of narrative can offer the oral historian a means of getting beneath the events described to reach some understanding of what those events mean to the narrator. The oral historian does not need to master the techniques of the scholar of linguistics to observe how people shape their narratives in order to make a point. We can identify how the telling of a story in a particular way – beginning perhaps with a complication or a problem and ending with a resolution – creates composure. We can see that a disconnected narrative might suggest a failure of the respondent to create coherence, a sense of comfort or well-being with a life story. We will also be able to see how people draw upon narrative models commonly employed in literature or film or even those present within historical or other publicly available narratives. The key to thinking about narrative is to remember that it is a communication strategy and that every element of that narrative – be it the repetition of certain words, the use of pauses or silences, the topping and tailing of stories, the use of direct speech – has a role to play in conveying meaning. In addition, the narrative created by the respondent is often only the first stage of a process by which the historian is intent on producing another narrative for an academic audience, one that weaves together the interview material gathered into a coherent and persuasive story of a different kind for a very different group of hearers. We need to be aware that the academic oral historian is wielding a power here – consuming and then transforming others' narratives. Ron Grele highlights the tension that exists between the 'power of the narrative' and the historian's tendency to 'destroy narrative'.[77] The historian is prone to do this at every stage – from interrupting a respondent's flow by asking a question, to editing, cutting and manipulating the recording or transcript for the purpose of supporting an argument. Remembering that narrative is part of the historian's art may prompt us to be more attentive to the art of narrative present within our respondents' stories. What is at stake is a form of power. We shall consider this issue in Chapter 8. In the meantime, we need to take stock of one aspect of narrative – that it is part of performance. We turn to this in the next chapter.

7   Performance

Introduction

When Ronald Blythe was undertaking the research for his book *Akenfield*, he asked one of the village men about the singing that accompanied the scything of the corn: 'What was the song Davie?' The man answered: 'Never you mind the song, it was the singing that counted.'[1] This chapter concerns this theme of performance by the narrator in the oral history interview. It starts from the assumption that an oral history narrative is first and foremost a performance of words, a way of speaking separated from ordinary speech, a speech act performed for an audience in a particular context.

With the shift from *what* is said to *how* it is said, there has arisen a general acceptance that oral history is a performance by a narrator for an audience. This means that we ought to be conscious of the performance shapes and forms that oral narratives assume. Furthermore, we should acknowledge that any narrative cannot be separated from its form – from its performance. Oral history is the performance of a speech act. This requires that as well as analysing its content, we might also want to consider its performance qualities. The singing – or the performance – is as important as the song. Orality or oracy – skilled orality – should be on the radar of the oral historian.[2]

Performance in early oral history

The early oral historians were as interested in the way people spoke and the shape of their stories as in the information they imparted. George Ewart Evans, the father of oral history in modern Britain, remarked that it was the speech of the people of Blaxhall, the village in Suffolk he spent so many years documenting, that 'alerted me to the age of the community ... and gradually persuaded me that this dialect or *variety* of speech ... was suitable as a vehicle for transferring the history of the East Anglian people to a new synthesis'.[3] And he describes the East Anglian variety of speech as giving oral history 'a proper and more durable clothing'.[4] This is a perfect way of describing the importance of acknowledging the way people speak. The words they choose, the cadences and volume of their speech, their decision to speak in dialect or not, the rhythm of their narrative, not forgetting their gestures, facial expressions and physical movements, are an intrinsic element of communication and contribute to the listener's interpretation of the words and their meaning.

Previous chapters have established that oral history narratives are, to quote Ruth Finnegan, 'of interest as structured aesthetic and personal creations in the present as well as (or even instead of) just a witness to the past'.[5] We have described how the narrative produced in an oral history interview is something intersubjectively created through an interaction between the interviewer and respondent. It assumes particular forms appropriate to the memory stories being produced, and the interview is an opportunity for the respondent to shape and present a sense of self. It follows then, that the oral history narrative is a performance, a speech act, a history-telling for an audience which occurs in a public context. And as a communicative act it involves not just language but also non-vocal articulation, performed by the body, for an interviewer who is usually both a listener and a viewer.

The significance of this understanding is nicely illustrated by the author Alex Haley in his well-known 1970s search for the origins of his family. Haley was an African-American whose knowledge of his family's African origins came via the oral transmission of stories. His search led him to Africa to uncover much about his ancestor, Kunte Kinte, a search subsequently published and partially dramatised as *Roots*.[6] Haley had been told the family narrative by family and friends since he was very young; he writes that he grew up hearing stories of his slave ancestors. He became aware of the importance of the language of transmission when Jan Vansina, the famous scholar of oral tradition, indicated that the sounds Haley had remembered from the family tales probably originated in the Gambia in West Africa. But he only recognised the significance of the performance aspect of history-telling when he encountered the African *griot*, or storyteller, who confirmed to him the story of the origins of his family. Haley could not understand the Mandinka tongue but he understood the significance of what he was being told by paying attention to the old man's performance:

> And there's a language that's universal. It's a language of gestures, noises, inflections, expressions. Somehow, looking at them, hearing them, though I couldn't understand a syllable, I knew what they were talking about ... The old man, the *griot*, the oral historian, Kebbe Kanga Fofana, seventy-three rains of age ... began to tell me the ancestral history of the Kinte clan as it had been told down the centuries, from the times of the forefathers. It was as if a scroll was being read. It wasn't just talk as we talk. It was a very formal occasion. The people became mouse quiet, rigid. The old man sat in a chair and when he would speak he would come up forward, his body would grow rigid, the cords in his neck stood out and he spoke words as though they were physical objects coming out of his mouth.[7]

Haley's vivid description of the *griot*, the context within which he performed the Kinte history, and Haley's and the audience's response to the telling, acts as a powerful reminder that the production of an oral history is an event which cannot be separated from the context in which it is performed. Story-telling of any kind, including oral history, is a social activity which cannot take place without an audience. Even if that audience consists only of the interviewer, the narrator is aware that he or she is communicating experience in a heightened encounter which requires a stylised mode of communication differing from everyday conversation.

So performance can be important to the oral historian. This chapter will introduce a number of ways of analysing what we might call memory per-formances using theories drawn from a range of disciplines, notably folklore research, ethnography, anthropology, linguistics and performance studies. We shall be considering two key ways in which the analysis of oral history may be informed by performance theory: first by analysing the performance element of the memory story itself – the performance that literally takes place before our eyes, and second by looking at how oral history may be transmitted through performance practice, for example by incorporating oral history into a staged drama. The chapter will go on to look at some instances where the application of performance studies has informed oral history practice, and, finally, it will offer some thoughts on how to apply some of these insights in one's own oral history practice and interpretation.

Theory

Performance theory and communication

A performance, in socio-linguist Richard Bauman's words, is an 'aesthetically marked and heightened mode of communication, framed in a special way and put on display for an audience'.[8] Using this definition, all oral history inter-views are performances. Indeed, Bauman notes that performance is con-stitutive of all the verbal arts (including oral history narratives).[9] Our narrators rarely speak in a conversational mode because they are responding to questions put to them and usually recognise that 'a bit extra' is needed. They sense that they are on a stage and performing for the interviewer and his or her sound recorder. Many narrators do indeed put themselves on display for their audience; they are conscious of the need to perform and thus they may moderate their language, adjust dialect or accent, elaborate stories, and so on. If we accept this proposition, then we can move on to consider how and why individuals adopt particular performance modes or styles, whether their performance is determined by a script or a score and if so from which repertoire these scripts are chosen, or whether he or she may exert creative choice. The oral history respondent might be compared to a musician in an orchestra: each understands what it is they are required to do, each is led by someone who desires a result, each will have a script that shapes the performance but each also may insert some individual choice or flair into their performance.

Bauman also notes a number of features which tend to characterise cultural performances. They tend to be scheduled, that is set up in advance at a specific time; they are temporally and spatially boundaried in that they have a defined beginning and end and are performed within a marked-off space; they are programmed or structured; and they are public occasions. Finally, they are reflexive: this means that they call attention to culture itself.[10] Clearly, the oral history interview does not necessarily exhibit all of these features, but there are sufficient similarities for us to make use of this typology when thinking about the oral history interview as a performance.

Performance in the sense of a special act of communication which is 'lifted out to a degree from its contextual surroundings and opened up to scrutiny by an audience' makes the act open to evaluation, according to Bauman.[11] He gives the example of the performance of a sea shanty. It may be sung in the context of work on a ship as a means to aid the coordination and enjoyment of a task so the performance element has a lesser importance. But it may also be sung on a stage in the context of a maritime folk festival. In this context, the performance of singing the shanty becomes the most important element. Likewise, an oral history respondent may relate in an interview a story he or she has told many times within the family group, perhaps as a means to convey family lore or to acculturate younger members of the kin group. When it is told to the interviewer, however, it becomes a performance to an external audience, and the performance element needs to be evaluated alongside the content of the story.

Performance then, is a form of communication but it is separated from everyday conversational ways of speaking because of the 'assumption of responsibility to an audience for a display of communicative competence'.[12] In other words, the performance of the narrator is evaluated by the audience (perhaps for its effectiveness, and the skill with which it is done). Bauman says: 'Performance thus calls forth special attention to and heightened awareness of the act of expression and gives licence to the audience to regard the act of expression and the performer with special intensity.'[13] A number of communicative acts might be considered a performance: a speech or oratory, the telling of a story or joke, or a life-history narrative. What is considered performance and what is regarded as everyday or conventional speech varies from culture to culture. In modern Western societies, we would instantly recognise some speech acts – joke-telling for instance – as performance acts that require a deviation from everyday speech patterns.[14] Roger Abrahams argues that in the USA black people constitute a different 'speech community' from white people in the way they use talk in everyday life.[15] Similarly, in St Vincent in the West Indies, a wide range of speech activities including gossip, storytelling and arguing, are judged as performance acts; that is to say that St Vincentians recognise that there is an art to engaging in gossip just as there is to telling a joke. In contrast, anthropologist Jack Goody has shown how the sixteenth-century Reformation in countries such as Scotland involved the denunciation of drama in all things, including religious worship, because it involved representation and detracted from the centrality of the word of God.[16] In accord with this, seventeenth-century Quaker culture restricted performance to very few speech acts in accordance with the spare or plain communicative style adopted by the Puritan movement.[17] The phrase 'let your words be few' summed up the Quakers' view that outward speech should be controlled because it was an act in the service of God. One of the consequences of this position in the seventeenth century was Quakers' refusal to utter what was then and now regarded as the everyday language of civility such as 'good day', 'good morrow' and 'God speed you'. Such greetings, for many seen as necessary aids to social interaction, were regarded as opening one up to the susceptibility of corruption, but of course their refusal to engage in this everyday etiquette attracted widespread condemnation.[18]

How then does one differentiate between everyday speech and communication which is deemed to be a performance? In order for communication to be understood as performance, it needs to fall within what is called the performance frame, a set of guidelines that signal to the audience that they are about to hear a performance. The performance frame will incorporate a number of conventions (which will be specific to each cultural community). The sociologist Erving Goffman described this as 'keying'.[19] These conventions might include the use of special codes or ways of saying things, special formulae (such as 'once upon a time'), particular speech styles and even contextual features such as the place in which the performance takes place or the clothes the performer is wearing.[20] All of these conventions 'key the performance', telling the audience that the communicative act is a performance which in turn conditions the audience response. These keys will differ according to cultural context. For instance, a stand-up comedy act – with its recognisable codes such as the one-liner joke, the pause for laughs, the picking on audience members – will be a performance that most modern Westerners could 'read'; we know what is going on and can respond accordingly. A political speech likewise contains codes such as the Churchillian use of repetition ('We will fight on the beaches, we shall fight on the landing grounds, we shall fight in the fields and in the streets, we shall never surrender') and oratorical devices such as those used to such winning effect by Barack Obama in his presidential campaign. 'It's about the tune, not the lyrics, with Obama', commented a speechwriter for former British Prime Minister Tony Blair.[21] In an entirely different context, that of the world of the African storyteller, the codes that key a performance are equally recognisable to the audience:

A good narrator uses his skill to develop and embroider the skeleton of the available plot with subsidiary details. His own vivid descriptions and songs, his actual style of delivery, gestures, mimicry and use of dramatic repetition are also skilfully interwoven. They way he presents his characters, his variation of speed and tone, vocabulary, persuasion of his listeners, vehemence and drama, are all knit into an aesthetic whole.[22]

It is only when these performances are situated in particular contexts or genres and in some cases performed by recognisable individuals in specific places, that they are meaningful within the performance system of a culture. In some cultures, storytelling is only recognisable as a performance when it is undertaken by the local storyteller, a specialist who may enjoy a high status in the community. For example, in the Jlao community of Liberia studied by Elizabeth Tonkin, certain individuals were identified as oral artists who were able to narrate long, complex narrative histories.[23] Henry Glassie was told of people in Ballymenone in Ireland who had 'the gift' of being able to spin a tale: 'It's a wonderful talent to be able to picture a long hot one and then fill it up, line by line. Oh now, it's wonderful.'[24] And the act of storytelling may be recognised by an audience when it takes place in a designated place and using particular linguistic devices. Likewise, the oral history is an event keyed by a number of conventions: it will normally take place in a private or semi-private space, it will involve a one-to-one conversation, and so on.

The fact that meaning may only be understood when the performance is enacted within the appropriate and commonly understood context leads to some interesting tensions. In everyday life we know the consequences when someone tells a joke or breaks into song at an inappropriate moment. The audience will often look embarrassed or try to ignore what has happened. In an oral history interview, the researcher can be thrown off balance when the expected framework of the event is broken, for instance when the interviewee bursts into tears or perhaps speaks about intensely personal matters which, to the interviewer, do not belong in the public domain. A more serious example concerns the deployment of oral tradition in a context unable or unwilling to incorporate or understand it. In north-western Canada, in the 1980s, First Nation communities used their oral traditions to support their land claims in the courts of British Columbia. Instead of hiring lawyers and engaging with the speech conventions of the Canadian courts they performed songs and dances which to them expressed the complicated relationships between peoples and place. Moreover they attempted to argue that their oral traditions demonstrated their ownership of the land. Their arguments were rejected by the court on the grounds that oral tradition, songs and reminiscences could not be evaluated in a legal context. Julie Cruikshank states that the lesson of this case is 'that removing oral tradition from a context where it has self-evident power, and performing it in a context where it is opened to evaluation by the state, poses enormous problems for serious understandings of its historical value'.[25]

So far we have been considering the idea of performance as something set apart from the everyday. But there is a branch of modern cultural theory called 'performativity theory' that finds performance in both everyday life and in every individual's identity. In this theory, everyday life involves practices

that constitute the site of the self. French theorist Jacques Derrida emphasised the performative speech acts that rework, tease and stretch language
with every usage. As we speak, we do not merely recirculate but minutely alter,
refresh and reassemble the meanings embedded in language, discourse and
signs. Judith Butler continued this approach in 1990 in her *Gender Trouble* in
which she argued that gender is not merely received in our genes and negotiated as a public discourse but is also *practised* in everyday activity, ritual
and learning. Every individual feels his or her way into gender roles, making
gender unfixed and uncertain. The very notion of 'identity' becomes with
Butler an interpretative danger that ensnares analysis in a struggle to define
and capture the individual. So, gender becomes a practice, not a prefigured
or constitutive category (such as 'woman'). We make our gender.[26] And, by
extension of this idea, we make our identity in thousands of everyday performances of speech, dress, gesture and deportment.

From this, Langellier and Peterson argue that even our everyday communication practices are performative in that they involve not just speech acts
but bodily/embodied communication too. The act of storytelling amongst a
group of friends or within a family context is a narrative performance,
embodied in the speaker and constituted by the relationship established
between the speaker and the audience. In Langellier and Peterson's words:

> The simple act of saying 'let me tell you a story' establishes a commu-
> nication relationship that constitutes the speaker as a storyteller and the
> listeners as audience. The utterance 'let me tell you a story' is, in other
> words, *performative* in that it does what it says it is doing. It performs the
> storytelling that it announces. 'Let me tell you a story' also establishes a
> story, the 'something that happened' that the storyteller re-enacts, recites
> or represents. The telling of the story is a *performance*. As a human
> communication practice, performing narrative combines the performative
> 'doing' of storytelling with what is 'done' in the performance of a story.[27]

The authors go on to illustrate how narrative performance in very ordinary
settings – a group of friends, family conversations – has, as one of its purposes, the solidification of group identities, the creation of imagined communities and the production of an idea of family. They suggest, for instance, that
the telling and retelling of 'classic' family stories – 'do you remember
when …?' has the effect of mediating struggles over the meanings of particular events in the course of which the identity and meaning of family is
renegotiated amongst its members. Through performing narratives the 'family
narrates itself'.[28] In a broader context, performing personal narratives is a
social bonding exercise in that it allows us to talk about ourselves whilst
simultaneously placing ourselves within the community – of friends, family,
neighbourhood, nation.

Performativity theory can be difficult to grasp, and is as yet little used by
oral historians. But new theoretical development in this area is likely to lead

to new ideas for practitioners. In the meantime, practitioners might find applicability to the oral history interview in a variety of ways. First, interviewees often retell stories they have told before; second, they often rehearse what they are going to say beforehand, especially if they know the questions in advance. Third and more broadly, according to performativity theory, every speech act is a performance through which identity is composed by the individual. This means that different interviews may produce different versions of that identity which can be compared and contrasted. This may be especially noticeable if a respondent is interviewed first on his or her own and then a second time with a partner or spouse present. Oral historians who have tried this technique often end up with interesting variation and even contradiction in both content and in the tenor of the performance. The narrator has no single identity in view to the oral historian – it can be constantly shifting – and by careful pursuit of its variations, important conclusions may be drawn.

Finally, one of the key elements of any performance – the voice – has been theorised.[29] The power of voice – its tone, timbre, intonation and so on – has long been recognised by broadcasters, actors and politicians, but theorists are also now interested in the voice as a route to revealing the identity of the speaker. For Anne Karpf, the voice:

> belongs to both the body and mind ... it bridges our internal and external worlds, travelling from our most private recesses into the public domain, revealing not only our deepest sense of who we are, but also who we wish we weren't. It's a superb guide to fear and power, anxiety and subservience, to another person's vitality and authenticity as well as our own.[30]

Karpf goes on to assert that the voice is embodied (it is not just a metaphorical thing). Voice, she says, 'has also become a common term for narrative authority and literary self-expression' but at the most basic level the voice is a sound one makes with the body.[31] And this means that the voice should be considered as part of the performance of an oral history.

Storytelling and performance

Attention to the performance element of oral history narratives has been influenced by analyses of storytelling. The storytelling tradition relies upon performance. A good storyteller knows that his or her communicative power derives not simply from remembering and retelling the stories but from knowing *how* to tell the stories to produce the desired effect. The storyteller is conscious of the importance of the performance and a skilled narrator will finesse the performance to suit the particular context and the expectations of the audience. Folklorist Linda Dégh terms this the etiquette of storytelling which incorporates a code of aesthetics, 'linguistic and semiotic formulas that include polished, structured speech and body language to create witty dialogues, to characterise actors and actions, and to elaborate traditional cadences'.[32] Tellers are also judged on the extent to which they use imagination and creativity, on the originality of their story development and structure and on their success in the 'bridging of everyday reality and fiction in the formulaic introduction and closure'.[33] The performance is an intrinsic part of a successful telling.

Storytelling, as it was understood and interpreted by folklorists, is the narration of a tale which may be 'traditional' in that it has been passed on orally. Collectors of stories in the nineteenth and early twentieth centuries, working in the ethnological tradition, tended to regard storytelling as a remnant of a disappearing or authentic culture, hence the many attempts to collect and catalogue tales before they disappeared. The most famous European example of this practice is the German Grimm Brothers' *Children's and Household Tales* and the Dane Hans Christian Anderson's fairytale collection. The social practices that sustained storytelling in many parts of Western Europe have largely disappeared. The evening house-visiting once commonplace in Highland Scottish communities which fostered storytelling and music-making rapidly declined after the First World War, thus limiting the opportunity for performance acts.[34] However, ethnological and anthropological approaches to storytelling have introduced analytical insights useful to the oral historian. Alongside the content of the story being told, these scholars have focused attention on the performance aspects of the tale-telling which means taking into account the precise context of the narration, not just the geographical and historical environment but also the context of the immediate performance, the teller's style, the nature of the audience, the purpose of the telling. The narrative event then is regarded as a social process rather than a product in itself or, in Cruikshank's words 'part of the equipment for living rather than a set of meanings embedded in texts waiting to be discovered'.[35]

The idea of what constitutes a storytelling narrative has been broadened by scholars working outside the folklore tradition so that our definitions of the storyteller and the tale are not confined to those narrators and tales identified as such in collections. Socio-linguists, for instance, have identified storytelling as a mode of speech rather than a formal performance event and have thus reconceptualised storytelling as a part of wider social discourse. In East European Jewish culture, for example, recognised storytellers did not exist, but stories were told in a variety of speech contexts including sermons, teaching, speeches and general conversation. Here, 'storytelling is not scheduled as an activity in its own right but always seems to occur as part of another activity'.[36] Furthermore, the stories are not ends in themselves but are means by which people achieve particular goals, be they rhetorical, educational or otherwise. Likewise in the Yukon territory of northern Canada, storytelling or the telling of stories serves a number of purposes: 'each performance is historically situated as the teller, the audience, and the intended meanings shift to meet the occasion'.[37] In the case of Angela Sidney, interviewed by Julie Cruikshank stories acted as 'cultural scaffolding' or a framework to aid the dialogue between the narrator and the investigator, but they had also been deployed by the narrator in a number of different contexts: for instance, at a son's homecoming as a 'gift' and at the opening of a new college as a means of representing the symbolic importance of the event. For Mrs Sidney, the narratives or stories she had learned as a child provided her with reference points and a means to say things about contemporary society as well as the past.

Clearly not all oral history interviews constitute stories or are told in the storytelling mode. A structured interview, where the interviewer poses the questions, is clearly not the same as a dialogue or a communicative event like the telling of a story. Yet many of us have conducted interviews in which the narrator has taken control and has chosen his or her own form to convey meaning which may include some features of the storytelling mode. To some extent, the degree to which this occurs is dependent upon culture. Some cultures more than others deploy storytelling devices as a means of communication. In the Yukon, Cruikshank discovered that the narration of stories was central to how her respondents communicated with her. Cruikshank's initial social-science approach to eliciting the history and experience of change was challenged by her respondents' approach to life history which had at its core the narration of a series of core stories.[38]

Performance as practice

So far we have been focusing on using performance theory as a way of analysing a speech act. But performance is also a practice, a creative event, a 'staged re-iteration of stories'.[39] So we also need to consider how a performance can be used to recreate or to stage a speech act, be it a folktale, a story or an oral history. I will restrict the discussion here to the staging of oral history narrative.

Performance of all kinds has become a recognised outcome of oral history production, ranging from the more obvious applications such as historical re-enactments and museum and heritage presentations to the less obviously congruent such as drama and dance. Practitioners in the field of performance studies have engaged with oral history as a means of representing memory acts 'in live representation as both a form (a container) and a means (catalyst) of social action'.[40] This does not mean the performance of staged re-enactments or heritage productions but rather the re-presentation of living memory in a public performance or what Della Pollock terms the translation of 'subjectively remembered events into embodied memory acts, moving memory into re-membering'.[41] In effect, this process of making an explicit performance (staged in public) out of an implicit one (the oral history interview) squares the memory circle; it can demonstrate how seemingly individual memories are amalgamations of communal ones through the engagement with an audience, and it can insert the private memory into public consciousness, thus creating new historical memory. In short, performing oral history can keep memory alive by providing a forum for an active engagement with remembering. It can also reorient our attention away from the primacy of the written or spoken word and towards 'doing-by-telling' or a focus on how the story is told.

The performance-studies approach treats oral history as a social activity and as such has much in common with the approach of ethnologists for whom the narrative is a living thing, with a purpose and a meaning (seldom fixed) that may be deployed in a variety of circumstances. This is helpful to oral historians who perhaps need to be reminded sometimes that oral history is not merely a means of collecting information but a communicative event with resonances beyond the interview.[42]

Application

Performance theories and oral history

The application to oral history of concepts and insights from the field of performance studies has been piecemeal and undeveloped. Historians have been slow to apply these insights to their analysis of oral narratives. But it is instructive to look to scholars from other disciplines who have used oral history methodology and who have paid attention to the performance aspect of the oral narrative, regarding this as much as the words spoken as essential to the expression of meaning. Barbara Meyerhoff argues that 'it is erroneous to think of performances as optional, arbitrary, or merely decorative embellishments' because they are in fact ubiquitous.[43] Focusing on the performance of an oral history narrative forces us to think about how the story works in the present because the performance is usually before our very eyes. The physical act of telling the story involving the combination of voice and gesture makes the performance something to be noticed and it gives the researcher clues on how to read or interpret the story being told.

The focus here then is on the idea of the oral history as a performance-oriented narrative rather than a content-oriented document and in some instances clearly the performance is paramount.[44] The narration of a folk tale or a song lyric for instance, makes little sense devoid of the performance because the performance makes them come alive, and, in many cases, the meaning is conveyed by the performance as well as and sometimes in place of the words. Alun Howkins' survey of the place of song in British life and as a source for the oral historian makes precisely this point.[45] But given the relative disappearance of song and indeed public storytelling in the oral culture of modern Western society it is not surprising that the most interesting research in this field draws upon non-Western cultural contexts. Robert O'Meally advocates listening to and watching African-American vernacular expressions of culture as a performance; indeed, he argues that all levels of that performance must be attended to – not just the lyrics in the case of blues music but also the musical structures, the context in which it is performed and the relationship between performer and audience – in order to reach a nuanced and multilayered understanding of the meaning of the event.[46] In an entirely different context, that of the southern African borderlands, Angela Impey's oral-testimony work with elderly women utilised music-making on the Jewish harp (*is'tweletwele*) as a means of evoking memories of the days when the women were young and had walked the landscape playing these instruments. Playing the instruments again elicited memories and stories. Impey notes that the instruments and the sounds they made carried 'referential functions' and 'index experiences, relationships, feelings and places'.[47] They participated in soundwalks along familiar routes, 'each cue prompting songs relevant to it, and the songs, in turn, elaborating their stories'.[48] Similarly, Megan Vaughan has used women's work and food-preparation songs as a form of oral testimony, charting women's changing experiences over time.[49] All these examples drive home the point that not only is performance an intrinsic part of history-telling but that oral historians should bear in mind that the spoken word is not the only or even necessarily the best form of narrating the past.

More commonly, oral narratives have been analysed for their performance elements: the tone of voice, the gestures, the expressions of emotion that give colour and meaning to the narration of a story. Rhonda Williams, in her interviews with two black American female activists in the public-housing sector, seeks to illustrate why we should pay attention to what she calls the 'voice of the narrative'.[50] Williams conducts a close analysis of the unspoken and verbal signals scattered throughout the women's narratives about their community advocacy work. Laughter, tone of voice, intonations and gestures are all noted and interpreted alongside the text. One of her respondents, Shirley Wise,

> did not tell her story nonchalantly, but with fire, a pensiveness, a commanding tone, and a serious face that bared her disgust and anger at the circumstances she found herself in and the conditions tenants faced. The way she spoke shaped the intensity of the words, and therefore – like her laughter – added another layer of knowing to the oral history.[51]

Similarly, in her rich and detailed analysis of the life of Ila Healy, hunter, 'cowboy' and rancher in Arizona, Kristina Minister is alert to her subject's performative self-representation in a series of oral history collaborations in which Mrs Healy narrates episodes from what Minister calls her 'performance career'. Her choice of work – hunting and ranching – permitted her to adopt a 'male performance style', taking the floor when telling stories for instance and positioning herself at the centre of stories. In adopting this performance style, Minister argues, she was creating a particular kind of self-image. While performing her all-action stories she was constituting a self in the present with which she felt comfortable and which she wished to project to her audience.[52]

For older people, as Meyerhoff suggests, there is a more elemental role for performance in the oral history encounter. It is a means by which they can become visible and attract attention to themselves. At a time of life when invisibility is an all-too-common experience, when many aspects of life are beyond a person's control, the oral history interview may be taken as an opportunity to demonstrate knowledge and to perform a version of the self that is not congruent with the image of the socially marginalised, physically limited, passive older person. Meyerhoff's work with elderly Jewish Holocaust survivors is a particularly apposite example: her respondents were desperate to tell their stories, not just as a way of keeping the memories alive but as a means of self-enrichment.[53] Reminiscence work with the elderly similarly has the potential to stimulate and invigorate. Taking the performance element of oral history one step further, the Age Exchange Reminiscence Theatre in East London not only incorporated older people's memories into a theatrical production but also involved those people in the production itself resulting in a transformation of older people's perception of themselves.[54]

Performance as event

The staging of oral history as a performance event is seen as a way of creating a creative, active and fluid space within which to debate and share memory. For Della Pollock, the leading practitioner in this field, performance:

> is an especially charged, contingent, reflexive space of encountering the complex web of our respective histories. It may consequently engage participants in new and renewed understandings of the past. It may introduce alternative voices into public debate. It may help identify systemic problems and to engage a sense of need, hope, and vision. As live representation, performance may in effect bring imagined worlds into *being and becoming*, moving performers and audiences alike into palpable recognition of possibilities for change.[55]

These are bold claims for what looks like a simple act of transferring oral history narratives to the stage. But Pollock's experience of organising a staged performance of *Like a Family*, a published history of cotton-mill workers in North Carolina based upon oral history interviews, clearly shows how the public performance of memory can facilitate the cultural or memory circuit.[56] When the performance toured the towns from which the original interview respondents had been drawn, they discovered how the public representation of memories fostered audience involvement in a number of ways, from individual interventions during the performance itself to lengthy informal discussions amongst and between audience members and performers at the event's close. The performance facilitated a 'retelling and reliving' and, most importantly, a dialogic exchange that fed into the performance each night. Pollock concludes that 'the most important meanings of any story or history are emergent in the performance of that story.'[57] The words spoken in oral history interviews engendered multiple meanings and interpretations when represented in a public forum that permitted exchange and intervention. Making oral history public through retelling in a performance event can sustain and reinvigorate memories of the past as Natalie Fousekis's students discovered when they produced performances based on oral history projects ranging from experiences of internment and concentration camps during the Second World War to conflicts between Vietnam War veterans and 1960s radicals.[58] And in Britain, the artist Jeremy Deller's re-enactment of the battle of Orgreave, a particularly violent event during the 1984–5 national miners' strike, based on oral histories with people on both sides and involving many of the original participants as well as battle re-enactment societies, was envisaged as a means of understanding the impact of the strike on strikers, their families, police and the mining communities at large.[59]

In Britain, Ronald Blythe's oral history-based tale of rural life in his book *Akenfield* of 1967 was turned into a dramatised film in 1974, followed thirty years later by a book sequel *Return to Akenfield* (by Craig Taylor) which itself was turned into a stage play. The original book presents a series of conversations with rural inhabitants, loosely based on interviews conducted by Blythe with farm labourers, craftsmen, village worthies and local professionals. At the heart of the book were the 'survivors', the men born at the end of the nineteenth century into rural poverty and who 'escaped' to the battlefields of the First World War. In 1974, *Akenfield* became a film of the same name, based on Blythe's screenplay and directed by Peter Hall. The film was an evocation of rural life past and present told through the story of Tom, a young man with dreams of escaping the claustrophobia and limitations of village life and poverty. The actors were residents of the villages and 'played themselves' (the actor who played Tom was a farm worker for instance), they extemporised the dialogue, and the film was shot at weekends over the course of a year, chronicling the changing seasons.[60] In 2004, on the thirtieth anniversary of the film, the BBC produced a documentary called *Akenfield Revisited*, which featured conversations with some of the original cast and crew. Thus, over a period of thirty-five years since the publication of the original book, private memories have become part of public memory, mediated by the on-screen re-enactments of the lives and reminiscences of the original characters.

The publication in 2006 of Taylor's *Return to Akenfield* once more awakened interest in the original book, and in 2009 this too became a performance, this time a stage drama produced by a theatre company located in the east of England. The play was toured around small villages in that part of the world, attracting local audiences, many if not most of whom would have been familiar with the original book. In an interview following the opening night: Taylor remarked: 'The best moment happened in the interval when people got up and began discussing what they had just witnessed. There were issues that were relevant to their own lives.'[61] On its fortieth anniversary, the present author wrote an appreciation of Blythe's original work.[62] His work in *Akenfield* demonstrated how oral history can take on a life beyond the interview, remaining fluid and negotiated rather than fixed on a page in a transcript or in an academic text.

The popularity of oral history at the community and popular level has also spawned the transference of oral history narratives from interview to performance event. In Shetland, where oral history has been since the 1980s an integral part of the way in which islanders imagine themselves and their past, a play performed by Shetland Arts entitled *It Wis Hard Work but* ... drew on oral histories with former female herring-gutters and was performed in front of an audience gathered at a conference to discuss Shetland women's history, sparking memory work amongst the audience members and between local women and visitors. The interaction between oral history and public performance of all kinds is now quite extensive – from using drama workshops as a forum for eliciting oral testimonies to incorporating oral history material into theatre productions. One example of the latter was *Sexshunned* about the experiences of lesbian, gay, bisexual and transgender people, a collaborative project between Ourstory Scotland which collects their life stories and the 7:84 Theatre Company.[63] Even more commonly, oral history is now widely incorporated into a range of public art projects and installations – from museum exhibits to public spaces. Many museums now have earphones for visitors to hear extract recordings to enhance the viewing of fixed exhibits. The installation of oral history recordings on lamppost transmitters along four miles of London motorway must count as one of the most imaginative uses of oral history in a public performance context.[64] In these ways, oral history often offers a 'pay-back' to the communities from which respondents come, stimulating other memories of the elderly whilst hopefully educating the young.

Practice

How might the historian apply these theories to the practice of interviewing and the analysis of oral history narratives? One might start with a series of considerations which could be applied to any form of verbal art. Finnegan lists the following:

> Questions for investigation thus include how or where performances takes place as actual events; how they are organised and prepared for; who is there, how they behave and what their expectations are; how the performers deliver the specific genre and the audience react to it; how it is framed within and/or separate from the flow of everyday life.[65]

Oral historians are frequently urged to make notes of the non-verbal elements of interviews and to take care when transcribing to include verbal tics and utterances so as to convey as far as is possible the narrative as a performance act, resting on the assumption that meaning is conveyed as much by non-verbal gestures and expressions as by the actual words spoken. Of course, both the recording (whether it is sound only or image and sound) and the transcription are both records of a performance, not the performance itself, so we should always be conscious that our analysis of a verbal text is at best one step removed from the act itself. So far we have been assuming that the person conducting the analysis also conducted the interview, thereby being able to draw on first-hand observations of the respondent's performance of a personal narrative. The increasing use of video recording of interviews, capturing the sound and the visual representation, does offer the researcher the opportunity to analyse the whole performance. As Dan Sipe observes, the power of the moving image reminds us that 'orality, at its core, is not purely a concept grounded in sound'.[66] Video can maintain the vibrancy, tonal inflections and presence of the original, capturing not only the 'unworded' elements of an interview but the very moment when memory is invoked or narrative created.[67]

Guidance on how to restore the aesthetic context to an oral narrative can be found in the works of scholars in ethnology, sociolinguistics and performance studies for whom a dissatisfaction with the failure to take full account of the performance element of verbal art prompted a turn to aligning the aesthetic or stylistic elements of a telling with the communicative. Dell Hymes provides a template for describing the important features of the speech event in a mnemonic, SPEAKING, which stands for Setting, Participants, Ends, Act-sequences, Keys, Instrumentalities, Norms and Genres.[68] Each of these can provide a heading for commencing the analysis of an oral history interview. It may seem a rather formulaic template, but in fact most oral historians already pay attention to these matters; the mnemonic merely serves as a handy reminder. For Elizabeth Fine, though, even this does not go far enough. She presents a model for making a 'performance report', a detailed textual representation of the complex vocal and bodily forms of communication that go into making a piece of verbal art. She terms it a 'performance-centred text' containing multiple marks and symbols to indicate paralinguistic features (that is, those elements of communication which communicate meaning such as tone and pitch of voice, emphasis, gestures and so on). This may strike the oral historian as excessively intrusive and detailed. While it certainly draws attention to the performance it perhaps can detract attention from what is said.[69]

The ethnologist Dennis Tedlock developed his own ethnographic approach to translating performance into a written text in response to his disappointment with existing printed collections of American Indian narratives which had been tidied up, decluttered and rendered devoid of their spontaneous performance qualities on the page, Using typography such as font size and capitals, notations for different kinds of pauses, split lines and italics, he is able to represent in print the poetic features of the performances that would otherwise be lost – the tone of voice, loudness and pausing.[70] As an example, let us take Tedlock's desire to represent the onomatopoeic words that were part of the linguistic style of the Zuñi narratives. Here is an extract where Tedlock transcribes the words in the native language and in translation:

'an suwe kululunan pololo
(low, hoarse voice) tuu – n teyatip,
'an papa wilo' 'anan pololo, wilo' 'ati
(low, hoarse voice) too – w teyatikya.
Sekwat lo'lii pottikya.
Laky'antolh Ihiton 'iya.
Lhiton 'ikya, ikyas
'isshakwakwa hish ky'aptom 'el'ikya.

His younger brother rolled the thunder
(low, hoarse voice) *tuu – n* it began,
his elder brother rolled the lightning, lightning struck
(low, hoarse voice) *too – w* it began.
Now the clouds filled up.
Here comes the rain.
The rain came, it came
'isshakwakwa the water really did come down.[71]

Following Tedlock's aspiration to make visible the sounds uttered as well as the words spoken, D. Soyini Madison adopts what she calls a 'poetic form of transcription' in order to convey the sound and rhythm of 'black language', informed by the understanding that 'words are alive with sounds that condition their meanings'.[72] To illustrate Madison's technique, consider her description of her respondent Mrs Alma Kapper, an elderly black woman. She conveys to the reader Mrs Kapper's demeanour, 'stately and authoritative', as she performs a story from her childhood. Mrs Kapper said:

I was on the porch by myse'f
I was jus' sittin on the porch
Mama was in the bed
I thought 'bout all I did
wokin' in the fiel'
takin' care ah Mama an' all lika that^^
an' all the res' ah the child'en
goin' off havin' fun on Sat'day
so I say "I caint go/I caint go!!!"
|| Jus' talkin' tuh myse'f ||
an'
(sits up in her seat straight and tall)
the WORD spoke tuh me
the WORD say

GO WHEN YO' CAIN AN' WHEN YO' CAINT
MAKE YO'SE'F SATISFIED!!
that was the spirit talkin' tuh/me
(she spoke with great confidence)
MAKE YO'SE'F SATISFIED!![73]

Madison notes, in order to aid our understanding of the meaning of
Mrs Kapper's narrative, that at the point when she uttered 'the WORD spoke
tuh me',

> her confidence rises in gestures and expressions of joy and excitement. As
> she speaks of the 'Lawd' she leans over toward me, smiling big and
> bright. She points her finger and waves her hands, her head moving back
> and forth to the rising pitch and volume of her voice. She is having a
> good time and the room is full of the joyful presence of Mrs Kapper.[74]

All of these solutions to the problem of how the researcher is to communicate
the performance element of a speech act pose problems. This is all the more
so when endeavouring to 'translate' a performance event from one culture to
another. In her sensitive analysis of what to do with the stories she was told
in Alaskan Yup'ik society, Phyllis Morrow suggests that the act of transferring oral performance to paper is problematic, and possibly unwise, not least
because of what she terms the 'authorship problem'.[75] The notion of authorship (who spoke) is culturally specific. In the Yup'ik context, storytelling is
not regarded as an individual act but as the outcome of the circulation of a
story by many storytellers, and, furthermore, meaning is not fixed in the
storyteller's version but has a fluidity that changes, for instance, with time,
with the teller and the context of the telling. Cultural differences between
Western and Yup'ik culture in the telling and interpretation of stories mean
that the Western desire to reduce stories to their meaning (through an analysis
of what was said and how it was said) conflicts with the native desire for
meaning to be invested in the performance act.

   This performance aspect of the oral history interview can be manifested in
many different ways. Some respondents will make elaborate preparations of
the interview setting – arranging chairs, side tables, laying out mementoes and
photographs and even inviting a friend or relative to sit in (an unplanned
eventuality that can disrupt the interviewer's preference for a one-to-one
interview). Others may present preprepared scripts or articulate a concern
that the story being told conforms to what is required by the interviewer.
They may moderate an accent or use of dialect for an interviewer who would
otherwise have comprehension difficulties or feel a standard pronunciation is
more appropriate for a public performance. The interviewee may adopt a
particular performance model (such as the storytelling mode) in order to
present a confident and practised narrative style whereby he or she takes
control of the 'interview' in order to muster the confidence for the event or as

an assertion of authority over it. Some respondents feel a responsibility to tell interesting or humorous stories. In all sorts of diverse ways, a performance may be prepared and 'laid on' for the interviewer.

The performance mode adopted will be to some extent determined by the 'script'; that is, the story or narrative the interviewee wishes to relate may suggest or require a certain form and style in order that it is heard in the appropriate way. To illustrate this, I will use the example of the narrative of a Shetland woman called Mary Manson. This example is also a reminder of the importance of producing a transcript that accurately records both the orality and the physicality of the interview, what Frances Good terms the 'humanity of the spoken word'.[76]

Mary Manson was interviewed twice in 1982 by a local folklorist and genealogist in her own home in front of two academics using a large old-fashioned reel-to-reel recorder, probably with her husband and the district nurse present. She was eighty-five years old and had lived on the island of Yell in Shetland all of her life. The interviews appear to have been undertaken to elicit information about Mary's knowledge of the local community, the work that was carried out in this crofting area, local customs and practices and characters. Mary was a fluent respondent, speaking in Shetland dialect, willing to engage in conversation, always ready to elaborate on names, places and experiences. But halfway through the second recording, the interview took an unexpected turn. From a question-and-answer routine, Mary suddenly took control of the interview. Mary was asked 'Now what wis that story aboot dee midder goin ta ... ?' (What was that story about your mother going to ... ?) Before the question was even finished, she launched into a long, uninterrupted narrative telling the tale of her mother and a friend, as two young and nervous girls, being sent on foot and by boat to another island to see a local 'wise woman' to fetch a cure for a sick relative. The journey was a perilous one, but the girls were befriended by local boatmen who took them from island to island. This is a coherent and practised tale, a story that Mary had told a number of times before. A short extract from the middle part of the story, as the girls arrive at the wise woman's house, provides a taste of this narrative. It appears below first in Shetland dialect, and then in English 'translation'.

> So dey got in here ta dis auld wife's hoose an da first that sho did wis ta come wi a basin o water ta dem ta wash dir feet in because I tink dir feet wis dat sore, travelling, my goodness, dey wir been travellin fae here da whole day an dan dey wir been travelling trow Unst. An sho got dem something ta eat, an I'll tell you whit sho got dem ta eat wis a bursteen brunnie, a piece o bursteen brunnie, I don't know if it wis tae or whit it wis bit onywye it wis a piece o bursteen brunnie, so dey got eaten dis. An so sho says, noo, I'll hae ta laeve you an geng furt an I'll maybe be a braw start awa, bit onywye sho says you'll geng ta bed an lay you doon, an I'll pit you ta bed afore I go. An da bed at sho hed wis a boxed bed, it wis a boxed bed ootbye at da partition, an dis door drew close, a widden door

at drew close in da bed. I mind Mammy sayin it wis a fine bed at sho hed,
sho hed a tauttit rug an a feather bed an of course, dan a days it wis laekly
supposed ta be a winderfil bed. Onywye dey got aff o dem an dey got intae
dis bed an sho drew da door across da front. So you can keen whit dey
wir likely tinkin, lockit in a dis black prison – black prison, didna know
whit wis going to happen efter dat. So anyway, sho left dem in yunder an
sho gied oot, an sho wis a braw while awa, an at last dey heard her comin
in, bit it had ta be kinda light, it hed ta be da spring do sees at sho could
see, anywye, daylight coming up or somethin. Bit dey heard her comin in
an dey heard her startin to get da fire up, it wis a fire in da middle o da
floor an dey heard her gettin doon da peats an gettin dis fire going, an a
pouring a water an a rattling o pans an tins an all dis. An dan efter a
while dey fan da smell o laek dis roots, laek a strong smell o roots boiling
So Mammy said dey could lie no longer for dey wir never fallen asleep in
yun, sho got up an sho tried, dir wis a chink in da door, an sho got up an
sho tried ta peep an see whit wis going on an sho said that da old wife
wis sitting ower da hertstane wi all dis pots an pans an a great pot
hanging in da crook, boiling with dis mixture. So eh, onyway sho said sho
raise up, Mam wid swear at sho never made ony noise at all ta peep oot dis
chink an of course dis old wife wis sittin wi her back till her an sho never
kent or sho let oot a shout, lie doon an faa asleep dis minute, sho says, I
keen ower weel at you're watching me, you're going ta destroy da medicine.[77]

So they got in here to this old wife's house and the first thing that she did
was to come with a basin of water to them to wash their feet in because I
think their feet was that sore travelling, my goodness, they had been travelling from here the whole day and then they were been travelling to
Unst. And she got them something to eat, and I'll tell you what she got
them to eat was a bursten broonie [corn cake], a piece of bursten broonie,
I don't know if it was tea or what it was but anyway it was a piece of
bursten broonie, so they got eating this. And so she says, now, I'll have to
leave you and go forth and I'll may be a good time away, but anyway she
says you'll go to bed and lay you down, and I'll put you to bed before I
go. And the bed that she had was a box bed [an enclosed bed by a wall],
it was a box bed outside at the partition, and this door drew close, a
wooden door that drew close in the bed. I remember Mammy saying it
was a fine bed that she had, she had a tatted rug [handcrafted knitted
rug] and a feather bed and of course, in those days it was likely supposed
to be a wonderful bed. Anyway they took their clothes off and they got
into this bed and she drew the door across the front. So you can know
what they were likely thinking, locked in this black prison – a black
prison, didn't know what was going to happen after that. So anyway, she
left them in there and she went out, and she was a long time away, and at
last they heard her coming in, but it had to be kind of light, it had to be
the spring you see because she could see, anyway, daylight coming up or

something. But they heard her coming and they heard her starting to get the fire up, it was a fire in the middle of the floor and they heard her getting down the peats and getting this fire going, and pouring the water and rattling the pans and tins and all this. And then after a while they found the smell like roots, like a strong smell of roots boiling. So Mammy said they could lie no longer for they had never fallen asleep, she got up and she tried, there was a chink in the door, and she got up and she tried to peep and see what was going on and she said that the old wife was sitting over the hearthstone with all the pots and pans and a great pit hanging in the crook, boiling with this mixture. So anyway she said she got up, Mam would swear that she never made any noise at all to peep out this chink and of course this old wife was sitting with her back to her and she never knew or she let out a shout, lie down and fall asleep this minute, she says, I know very well that you're watching me, you're going to destroy the medicine.

This is a remarkable and revealing story (of which this is only a small extract). It has a momentum and a drive that sees the narrator Mary Manson in control, and her hearers are in thrall. The 'story about her mother' is a performance on a number of levels. To begin with, the story is not narrated in answer to a question about some aspect of island life; rather it is told as a bounded tale with a symmetrical structure (the girls travel there and back, there is a focus on inside and outside, light and dark, health and illness, then and now).[78] Indeed, the story contains many of the elements of narrative identified in Chapter 6. Notably, it had begun with a statement about the medical provision as it was in her mother's day, thus orientating the listener:

> Weel, I canna mind whin it would have been, but onywye I just tink da difference noo, although we are never thankful enough, two nurses an two doctors here in Yell, an you just need ta feel a pain or anything, lift da phone an call da doctor an he's here afore you get da phone laid doon, at da door ta see what's wrong wi you. An dan ta think aboot da old folk, whit a life dey had if anything wis da maitter wi them, aha.

> Well, I can't remember when it would have been, but anyway I just think the difference now, although we are never thankful enough, two nurses and two doctors here in Yell, and you just need to feel a pain or anything, lift the phone and call the doctor and he's here before you put the phone down, at the door to see what's wrong with you. And then to think about the old folk, what a life they had if anything was the matter with them, yes.

And the story is concluded with a resolution: the sick relative is restored to good health with the help of the medicine, there is a 'happily ever after' ending and a return to the present: 'An sho never lookit back, sho never lookit back fae that day. No ... Sho married an had nine of a family, an lived to an old age, so dat's da story o da bottle o medicine, bit look noo a days.' (And she never looked back, she never looked back from that day. No ... She married and had nine of a family, and lived to an old age, and that's the story of the bottle of medicine, but look nowadays.)

Second, Mary employs a number of storytelling devices – the use of reported speech, vivid detail, repetition ('lockit in a dis black prison – black prison') and suspense – to keep the listener's attention. Third, the narrative has all the ingredients of the classic fairytale: young girls on a transformative journey, a 'witch'-like woman, magic potions, taboos (the girls were not permitted to look at the mixture or to let the bottle touch the ground), and juxtapositions of light and dark, young and old, good and evil. And finally Mary possesses the storyteller's authority: she takes the stage and holds it while she skilfully tells the story. Interruptions by the interviewer are not allowed to disrupt the telling. In fact she maintains authorial control over the narrative at all times, even at the end asserting her own ownership of this story by referring to it as the 'story o da bottle o medicine' rather than the 'dat story about dee midder'. Mary Manson's story is a creative act; the performance cannot be separated from the words spoken because it is the performance that gives the story meaning or significance.

It is rare to encounter such a perfectly formed narrative performance within an oral history interview – few of our respondents are natural storytellers – but many respondents will narrate short pre-prepared or composed stories that enable them to assume narrative competence and authority. And when they do this, we must pay attention because a story well told almost invariably possesses meaning for the respondent and it is being told for a reason. Ultimately, though, performance is implicit in every oral history interview. The heightened occasion demands it of our respondents. It is the task of the researcher to notice and to interpret the elements of the performance that add meaning to the words said. The act of telling a story is, according to Cruikshank, a form of communication-based social action.[79] Our oral history interviewees use the opportunity of the oral history interview to act or speak out in words and gesture what they believe to be significant. Performing is a means of self-revelation, an opportunity for proclamation, not an optional extra but an intrinsic part of any oral narrative.

Conclusion

Consideration of performance adds an exciting dimension to the analysis of oral history testimony. It raises the eyes of the practitioner from the words of the transcript to the significance of the interview event as a communicative act. We are reminded that narrators finds status, meaning and significance in the performance. More than that, the performance act becomes part of their contemporary identity; they are a repository of knowledge about the past, according them a significance which the oral historian, by asking for their memories and placing the microphone in front of them, is according them.

The oral historian can sometimes be fooled by all the textbooks, rules and procedures of our work, and by the emphasis upon analysis, into thinking this to be a dry-bones exercise in which the performance is a distraction. It is not. It is central. And from it we learn not only a sense of the significance of the story and the event to narrators but also that our analysis needs to convey the emotions and effort which our respondents invest in recalling their past.

8 Power and empowerment

Introduction

In 1988 Paul Thompson made a case for the transformative and empowering potential of oral history:

> oral history certainly can be a means for transforming both the content and purpose of history. It can be used to change the focus of history itself, and open up new areas of enquiry; it can break down barriers between teachers and students, between generations, between educational institutions and the world outside; and in the writing of history ... it can give back to the people who made and experienced history, through their own words, a central place.[1]

This argument has lost little of its allure today. Indeed, since then, the use of oral history as a means of empowerment (of individuals, social groups and communities) and of change (social, political, academic) has expanded markedly. As we shall see shortly, in the early years of oral history practice in the 1960s, 1970s and 1980s, scholars – mainly those sympathetic to the political left and involved in feminist politics – used this methodology to make visible those groups who traditionally had been silenced in historical narratives. This would enable an engagement with liberationist politics through an understanding of a history of oppression. In the words of Michael Frisch, oral history in the 1970s was regarded as a 'challenge to all the assumptions of conventional scholarship, a way for a new kind of history from the bottom up and the outside in to challenge the established organisation of knowledge and power and the politics that rested on it'.[2]

More recently though, oral history has been utilised in different activist contexts around the world, from recording the life histories of refugees to conducting oral history in the name of advocacy amongst aboriginal and tribal communities as a way of documenting their land rights in the absence of written documents. Oral history has moved a long way in terms of the arenas in which it is practised, from the factory floor to the indigenous community. But it has largely retained its role as a tool of advocacy for groups marginalised or excluded from formal channels of power. In this way, oral history has remained at the intersection of academic research and the political sphere. Oral history was intended to give a voice to the voiceless, a narrative to the story-less and power to the marginalised. While its field of operation may have shifted, these aims are still present in much oral history work at both the academic and the grass-roots level.

However, the claim that oral history is in itself empowering for the respondents must not be accepted uncritically. What Grele terms an 'enthusiastic populism' can all too easily transmogrify into academic privilege.[3] Issues of power relations in the interview setting, and the gap between the words spoken and the interpretation drawn from them by the scholar, are just two concerns. Oral historians, many of whom retain the democratic and emancipatory impulses of earlier generations of practitioners, have striven to find ways to diminish power gaps, to democratise their academic practice and to find public use for their research practice. In the process they have found new ways of ensuring that oral history retains its critical edge and acts as a power base for change.

Empowering the silenced: the first wave

The first major group in the world to be systematically recorded on tape were the survivors of the Jewish Holocaust in the 1940s. This began in 1953 with an official Israeli government project to record testimony by the Yad Vashem Holocaust Martyrs' and Heroes' Remembrance Authority, which today provides not merely a recording and deposit facility but also has a remembrance principle as central to its work.[4] As well as its museum to the Holocaust, the Yad Vashem maintains a database of all victims of the *Shoah* and receives and stores testimony from survivors from around the world. In this way, an oral history undertaking is centrally located in a national and religious act of remembrance and identity. Later, in the 1960s and 1970s, many academics conducted oral history projects amongst survivors of the Nazi death camps, including non-Jewish victims, contributing to an area of academic history in which oral remembrance achieved a central place. But a significant number of large public oral history projects have developed in the decades since, most putting oral testimony (both in recorded and transcribed form) online, and many of them located in the USA.[5] With between 6 and 11 million dead, and millions of surviving victims, such projects have been vast in scale, often with aims of promoting, as with one archive, 'cultural, racial and religious understanding through unprecedented worldwide access to its collection of Holocaust survivor narratives'.[6] Oral history remembrance is in this case about empowerment, including religious, ethnic and national identity, but is also part of a more general move to encourage 'victims' to see themselves as 'survivors'.

Oral history, as a means of empowering the weak, the disenfranchised and the victim, has grown in many directions since the middle of the twentieth century. Facilitating those who rarely featured in mainstream histories to 'speak for themselves' was a noble aim of many of the first wave of professional oral historians and community activists. In the USA from the 1950s, Studs Terkel was providing ordinary people with a voice through broadcasting oral history in his radio shows, and for five decades he published books of extracts that revealed the hopes, fears and suffering of American working people. He tackled big themes: experience of the economic depression of the 1930s, of the Second World War, of race relations and hope. In his work was to be found the philosophy that the testimony speaks for itself; he provided limited analysis and editorial and just let the words be heard.[7] To an extent, this philosophy permeates much oral history work, but more analytical, abrasive and dialectical techniques were also being developed. This was especially the case in the UK, where many early oral historians had strong links with the emerging new social and labour history in the 1960s and 1970s which advocated 'history from below'. Exemplifying this approach was the work of Raphael Samuel for whom 'oral tradition' was an antidote to the introspective, sectarian and elitist history that dominated the corridors and publications of academe.[8] In his study of the labouring community of Headington Quarry, Samuel argued that even basic research on the village was impossible without recourse to 'the spoken word of oral tradition'.[9] Oral history was necessary because it directed 'the historian's attention to the fundamental common things of life: the elements of individual and social experience rather than upon administrative and political chronologies'.[10] Samuel's subsequent publications exemplified this approach, focusing on hidden lives of labouring men, highlighting the importance of people's own interpretations of their lives.[11]

For historians who identified with this critical and often socialist standpoint, oral history was a means of subverting the dominant historical narrative or at least suggesting an alternate one from the point of the view of the respondents who might represent the voice of the people (meaning ordinary or labouring folk). In the USA and in the UK, oral history has been deliberately deployed to understand and illuminate class relationships by accessing the experiences of workers in a variety of industries – from Paul Thompson's work on Coventry car workers to New York University's project beginning in 1976 to document the history of the American left by means of oral history interviews with veteran political activists.[12] In Britain, oral history was used to notable effect following the 1984–5 miners' strike when the Conservative government attempted to break the power of the National Union of Mineworkers over the issue of pit closures. Oral histories conducted within the mining communities affected have presented the story of the strike from the standpoint of miners and their wives and families, as well as revealing the fissures within communities.[13]

Similarly, in Germany, a new generation of labour historians including Lutz Niethammer and Detlev Peukert, saw oral history as a means of transforming the relationship between historians and workers – it became 'a channel for the communication of experience' and a way of bringing together academic practice with political engagement in scholarly but also practical ways.[14] And this tradition continues in the work of oral historians such as Ian McDougall of the Scottish Working People's History Trust, who is committed to recording and publishing the memories of labouring Scots.[15]

But this approach was taken further by many oral historians in the 1970s and 1980s. In the USA, Michael Frisch and his collaborators were interested in the potential of oral history to provide a platform for political change but understood the problems implicit in this approach. The 'voice of the people' could not be, on its own, a force for radical change.[16] Once recorded, transcribed, edited and analysed by researchers, those voices were not neutral narratives offering a 'pure' vision of the past but were elements in a political project of resistance. In a critical analysis of his own involvement in a project based on oral interviews with the city of Buffalo unemployed, designed to produce a documentary article for the *New York Times Magazine*, Frisch described the conflicts that arose between the demands of publication and the researchers' agenda. While the editors of the magazine were happy to feature 'the pain and the suffering of the working class, they were less inclined to open their pages to the ideas, values, reflection, advice and social consciousness of these people'.[17] Power and 'authority' are keys to understanding this tension. 'Those truly interested in a history from the bottom up, those who feel the limits of historical reality defined by the powerful, must understand that presuming to "allow" the "inarticulate" to speak is not enough.'[18]

At the same time a parallel development emerged out of the women's movement and feminist politics. Concerned at the invisibility of women in the writing of mainstream histories, historians and activists sought to place women in the historical record, to listen to women's own voices and to use oral history as a tool of feminist research. Gluck and Patai remarked, in what is widely acknowledged as the most influential book in the field of feminist oral history, *Women's Words*, oral history conducted by women, with women, conformed to one of the key principles of feminist research – namely to conduct research 'by, about, and for women'.[19] Oral history seemed to fit well with the feminist aim to conduct an 'egalitarian research process, characterised by authenticity, reciprocity, and intersubjectivity'.[20] Though these authors recognised some of the inherent contradictions contained within this agenda, nonetheless it was an approach that resonated throughout the women's movement and feminist research practice. *Our Work, Our Lives, Our Words*, a collection of studies of women's work in England informed by oral history met the desire not only to place women in the historical record and to make women's lives historical but also to forge a link between the past and present in the lives of women, thus touching on one of the emancipatory discourses of feminist oral history.[21] In this way, women were encouraged to see women's experience in the past as relevant to their position in the present. Likewise, *Dutiful Daughters*, a collection of autobiographical narratives about women's private lives, was conceived as a feminist project to bring the oppression experienced in the private sphere into the public, in the process challenging male interpretations of women's experience.[22]

In this emerging rationale, in order to make sense of lives in the present day, women (and other oppressed or subordinated groups) needed to have knowledge and understanding of the oppressions of the past. In the words of Sherna Gluck in 1977:

> Women's oral history is a feminist encounter, even if the interviewee is not herself a feminist. It is the creation of a new type of material on women; it is the validation of women's experiences; it is the communication among women of different generations; it is the discovery of our own roots and the development of a continuity that has been denied us in traditional historical accounts.[23]

One of the key principles underpinning this agenda was women's common experience *as women*; oral history would illuminate this commonality as a means of informing the development of a shared female/feminist consciousness which in turn would act to bring about change, not only to the writing of history but in a bigger political context. In the words of Joan Sangster: 'As feminists, we hoped to use oral history to empower women by creating a revised history "for women", emerging from the actual lived experiences of women.'[24] The message was that oral history could be empowering for women themselves, drawing on a tradition borrowed from black historians in the USA who, as early as the 1920s, began to interview former slaves. For these first women's oral historians the practice was both an academic and a feminist-activist project, something to which many, including Gluck, remain committed in the belief that 'it can advance our knowledge but also empower people and contribute to social change'.[25] From this point on, oral history has been central to women's history research on the twentieth century, stimulating the search for older forms of personal testimony (from diaries, autobiographies, court records and so on) for earlier centuries.

A further stage in the politicisation of oral history work occurred in Britain in the 1980s and early 1990s. At the time of Margaret Thatcher's right-wing Conservative government, members of the Popular Memory Group at Birmingham's Centre for Contemporary Cultural Studies put the case for oral history having transformative potential.

> History – in particular popular memory – is a stake in the constant struggle for hegemony ... [A] sense of history ... is one means by which an organic social group acquires a knowledge of the larger context of its collective struggles, and becomes capable of a wider transformative role in the society. It is the means by which we may become self-conscious about the formation of our own common-sense beliefs, those that we appropriate from our immediate social and cultural milieu. These beliefs have a history and are also produced in determinate processes. The point

is to recover their 'inventory', not in the manner of the folklorist who wants to preserve quaint ways for modernity, but in order that, their origin and tendency known, they may be *consciously* adopted, rejected or modified. In this way a popular historiography, especially a history of the commonest forms of consciousness, is a necessary aspect of the struggle for a better world.[26]

For the Popular Memory Group, oral history had radical potential for socialists, feminists, anti-racists and for the 'people'. But they were under no illusions about the difficulties of translating oral history practice into popular consciousness and political change.

In the wake of oral history's popularity in the 1970s amongst labour and women's historians, other marginalised and silenced groups began to see its potential for their fields: gay and lesbian history, the history of black, ethnic and migrant communities and the history of the learning and physically disabled amongst others.[27] Oral history method was a means by which the histories of these groups could be collected and knowledge gained in the absence, often, of printed records containing the subjective experiences of individuals and groups. Historians of black and other non-white communities in the USA in particular began to gather oral testimony. For instance, the Samuel Proctor Oral History Program was initiated at the University of Florida in 1967; it now holds more than 4,000 testimonies.[28] And in Washington State a project initiated by the Black Studies Department in 1972 collected oral histories from African-American pioneers.[29] Lesbian, gay, bisexual and transgender (LGBT) communities and latterly the learning and physically disabled, also welcomed oral history as a means whereby individuals could 'speak for themselves', going some way towards negating the power structures within academia and in society more generally that suppressed the authentic experiences of those who did not conform to societal norms in terms of ethnicity, sexual orientation or ability. And those who championed the rights of disadvantaged groups have regarded oral history as one of the ways by which the perspectives of the poor, the underprivileged and disenfranchised could be integrated into campaigning for social and policy change. As Hirsch explains in the disability-studies context, it is important to 'uncover the history of disabled people, to explore the cultural meanings of disability, to end the oppression of people with disabilities'.[30] Oral history then was invested with a great deal of optimism.

Alongside the academic engagement with oral history there developed a movement in the 1970s amongst community groups and the social-care professions. The latter began to use oral history to enhance existing ways of communicating with and gaining information about client groups but soon became a strategy for allowing individuals and groups to ascribe their own meanings to experiences and events. In Ruth Martin's words, oral history 'can provide a bridge between the problems social workers and their clients seek to confront and the clients' own solutions'.[31] Amongst older people, oral history was identified as a positive, affirming activity. It not only elicited information about times gone, providing legitimation of a past life, but it also acted as a therapeutic technique, especially in the case of residents in residential homes and those suffering low self-esteem.[32] This practice is often termed reminiscence therapy. This approach directly challenged earlier attitudes to the elderly's tendency to reminisce about the past which regarded it as a symptom of mental deterioration, of regression and a denial of the immediacy of the present.[33] Given the almost complete absence, until very recently, of the elderly as a recognised group within historical accounts, oral history's focus on talking to older members of the community was in itself seen as a validating activity, not merely a means of gathering material about past times.[34] Reminiscence work was given support in Britain by the government's Department of Health and Social Security which funded the Reminiscence Aids Project in 1978–9. This project produced visual and aural aids to stimulate recall amongst the elderly, particularly those with mental impairment, and its widespread application raised awareness amongst those working with elderly people of the value of reminiscence and prompted life-history work to be used as an assessment tool in order to cater better to people's individual needs.[35]

Recent approaches have focused more on what may be achieved for the older people themselves from their participation in life-history and reminiscence projects. Reminiscence, it has been argued, has an important role to play in the validation of a coherent self and for the maintenance of self-esteem at a time when a person may be experiencing loss of independence. Oral history can have a place in eliciting older people's needs and desires in respect of care solutions; it may aid the preservation of a sense of autonomy or identity; and it may give the older person a voice to challenge or shape his or her environment, in short shifting the power imbalance that can so often exist within care settings. A recent project interviewing elderly lesbian, gay, bi-sexual or transgender individuals, for instance, demonstrated how many were very concerned about their future in places such as the care environment in which open expressions of sexuality were regarded as inappropriate and where services were unable or unwilling to meet the needs of this group and their carers.[36]

At the core of many of these studies was the acknowledgement, tacit or otherwise, that the control of memory (and therefore history) is the subject of a power struggle between those who wish to claim the right to the 'truth' about the past and those who challenge that interpretation. The view is now widespread that the writing of history itself is a perpetual power struggle as competing interpretations make claims to superior knowledge, authenticity and strength of argument. This is exceptionally clear in the case of totalitarian regimes that attempt to control memory – both individual and collective – by maintaining a version of the past through official acts of silence, commemoration, oppression and manipulation. Irina Sherbakova's interviews with those who lived through the era of the Stalinist prison camps in the

Soviet Union from the late 1930s to the 1950s show how state power rewrote history so that individual memories of that time and of the experiences of the labour camps and exile were confused and thus effectively silenced.[37] Likewise, Orlando Figes' study of private life in the same country employed oral history to liberate personal stories which had been silenced by the insidious power of the Stalinist system.[38] The fear of speaking and even remembering the past is vividly illustrated in a deluge of personal reminiscences, letters and diary entries mined from the silence of the Soviet and post-Soviet era. People had learned not to talk about their past, as this woman whose father was arrested in the 1930s explained:

> We were brought up to keep our mouths shut. 'You'll get into trouble for your tongue' – that's what people said to us children all the time. We went through life afraid to talk. Mama used to say that every other person was an informer. We were afraid of our neighbours, and especially of the police ... Even today, if I see a policeman, I begin to shake with fear.[39]

Since 1989 and the fall of Communist governments in Eastern Europe oral history has been widely used to reveal the hidden aspects of life behind the Iron Curtain.[40]

In situations such as this, oral history can be seen as one way of liberating personal and group memory and in the process providing the opportunity for a collective reinterpretation of the past. The work of the Truth and Reconciliation Commission in post-apartheid South Africa in the 1990s and 2000s, although not strictly 'oral history', is an example of a similar process – albeit with the blessing of the government – that allowed a history to be told which had hitherto been silenced by an oppressive regime. One of the key objectives of the Commission was what is called 'restorative justice', a process in which both survivors' and perpetrators' voices are heard in order to bring about accountability and also restitution.[41] Similar projects have been instituted in other parts of the world affected by internal conflict such as Northern Ireland and Rwanda. Clearly it is a process which may go some way towards shifting the balance of power from oppressors to oppressed though it is not without criticism. In the case of South Africa's Truth and Reconciliation Commission, its commitment to hearing the voices of the perpetrators as well as those of the victims produced the potentially dangerous scenario in which, in one commentator's opinion, the institutional effects of apartheid were silenced and the achievement of justice (for the victims) was sacrificed on the altar of reconciliation.[42]

Oral history has thus emerged with advocates variously promoting political aims, and the telling of life stories as a means to achieving personal coherence or composure. Oral history has been deployed to convey international shame for genocide, to foster religious and ethnic identity, to advance the power of marginalised groups, to diminish the power gap between academics and society and to contribute to the writing of alternative histories. Groups of victims or hitherto-silenced groups could be empowered to advance their interests. In most cases, the impetus came from the historians with political and radical agendas, working within and outside the academy, who saw oral history as a way of making a difference, of effecting political or social change. In some cases, oral historians have direct links with governments in this work. But in others the links forged between academics and community groups, trade unions, women's organisations and later all manner of groups with an equality agenda, were oppositional rather than official and founded on sound political and academic principles, and in many cases they have made a difference.

Elite oral history

Power resides not solely amongst the people en masse; it is also located amongst elite groups in positions of authority and control in government, the economy and society. Oral history research must engage with these groups; speaking to those who made the decisions that affected the many is one way of discovering how power is distributed in society and how those with political, economic or cultural power use it to their or others' advantage or disadvantage.

Some describe the interviewing of eminent people – politicians, military leaders, leading intellectuals and the like – as elite oral history, implying that it is a different category of oral history practice.[43] And certainly it may be in some respects. Few of those in power have been silenced or marginalised by the historical narrative. Generally, they have had ample opportunity to have their voice or viewpoint heard. Some will have published memoirs or autobiographies, thereby fixing their memory of events in print and in public consciousness, or their views will be recorded in official documents, reports and publications. Moreover, the power relations between the interviewer and interviewee throughout the course of the oral history encounter – from first contact to the production of an output – are likely to look different from most other scenarios we have described in this book.

Eva McMahan, in her analysis of oral history as a communicative event, argues that interviewing powerful elite respondents usually involved eliciting information and evaluating it for the record; therefore interviewers and respondents use particular discursive strategies to achieve cooperation and coherence.[44] Following a question-and-answer format, both parties deploy particular communicative strategies. For instance, the interviewer might adopt the role of neutral elicitor of information and employ what is called topic management in order to keep the interviewee on track and move the interview forward.[45] In this scenario, the respondent may hold most of the cards, being able to avoid answering or providing partial answers. However, if an interviewer is both information elicitor and assessor of that information, the dynamics of the interview subtly shift as the interviewer may challenge the information provided or the respondent's interpretation. McMahan's analysis merely describes the communicative strategies deployed in this kind of situation, but we can easily imagine the consequences for the interview dynamics, especially in the case of a significant power gap between the parties.[46]

Researchers aiming to interview prominent individuals are often forced to approach them through intermediaries in the first instance, providing the potential interviewee with the opportunity to turn down the request or at least to vet the interviewer before agreeing to meet. Interviewees in the 'elite' category are more likely to be short of time, to wish to take some control of the interview (maybe by agreeing questions or areas to be covered in advance) and may be more concerned about how their words are used and interpreted in print. It is likely that an elite interviewee will have prepared his or her memory frame in advance, will produce a composed narrative and will be less willing to be sidetracked or diverted onto tangential issues. Thus the potential power imbalance may tip towards the interviewee, especially when the researcher is young, a student or an inexperienced oral historian. Thorough preparation is key to a successful interview in these circumstances. A student in my own department who interviewed the former British ambassador to the Soviet Union for her doctoral research was adamant on this point, emphasising that one is likely to conduct a more successful interview (from the point of view of both parties) if the interviewer is well informed and able to respond intelligently to the interviewee's answers.[47] Another research student was told by one of her potential informants to come back to him when she had done some research – wise advice that meant that when the interview did take place she was in a position to conduct it from a more informed position which in turn had an impact on the power relations within the interview relationship.[48]

Though there is a distinct literature on elite oral history interviewing, it is important to also consider how *undifferent* is the act of interviewing supposedly 'powerful' people. The assertion of power is equally possible from an elderly widow from a working-class home as it is from a politician or banker. The acts of preparing an interview space, controlling the time available and who is present, verbal domination of the proceedings, and avoidance of questions through misremembering, disinformation, insolence or silence can and often do come from respondents in high or low 'stations' in society. The very nature of the interview lends itself to differential power relations, and the awareness and strategies of the interviewer are rarely fundamentally different.

The complexities of empowerment: criticisms and solutions in the second wave

In 1979 in her seminal article 'Work, Ideology and Consensus under Italian Fascism', Luisa Passerini was outspoken in her criticism of a populist tendency in oral history, 'that is, to replace certain of the essential tenets of scholarship with facile democratisation, and an open mind with demagogy'.[49] She was referring to the understandable, if naive, belief that oral history could be a means by which people 'spoke for themselves'. This naivety was founded on a simplistic notion that an untainted 'true voice' would be heard in the oral history interview. Passerini pointed the way to observing the interview as a complex power play with many possible voices.

Since the 1980s, historians have developed a more critical approach to the issue of empowerment. They quickly recognised that many of the claims made for the democratising and emancipatory power of oral history were compromised by a series of methodological and theoretical problems. These were, first, the inequalities of power embedded in the interview relationship itself; second, the power imbalance that arises at the point of interpretation and publication; and third the assumption that respondents are able to speak with an autonomous voice (that is that they can 'speak for themselves'). The Popular Memory Group summed up in 1982 – admittedly in an exaggerated way – the dilemma of those who seek to use oral history as a tool of political change:

> the historian may assert that he [or she] has 'sat at the feet of working-class witnesses' and has learnt all he knows in that improbable and uncomfortable posture. It is, however, *he* that produces the final account, *he* that provides the dominant interpretation, *he* that judges what is true and not true, reliable or inauthentic … In all this, at best, the first constructors of historical accounts – the 'sources' themselves – are left untouched, unchanged by the whole process except in what they have given up – the telling.[50]

In what follows we will focus on two critical approaches to these problems, the first emanating from feminist scholars, the second advocating a redistribution of authority.

Feminist approaches

Feminist researchers in the 1970s were quick to point out that the oral history interview was not necessarily an equal relationship. Indeed, what they described as the masculine paradigm of objective interview practice – predicated on the idea that the interview was a means to gaining information and that it should be conducted in as neutral or objective a manner as possible – necessarily incorporated a power imbalance between researcher and subject. The very fact that we arrive at an interview armed with recording equipment and research questions gives us legitimacy and thus power. Hence a new feminist methodology emphasising empathy, mutual respect and a recognition of the positive intersubjective relationship between researcher and subject was promoted as the key to eliciting meaning as well as to facilitating agency on the part of the respondent.[51] Some also advocated that interviewees should become collaborators in the research process. Similar invocations to inclusivity have been heard from the disability-history community.

Since then, however, feminist scholars have reined their optimism back somewhat for a new kind of research practice. As Joan Sangster remarks, 'while a detached objectivity may be impossible, a false claim to sisterhood is also unrealistic'.[52] As she and others have pointed out, the majority of attempts to equalise the relationship between researcher and subject founder because, in the final analysis, the researcher holds a privileged position, especially if she is a professional or academic scholar. We are trading on our position to gain access to individuals and their memories, and in the interview setting that inequality is ever present. Furthermore, as Judith Stacey graphically describes from her own research practice amongst families in California's Silicon Valley, an ethnographic approach that prioritises empathy and connection between researcher and respondent carries its own dangers. Getting close to one's subjects and moreover, suggesting that one's relationship with them exists on an equal footing, places the researcher in an impossible situation because 'fieldwork represents an intrusion and intervention into a system of relationships ... that the researcher is far freer than the researched to leave'.[53] Stacey concludes that in attempting to position oneself as researcher on an equal footing with one's subjects is exploitative, intrusive and ultimately treacherous.

Feminist researchers have been liable to downplay other structural relationships such as class or race in the attempt to establish a research practice that equalises power between women. Stacey remarks that feminist scholars are 'apt to suffer the delusion of alliance (amongst women) more than the delusion of separateness' (between middle-class academics and working-class interviewees for example), an astute observation that is taken up by Diane Reay in the context of interviews with middle- and working-class women in London. Central to her analysis is Reay's self-positioning as an educated working-class woman and her use of the concept of 'hierarchies of knowledge' to explore how power operates at a number of levels. First, she notes that although adopting a feminist position in her research practice was acceptable within the academy (and to some extent unproblematic), much more at issue was the adoption of a working-class stance given that working-class knowledge does not have a place within academic discourse. Second, she experienced a tension between her own subject position (educated working-class woman) and her evident power in analysing the data drawn from the interviews. Interpretation was often difficult, she writes, because 'neither my "truth" nor those of the working-class women I interviewed fit easily into academic "truths"'.[54]

Reay's observations indicate to us that the power gap in the research arena is multilayered; it cannot simply be countered by trying to equalise the relationship between the academic and the subject or by applying feminist research principles because there are too many other variables at work. Sondra Hale worked with women in the Sudan, a developing country in which the visiting feminist historian is imposing a Western woman's priorities in a wholly different context; she shows how the application of feminist research principles may be inappropriate, a case of prioritising the process over the product, to use Hale's words.[55] As she explains, 'when there are class differences and/or racial differences, or when the interviewer represents the colonizer and the narrator the colonized, it is not appropriate for the interviewer/biographer to want "equal time", or expect to be equally affirmed'.[56]

Even if we overcome the power imbalance within the interview setting, problems may still arise at the point of use of the output – the recorded interview or the transcribed words. At every stage of the process – from transcription and interpretation to publication – the researcher effectively holds the power, whatever one's intentions to maintain a collaborative relationship with one's subject. Increasingly the narrator's voice fades and the researcher's gains prominence as we move further away from the direct relationship with the subject. The process is nicely described by Katherine Borland in the context of her own experience of interviewing her grandmother and the interpretive conflicts that arose. She observes that we, the researchers,

> identify chunks of artful talk within this flow of conversation, give them physical existence (most often through writing), and embed them in a new context of expressive or at least communicative activity (usually the scholarly article aimed towards an audience of professional peers). Thus, we construct a second-level narrative based upon, but at the same time reshaping, the first.[57]

Again, feminist oral historians have been most alert to this issue and have attempted to offer solutions to counter the tendency for the researcher to abrogate her responsibility to the narrator. It has become good practice to share the interview material with one's interviewees, at least offering respondents the opportunity to see the transcript in order to correct errors and to have a final say over whether the material is permitted to be used by the researcher. Many of us have experienced a situation whereby a respondent is unhappy with the transcript and refuses to sign a release form, but that is the price one pays for offering a respondent some control over the use of their material. But while collaborating on the production of the data may be a useful strategy in some contexts, it rests on the assumption that our respondents are interested in being involved at this level or that they are able to engage with us in this way.

But it is at the point of interpretation that scholars are likely to experience the greatest anxiety. There can be few oral historians who have not felt slightly uncomfortable when, in the safety of their own studies, and at some physical and intellectual distance from their subjects, they begin to place interpretations on narrators' words which may derive from theoretical positions or conceptual frameworks far removed from the interview itself. Penny Summerfield acknowledges the problem, noting that she took the decision to anonymise the names of her respondents in order to 'protect them from the embarrassment which my mediation between their words and "the public" might cause'.[58] She goes on to say that this strategy 'screens interviewees from the ultimate manifestation of the power imbalance in the oral history relationship, the historian's interpretation and reconstruction in the public form of print of intimate aspects of their lives'.[59] But given that many interviewees would recognise themselves in a published text despite being given pseudonyms – several of my own respondents were only too pleased to tell me they had spotted their alter egos – this approach only really deals with the issue of public recognition. It does not effectively change the power imbalance in the eyes of the respondent or at a structural level.

One might conclude at this point that there can be no feminist solution to the problem of the evident inequalities that exist between researcher and subject, that all attempts to foster greater collaboration and subject involvement in the project are bound to fail because none of the strategies employed do anything to counter the structural inequalities that are implicit in the research project.[60] As Daphne Patai memorably states: 'The world will not get better because we have sensitively apologized for privilege.'[61] Her own self-reflexive observations on her research practice amongst Brazilian slum-dwellers places our navel-gazing about collaboration and power-sharing in perspective. A vignette drawn from Patai's encounter with her respondent Teresa encapsulates the issues discussed above. Despite Teresa's evident poverty, she offered Patai something to eat – a piece of cake – indeed what appeared to be the only foodstuff she had available in the house. And this act of generosity sparked in Patai a series of questions about her research practice and the inadequacy of her responses in dealing with vastly unequal power relations.[62] Perhaps if we want to maintain oral history's place in the academy *and* as a means for political and social change we have to acknowledge the power imbalances and do our best to minimise them whilst not becoming frozen in the face of the difficulties.

Sharing authority

It is not only feminist oral historians who have struggled to address issues of power. The notion of a shared authority between researcher and subject, articulated by Michael Frisch in 1990, owes much to the feminist debates summarised above. Frisch was excited by the prospect of oral history's 'capacity to redefine and redistribute intellectual authority', in order to achieve an interpretive synthesis that works to the benefit of scholars and the public.[63] Thus, collaboration and the devolving of intellectual power to 'the people' or communities has to be done, Frisch argues, by drawing on the best practices and traditions of both professional scholarship and grass-roots activism. A shared authority praxis can be empowering for all parties interested in the place and power of historical understanding in society. Frisch writes:

If oral historians need to understand that their method can do much more than the extraction of knowledge from human history mines, public historians need to realize that their method can do much more than merely redistribute such knowledge. It can, rather, promote a more democratized and widely shared historical consciousness, consequently encouraging broader participation in debates about history, debates that will be informed by a more deeply representative range of experiences, perspectives and values.[64]

And, connecting the historical with the political, Frisch notes that this is important because knowledge of history has great import in our present-day lives. 'It is history ... that can provide the basis for shared re-imagination of how the past connects to the present, and the possibilities this vantage suggests for the future.'[65]

Frisch's vision was intended to apply to the interview situation itself, but practitioners have picked up the baton of shared authority and applied the concept much more extensively beyond the immediate encounter and into a deep and sustained collaborative practice that encompasses the design of the project, the conduct of the interviews, the interpretation of the material and the distribution of the product. This kind of shared authority is a tall order to meet. It is time-consuming, long-term, personally demanding, involves moral and ethical issues regarding interpretive and critical control and in many cases may not be an appropriate methodology.[66]

At this point it may be helpful to provide two instances of shared authority or collaborative working in practice in order to illustrate the advantages and the pitfalls: first the work by those researching in the field of learning disability and second Lorraine Sitzia's collaboration to produce an oral history-based autobiography.

Jan Walmsley, one of the leading researchers in the field of oral history and disability, pioneered collaboration with her research subjects in part as a necessary adaptation to the special needs of research participants with learning disabilities but also as a strategy to circumvent some of the obstacles that prevented the voices of the disabled being heard and thus having an impact on the policies that affected them. In Walmsley's words, collaboration is a 'step towards empowerment' for people who are amongst the most powerless in our society.[67] Using life maps (an illustrated or pictorial summary of an individual's biography), Walmsley used information from an initial interview to help respondents create narrative accounts of their life stories. She also tried to use terminology that would have been familiar to her respondents rather than the jargon preferred by those in charge ('looked after' rather than 'caring' for instance). However, despite making every effort to explain her research to interviewees and to achieve a degree of shared ownership, Walmsley concluded that this was almost impossible to attain largely because of the comprehension gap between herself and her interviewees.

Michelle McCarthy, who conducted research into the sexual experiences of people with learning disabilities, took the collaborative agenda a step further, by involving her respondents in the design of the project, data collection and so on.[68] In Lindsay Brigham's life-story work with young women with learning difficulties, her attempts to involve the women more fully in the project resulted in some of the women taking control – in one instance by interviewing each other and in another by taking the camera from the researcher and taking photographs themselves.[69] Brigham argues that collaborative working in this field is the only way in which people with learning difficulties can take control of the research whilst also recognising that academic researchers may be their allies – acting as 'academic advocates' rather than their spokespeople.[70] This is the kind of approach advocated by the People First movement in Britain – a self-advocacy movement that aims to empower people with learning difficulties to be active and engaged in such projects and to contribute to research that will have an impact upon their lives.[71]

If researchers working in the field of learning disability are finding ways to share power, Lorraine Sitzia's close collaboration with one man in the production of a published autobiography based on oral history demonstrates the difficulties that may arise in truly collaborative ventures.[72] In an honest and self-critical account, Sitzia explores how her work with Arthur to produce his autobiography – whereby Arthur played an equal role in the decision-making – was not only creative and fulfilling but also difficult as the shared authority framework created tensions over ownership and control of the material. Sitzia admits to feeling uncomfortable at sharing a public platform with Arthur to talk about the project, his presence inhibiting to the scholarly freedoms one associates with presenting one's material to an audience. She also cites the problems arising from establishing such a close working relationship with someone – collaboration in this case involved friendship and mutual benefit but also the tensions that almost inevitably arise when boundaries are not clearly established. Sitzia concludes that although shared authority may be desirable, there are limits to its reach in practice.

For academics at least, shared authority has limits. Our research is inevitably shaped by an unavoidable fact: we are engaged in an unequal relationship with the sole purpose of obtaining other people's memories for our own use. The researcher is likely to benefit in terms of accessing useful primary source material to be used for academic self-advancement. If the subject benefits from the process this is a happy but unintended outcome. Most oral history encounters probably pass with little comment: the interview goes well, both parties are content, and each goes away with the assumption that the other got what they wanted – the opportunity to tell a story to a captive audience on the one side and the collection of research material on the other.

But on occasion this unspoken contract falls apart, most especially perhaps when the respondent is unhappy for the researcher to take interpretive control of the material and wishes to assert his or her authorial power. When Tracy K'Meyer and Glenn Crothers interviewed Marguerite Davis Stewart, a light-skinned African-American woman who 'repeatedly crossed the color-line' during her life in racially segregated Kentucky, they encountered a conflict between their desire to conduct a rigorous interpretation of the material she provided and their ethical concerns when Stewart sought to control what material was included and excluded in the final publication. The authors' solution was a compromise. The transcript of the interview respected Stewart's wishes whilst the authors held to their belief that historians should 'have the right and responsibility to bring to [the transcript] their own interpretive skills'.[73] Thus, while Stewart repeatedly stated that race was not important to her, K'Meyer and Crothers, through an analysis of her language and the content of her stories, assert a contrary conclusion, that colour and racial identity were crucial factors in her life story.[74] At the conclusion of this project it seems that authority was not exactly shared; rather, it was distributed differently according to the interests of the parties involved. Stewart got to tell her story and, according to the authors, 'ultimately embraced her multiculturalism'.[75] The researchers accessed information about racial identity and learned how to implement ways of collaborative working.

Advocacy: the third wave

The current preference within oral history practice is to speak of advocacy rather than empowerment. The difference between the two is nicely described by Sherna Gluck in the context of her own work with Palestinian women in the Occupied Territories. She notes that whereas in her earlier oral history work her interviews with women were informed by her desire to 'give them a voice – or rather to make their voices heard', in this project she aimed to use their voices in order that she might advocate on their behalf.[76] What we are seeing is oral history being used by historians and others such as anthropologists and development workers as a political tool but one that harnesses the knowledge and skills of both parties: the researcher and the respondents. 'A major obligation of the oral historian is to "return the compliment"' write Nigel Cross and Rhiannon Barker in reflecting upon the deployment of oral history methods in a development context, in this case the Sahel oral history project, a large-scale enterprise that interviewed more than 650 respondents in eight countries in the Sahel region of Africa.[77] In this kind of practice, the practitioner is the person using the oral history in order to advocate on another's behalf but at the same time those telling their stories also develop capacity in the sharing of information about past practices and experiences within their own communities. Advocacy oral history then is regarded as a means by which participants themselves are empowered to transform their lives. This methodology has been practised in a wide variety of settings, from the health-care professions to the native land-claim courts.

In this context, oral history narratives are part of a range of strategies employed by researchers or key workers to highlight communities' own interpretations and understandings of a situation. For instance, the worldwide network of Panos Institutes has as its aim the promotion of the 'participation of poor and marginalised people in national and international development debates through media and communication projects'.[78] They use the collection of oral testimony as a key way of prioritising voices in development debates, as a means of capacity-building amongst marginalised communities, and as a way of communicating to policy-makers the needs and experiences of those who are the recipients of development policies. One Panos project on the consequences of drought and desertification spoke with nomadic pastoralists in Ethiopia whose livelihood has been seriously threatened by the destruction of grazing and water sources. A series of narratives highlights the contrast between past and present, as expressed here by Chuqulisa, a divorced mother of six who said:

> There is a big difference [nowadays]. Love is lacking among people now. Those who have something do not share with those who have nothing. Individuals do not help one another ... Life is also difficult now. Cows do not give milk. The reason is that they do not get sufficient pasture.[79]

Referring to a project assessing poverty-reduction strategies in Pakistan, Zambia, Kenya and Mozambique, the Panos Institute argues for the importance of listening to people's narratives which:

> vivid and direct, full of detail ... are a powerful reminder of the human indignities that lie at the heart of poverty and why effective approaches to poverty reduction matter. They illustrate the many different ways that poverty affects people and reveal the ingenuity and resourcefulness they have to employ simply to meet basic needs, and the challenges they face in pursuing their rights. Through these stories, men and women in rural and urban communities present their own perspectives on the factors that keep people poor.[80]

Similarly, in the wake of the devastation wrought by Hurricanes Katrina and Rita in the American South, the National Policy and Advocacy Council on Homelessness – a grass-roots anti-poverty organisation with a mission to 'ensure that national homelessness policy accurately reflects the needs and experiences of local communities' – has recorded oral narratives with a range of participants from survivors to church representatives and charity workers as a means of conveying an understanding of the difficulties experienced by those caught up in the disasters.[81]

Oral history is also widely employed as a political tool amongst refugees and displaced peoples. The outstanding example in this respect is the work undertaken with and by Palestinian refugees since the 1948 Arab–Israeli War when hundreds of thousands of Palestinians fled or were driven from their lands. This moment in Palestinian history has come to be called *al-Nakba* (the Catastrophe), and 1948 and its consequences have assumed pivotal importance in the narrating of Palestinian identity in the decades since.[82] Thus, a number of organised programmes such as the al-Nakba oral history project, have conducted interviews amongst Palestinian refugees about their experiences before, during and after the creation of Israel and the Palestinian exodus, aiming to 'retain and enhance Palestinians' sense of community and belonging', to maintain connections amongst diasporic Palestinians and to communicate the plight of displaced Palestinians to the rest of the world.[83]

Indeed, oral tradition is one of the few remaining points of common identity available to displaced groups. As Randa Farah notes:

> Needless to say, refugees did not wait for us (researchers, activists, 'intellectuals') or for the PLO to reminisce about the past and recount their histories. They have been orally transmitting their pre-Nakba, Nakba, and post-Nakba stories since their expulsion, retelling and reinterpreting events and experiences to each other and to their children, often against the ways that larger powers, and frequently we as researchers, have organized and/or sometimes imposed history upon them.[84]

Certainly, oral history, or the circulation of oral narratives has, according to Diana Allan, permeated everyday life in some Palestinian communities to the extent that the memorialisation of 1948 'has thus become an assumed part of everyday practice, merging personal memory with pedagogical commemoration to the point where the past so thoroughly permeated intersubjective relations that even generations who did not experience these events are, in some sense, expected to claim them as their own'.[85] The words of a young Palestinian living in the Shateela refugee camp illustrate this process: 'Although we are still living the results of al-Nakba, my generation didn't experience it, and I refuse to inherit it ... it is as if all Palestinians here have to have the same memory, and the same perspective on who we are and how to resist.'[86]

Amongst settled migrant communities, oral history has been used to counter racist propaganda and stereotypes and as a means of communicating the culture and history of a group to the dominant society. In Britain, for instance, numerous agencies have utilised oral history techniques amongst refugee and asylum communities yielding results which are then communicated to government. In 2003, Refugee Action and the Museum of London conducted interviews with 100 Vietnamese refugees around the country with the aim of bridging the gap between three generations of the Vietnamese community, helping them share their experiences with the British public and providing useful data for resettlement and integration policies.[87] In the process, the authors note the project stimulated considerable community awareness. Alistair Thomson commented in 1999 that the 'process of "bearing witness" – by migrants, refuges and other victims of social and political oppression – is thus empowering for individual narrators and can generate public recognition of collective experiences which have been ignored or silenced'.[88]

Advocacy then, implies that the research subjects have an active engagement with the oral history project and understand that their involvement can have real benefits in community and political terms. The most striking example of the impact of oral history in a claim for political legitimacy is the case of aboriginal or First Nations land claims in Australia, New Zealand and Canada. In Australia, the 1976 Aboriginal Land Rights (Northern Territory) Act permitted a claim to land title if the claimants could provide evidence of continuing traditional association with the land. But of course aboriginal peoples were the least able to provide this evidence in the absence of written documents proving ownership or continuous settlement. Rather, aboriginal peoples, who traditionally had low literacy levels and for whom oral traditions establish identity and relationship to place, express their connection to the land via stories which rarely recognise modern land boundaries and which have few concrete markers recognisable by modern courts.[89] Thus, it was necessary for indigenous peoples to convince the State, through the courts, of the legitimacy of their oral traditions for, as David McNab has written in relation to the land-rights struggle in Canada, oral tradition is the means by which native peoples see themselves and their relationship with the environment; they are 'facts enmeshed in the stories of a lifetime' with no obvious relationship to the ways in which those with European antecedents understood their history.[90] One of the first attempts to convince a court of the legitimacy of oral tradition as evidence was undertaken by the Gitksan and Wet'suwet'en First Nations in British Columbia, Canada in the 1980s. They argued that their claim could be supported by expressions of ownership through public narrative, song and dances, and they enacted these in court. In this case, the judge rejected their claim on the basis that this kind of evidence could not be evaluated against 'positivistic definitions of "truth".'[91] But in 1997, the Canadian Supreme Court argued that aboriginal oral tradition had to be treated on an equal footing as evidence with traditional forms such as historical documents.

Likewise, in Australia, oral evidence has been accepted in land-claim cases though here, the Commonwealth Native Title Act and subsequent case law require that oral claimants prove a direct genealogical link with the indigenous people who held native title of the land at the time of the declaration of British sovereignty. In order to meet this requirement, indigenous peoples have relied on a combination of documentary and oral evidence.[92] Describing the evidential submissions in Australian land-claim cases, Deborah Bird Rose states:

> Most of the claimants, most of the time, do not validate their knowledge by testing it against other frames of reference, and certainly not by validating it with reference to the written word. Rather, they validate their knowledge by demonstrating that its authority derives from previous generations: they know, and they have the authority of knowledge, because they were told. Authorised knowledge, in short, has a human genealogy and is orally transmitted.[93]

Power and the output

One of the ways in which oral historians have sought to shift the balance of power from researcher to respondent is through democratisation of the output of a project. The ability to distribute oral history material – both the digital recording and the transcript – on the World Wide Web has opened up a new debate about accessibility and ownership. The digital revolution has catapulted oral history into a new world where almost anyone can conduct oral history facilitated by relatively inexpensive and easy to use sound and video recorders, and many more can access the output if it is placed on a website than if it is deposited in a traditional archive. Many of the projects referred to in the last section on advocacy have placed either extracts or full versions of interviews on their websites for a number of purposes: accessibility, publicity, transparency and for the immediate impact such material can have on the viewer or listener. The Panos Institute argues that the short films, photographs and spoken narratives featured on its website 'empower their subjects and ... inform and influence decision makers'.[94] The UK advocacy organisation Patient Voices states on its website that its digital storytelling project feeds patient experience into the health service.[95] Similarly, although with a more rigorous academic input, the project Healthtalkonline records, using in-depth qualitative research methods (notably the interview), patients' experiences of a range of health-related conditions in order to provide not only an 'evidence-based approach to patient experience' for the use of researchers and health practitioners but also, via audio clips on the website, for wider patient use, helping them to make informed decisions about their own health management.[96]

The growth of community-led oral history projects has also shifted the balance of power in terms of who controls the output of research. In the early days of community projects in the UK, for instance, the lead was taken by academic researchers, but since the 1980s volunteer-led projects, with their roots in community advocacy and regeneration, have predominated, with consequences for the types of output produced and the interpretations contained therein.[97] The round-up of 'Current British Work' in the British journal *Oral History* provides a snapshot of the range of local and community projects flourishing under the auspices of local-history groups, heritage societies, schools and community organisations. And the support that many of these projects received from the UK Heritage Lottery Fund meant that they were honour-bound to distribute the results of their work in a democratic and inclusive fashion, hence exhibitions, CD-ROMs containing audio clips, DVDs and websites, all of which have the potential to reach a wider sector of the population than the traditional book.

Conclusions

Oral history's journey from empowerment to advocacy mirrors the expansion in the use of oral history methodology across disciplines and territories and, more significantly, in contexts far removed from academia – the courtroom, the development project, the disaster aftermath, the multicultural community. Oral history has thus diversified with the times. The difference between the aims and practices of the early practitioners who wanted to give people a voice, who wanted to challenge standard historical narratives and in the process empower the disadvantaged and silenced in our societies and today's advocates of oral history who regard oral history as a means by which the subjects might empower themselves, is not in terms of ambition but context. While community-based oral history is still practised and academics and researchers do still 'dig where they stand', the reach of oral history reflects its success as a weapon in the armoury of those who want to make a difference on a larger global stage. It may still be too early to evaluate the results of this shift in emphasis. Certainly, the amount of material produced from such projects has aided our insight into the self-understanding of individuals and groups traditionally marginalised by development projects or state-implemented policies. But it is hard to tell at this stage whether the groups and communities themselves have benefited in material or psychological ways from the opportunity to tell their stories.

Advocacy oral history seems to counter the charges made by those who criticised the empowerment agenda for its tendency to reinforce the power imbalance between the researcher and subject. It is notable that much advocacy work is often undertaken by community and development workers rather than by academics so the power dynamics are subtly different. Such workers are employed by organisations who are explicitly working to further the needs and interests of others, unlike academics for whom an altruistic agenda is often hard to disentangle from self-advancement. Ultimately though, the advocacy movement is testament to the flexibility, popularity and reach of oral history at all levels – from the community to the global.

The aim of this book was to provide oral historians with a user-friendly introduction to the theories that inform analysis of oral history material. Along the way we have charted the journey that this methodology has taken – from recovery history to advocacy and from marginal practice to mainstream. The exciting aspect of oral history practice is not only the ability to get up close and personal to one's primary sources but also the opportunity to develop new interpretive and analytical approaches deriving from the will to understand our respondents' meaning. Oral history is a constantly evolving practice that sits at the interface between the personal and the social, between past and present, and theory merely helps us to negotiate a route towards a better understanding of the significance of people's memories. Henry Glassie remarked of the people of Ballymenone that when they tell stories 'they say what they know to discover what they think'.[98] Oral history is a bit like this; our respondents tell us stories and in the process of the telling and its afterlife, the significance of those stories is illuminated to the teller and the listener. The theories and their applications outlined in this book hopefully make the process of understanding a little easier.

Glossary

agency The power (of an individual) to change or affect events or to make choices that influence the course of history.

autobiographical memory This refers to the personal reconstruction of the events of one's life. An autobiographical memory typically contains information about place, actions, persons, objects and thoughts which one believes have been personally experienced. An example of an autobiographical memory might be one's first day at school or one's first kiss. Also sometimes called episodic memory, that is the memory of autobiographical events.

collective memory A collective memory is a shared memory of an event or experience. It is distinguished from autobiographical memory by virtue of it being commonly shared and circulated amongst a group, and it might shape individual or autobiographical memory.

composure This has two meanings. First it refers to the striving on the part of an interviewee for a version of the self that sits comfortably within the social world, an account that achieves coherence, with which the interviewee can be content. The second meaning refers to the creation of an account of experience, 'to compose' a story about the past.

cultural circuit The process by which personal memories of events and experiences draw upon popular or public constructions of the past, and in turn popular accounts draw on the memories of individuals.

discourse A message or injunction expressed via a language system (words, texts, images, etc.) and circulated within culture.

intersubjectivity This refers to the relationship between the two subjectivities in the interview: those of the interviewee and the interviewer. It concerns the interpersonal dynamics of the interview situation and the process by which the participants cooperate to create a shared narrative.

life history a chronologically told narrative of an individual's past. It typically contains recognisable life stages and events such as childhood, education, marriage and so on.

life story A narrative device used by an individual to make sense of a life or experiences in the past. A life story is not a telling of a life as it was but a creative version of a life which has been interpreted and reinterpreted over time. It is the creative and constructed elements of the life story that distinguish it from the life history.

methodology The methods, the principles of research or the ways of doing adopted by a discipline.

narrative An ordered account created out of disordered material; narrative is the means by which we communicate experience, knowledge and emotion. A narrative is also a story told according to certain cultural conventions.

narrative analysis The identification and interpretation of the ways in which people use stories to interpret the world; narrative analysis involves the identification of structures within texts (verbal or written) by means of linguistic or literary analysis.

narrator A term used for the interviewee often preferred by oral historians who regard the interview as a communicative event or dialogue rather than a question-and-answer session.

oral tradition Messages or stories transmitted orally from one generation to another. It is dynamic and historical; it is continually passed on and in the process the message is transmuted. Each rendering of the oral performance will be influenced by the circumstances in which the telling occurs.

performance A heightened mode of communication, differentiated from everyday speech by its aesthetic qualities. A performance tends to take place in a special place, for an audience and displays particular features that mark it off from ordinary conversation.

personal testimony An umbrella term that incorporates all forms of the expression of personal or individual experience including diaries, letters, memoirs and oral history.

popular memory This refers to the production of memory of the past in which everyone is involved and which everyone has an opportunity to reshape. Popular memory involves a dialogue or struggle between individual and collective memory.

reflexivity The act of consciously thinking about one's presuppositions and how these might impact upon the conduct of one's research.

respondent A term often used in place of 'interviewee' in the social-science tradition. Sometimes criticised for implying the passivity of the interviewee (*see* 'narrator').

self The notion of a unique identity, distinguishable from others. It is usually seen as socially constructed by culture and the product of mediation between cultural discourses and material experience.

subjectivity This refers to the constituents of an individual's sense of self, his or her identity informed and shaped by experience, perception, language and culture – in other words an individual's emotional baggage.

Notes

Introduction

1 A. Portelli, *The Death of Luigi Trastulli and Other Stories: Form and Meaning in Oral History* (Albany, NY, 1991), p. vii.

2 A. Portelli, 'Oral History as Genre', in M. Chamberlain and P. Thompson (eds), *Narrative and Genre: Contexts and Types of Communication* (London, 2004), pp. 23–45, here p. 23.

3 P. Thompson, *The Voice of the Past* (3rd edn, Oxford, 2000), pp. 25–81. All future references to this book refer to the 2000 edition unless stated otherwise.

4 The FWP archive is held at the Library of Congress, Washington, DC; a selection of the materials are available online at http://memory.loc.gov/ammem/wpaintro/wpahome.html (accessed 21 July 2009). See R. Rosenzweig and B. Melosh, 'Government and the Arts: Voices from the New Deal Era', *Journal of American History*, 77 (2) (1990): 596–608, and, for a re-evaluation of the FWP, see J. Hirsch, 'Before Columbia: The FWP and American Oral History Research', *The Oral History Review*, 34 (2) (2007): 1–16.

5 See www.columbia. edu/cu/lweb/indiv/oral/about.html (accessed 10 July 2009).

6 For a detailed and extensive survey of the growth and antecedents of oral history on the international stage see Thompson, *The Voice of the Past*, pp. 65–81.

7 S. Terkel, *Hard Times: An Oral History of the Great Depression* (London, 1970); *Working: People Talk About What They Do All Day and How They Feel About What They Do* (London, 1975); *The Good War* (London, 1984); *Race: What Blacks and Whites Think and Feel About the American Obsession* (New York, 1992). For biographical background on Terkel and links to sound clips from some of his interviews see www.studsterkel.org/ (accessed 12 August 2009).

8 R. Blythe, *Akenfield: Portrait of an English Village* (London, 1969). L. Abrams, 'Akenfield: Forty Years of an Iconic Text', *Oral History*, 37 (1) (2009): 33–42.

9 G. E. Evans, *Ask the Fellows Who Cut the Hay* (London, 1956). A. Howkins, 'Inventing Everyman: George Ewart Evans, Oral History and National Identity', *Oral History*, 22 (2) (1994): 26–32.

10 R. Grele, 'Directions for Oral History in the United States', in D. K. Dunaway and W. K. Baum (eds), *Oral History: An Interdisciplinary Anthology* (Walnut Creek, Calif., 1996), pp. 62–84; p. 63.

11 Paul Thompson's Edwardians project at Essex University was typical of this approach. For details of the sampling and data-collection methods employed see http://www.esds.ac.uk/qualidata/online/data/edwardians/introduction.asp (accessed 31 January 2010).

12 H. Newby, 'Akenfield Revisited', *Oral History*, 3 (1) (1975): 76–83; p. 80.

13 Thompson, *The Voice of the Past*, pp. 101–2. For a rebuttal see Abrams, 'Aken-field' and see Blythe's very honest statement about his methodology in the preface to the second edition of *Akenfield* (London, 1999).

14 This approach is best seen in the work of A. Portelli, especially *The Death of Luigi Trastulli*, but a similar message can be found in R. Grele (ed.), *Envelopes of Sound: The Art of Oral History* (New York, 1991).

15 L. Passerini, 'Work, Ideology and Consensus under Italian Fascism', *History Workshop Journal*, 8 (1979): 82–108.

16 Passerini, 'Work, Ideology and Consensus', p. 84.

17 Passerini, 'Work, Ideology and Consensus', p. 84.

18 Passerini, 'Work, Ideology and Consensus', p. 84.

19 Passerini, 'Work, Ideology and Consensus', p. 91.

20 For an extended analysis, see L. Passerini, *Fascism in Popular Memory: The Cultural Experience of the Turin Working Class* (Cambridge, 1987).

21 S. Schrager, 'What Is Social in Oral History?', *International Journal of Oral History*, 4 (2) (1983): 76–98; here, p. 77.

22 Grele, *Envelopes of Sound*, p. 245.

23 E. Roberts, *A Woman's Place: An Oral History of Working-Class Women, 1890–1940* (Oxford, 1984).

24 E. Roberts, *Women and Families: An Oral History, 1940–1970* (Oxford, 1995), p. 3.

25 D. James, *Doña María's Story: Life History, Memory and Political Identity* (London, 2000), p. 124.

26 A. Oakley 'Interviewing Women: A Contradiction in Terms', in H. Roberts (ed.), *Doing Feminist Research* (London, 1981), pp. 30–61; here p. 31.

27 See the collection of articles on interviewing for a taste of this research in R. Perks and A. Thomson (eds), *The Oral History Reader*, 2nd edn (London, 2006). All subsequent references to this book are to this edition unless stated otherwise.

28 For an excellent overview of these issues see V. R. Yow, *Recording Oral History: A Guide for the Humanities and Social Sciences* (2nd edn, Walnut Creek, Calif., 2005), pp. 157–87.

29 A. Portelli, 'Deep Exchange', in A. Portelli, *The Battle of Valle Giulia: Oral History and the Art of Dialogue* (Madison, Wisc., 1997), pp. 72–8.

30 James, *Doña María's Story*, p. 132.

31 James, *Doña María's Story*, p. 132.

32 James, *Doña María's Story*, p. 133.

33 James, *Doña María's Story*, p. 135.

34 R. Samuel, 'The Perils of the Transcript', *Oral History*, 1 (2) (1971): 19–22.

35 R. O. Joyce cited in Yow, *Recording Oral History*, p. 317.

36 Interview with Agnes Leask by L. Abrams, 2002.

37 Shetland Archive: 3/1/162/1: interview with Agnes Leask, 1986. A standard English transcription would read something like this: 'It was a croft probably about maybe twelve or fourteen acres, it was a very good croft, the Twatt crofts was very good quality, but they weren't excessively big. But it was a croft that was big enough to have like milking cows for the house and rare young beasts for sale and that sort of thing, plus their own corn for meal and such like as that. But of course a wife with a lot of young bairns couldn't work it to the same extent as if they'd both been working.'

38 D. Dunaway, 'Transcription: Shadow or Reality?', *The Oral History Review*, 12 (1984): 113–17; here p. 116.

39 Dunaway, 'Transcription', p. 116.

40 Blythe, *Akenfield* (Penguin Classics edition, London 2005), p. 31.

41 Blythe, *Akenfield* (Penguin Classics edition, London 2005), p. 37.

42 C. Borland, '"That's Not What I Said": Interpretive Conflict in Oral Narrative Research', in S. B. Gluck and D. Patai (eds), *Women's Words: The Feminist Practice of Oral History* (London, 1991), pp. 63–76, here p. 63.

43 James, *Doña María's Story*, pp. 31–116.

44 Examples include the series of books published in the Scottish 'Flashbacks' series published in association with the Scottish Ethnological Research Centre and the work of Ian MacDougall for the Scottish Working People's History Trust such as Ian MacDougall, *Voices of Leith Dockers: Personal Recollections of Working Lives* (Edinburgh, 2001). Also see E. Marcus, *Making History: The Struggle for Gay and Lesbian Equal Rights, 1945–1990* (New York, 1992) which contains forty-five lengthy extracts from transcripts and minimal commentary.

45 Roberts, *A Woman's Place;* P. Thompson, T. Wailey and T. Lummis, *Living the Fishing* (London, 1983); L. Abrams, *The Orphan Country: Children of Scotland's Broken Homes, 1845 to the Present Day* (Edinburgh, 1998).

46 R. Finnegan, *Tales of the City: A Study of Narrative and Urban Life* (Cambridge, 1998).

47 P. Summerfield, *Reconstructing Women's Wartime Lives: Discourse and Subjectivity in Oral Histories of the Second World War* (Manchester, 1998); A. Thomson, *Anzac Memories: Living with the Legend* (Oxford, 1994); James, *Doña María's Story.*

48 C. Joyner, 'Oral History as Communicative Event', in Dunaway and Baum, *Oral History*, pp. 292–7.

49 R. Grele, 'History and the Languages of History in the Oral History Interview: Who Answers Whose Questions and Why?', in E. M. McMahan and K. L. Rogers (eds), *Interactive Oral History Interviewing* (Hove, 1995), pp. 1–18; here p. 2.

The peculiarities of oral history

 1 R. Rosaldo, cited by J. Cruikshank, 'Oral Tradition and Oral History: Reviewing Some Issues', *The Canadian Historical Review*, 75 (3) (1994): 403–18, here p. 409.

 2 A. Portelli, 'What Makes Oral History Different?', in A. Portelli, *The Death of Luigi Trastulli and Other Stories: Form and Meaning in Oral History* (New York, 1991), pp. 45–58.

 3 Portelli, 'Oral History as Genre', p. 25.

 4 Portelli, 'What Makes Oral History Different'. He gives slightly different names to some of these elements.

 5 Shetland Archives, AD 22/2/1/55: Agnes Hawick, child murder or concealment of pregnancy, 25 May 1854.

 6 National Archives of Scotland, AD 14/91/169: Precognition: Elizabeth Brymer – High Court Dundee, 1891.

 7 Portelli, 'What Makes Oral History Different?', p. 48.

 8 H. White, 'The Value of Narrativity in the Representation of Reality', *Critical Inquiry*, 7 (1) (1980): 5–27; here p. 5.

 9 N. Wachowich, *Saqiyuq: Stories from the Lives of Three Inuit Women* (Montreal, 1999), p. 18.

10 Portelli, 'What Makes Oral History Different?', p. 50.

11 Portelli, 'What Makes Oral History Different?', p. 55.

12 Portelli, 'What Makes Oral History Different?', p. 56.

13 Portelli, 'Oral History as Genre', pp. 24–5.

14 Portelli, 'Oral History as Genre', p. 32.

15 J. Vansina, *Oral Tradition as History* (Madison, Wisc., 1985), pp. 12–13.

16 Vansina, *Oral Tradition as History*, pp. 27–31. On the value of oral tradition for history see J. Vansina, *Oral Tradition: A Study in Historical Methodology* (London, 1965).

17 D. Schacter, *Searching for Memory* (New York, 1996), p. 16.

18 Vansina, *Oral Tradition as History*, p. 29.

19 See Cruikshank, 'Oral Tradition and Oral History', p. 404.

20 Portelli, 'Oral History as Genre', p. 28.

21 M. Frisch, *A Shared Authority: Essays on the Craft and Meaning of Oral and Public History* (New York, 1989).

22 J. Bornat, 'Is Oral History Auto/Biography?', in *Auto/biography*, 3 (2) (1994): 17–30.

23 This point is discussed at greater length in Chapter 6 but see K. Langellier and E. E. Peterson, 'Spinstorying: An Analysis of Women Storytelling', in E. C. Fine and J. H. Speer (eds), *Performance, Culture and Identity* (Westport, Conn., 1992), pp. 157–80; and R. Ely and A. McCabe, 'Gender Differences in Memories for Speech', in S. Leydesdorff, L. Passerini and P. Thompson (eds), *Gender and Memory* (London, 2005), pp. 17–30.

24 M. Chamberlain, *Fenwomen: A Portrait of Women in an English Village* (London, 1975), p. 100.

25 Portelli, 'Oral History as Genre', pp. 26–7.

26 The reference is to M. Bloch, *The Historian's Craft* (Manchester, 1992).

27 R. Dorson, 'The Oral Historian and the Folklorist', in D. K. Dunaway and W. K. Baum (eds), *Oral History: An Interdisciplinary Anthology* (Walnut Creek, Calif., 1996), pp. 283–91.

28 H. Glassie, *Passing the Time in Ballymenone: Culture and History of an Ulster Community* (Bloomington, Ind., 1995), p. 13.

29 Glassie, *Passing the Time in Ballymenone*, p. 14.

30 D. James, *Doña María's Story: Life History, Memory and Political Identity* (London, 2000), p. 135.

31 R. Grele cited in James, *Doña María's Story*, p. 135.

32 B. Allen, 'Re-creating the Past: The Narrator's Perspective in Oral History', *Oral History Review*, 12 (1984): 1–12.

33 Portelli, 'Oral History as Genre', p. 35.

34 A. Portelli, *The Order Has Been Carried Out: History, Memory and Meaning of a Nazi Massacre in Rome* (Basingstoke, 2007).

35 A. Krog, *Country of My Skull* (London, 1999).

36 On the implications of the digital revolution see M. Frisch, 'Oral History and the Digital Revolution: Towards a Post-Documentary Sensibility', in R. Perks and A. Thomson (eds), *The Oral History Reader* (2nd edn, London, 2006), pp. 102–14.

37 S. Cole, *Women of the Praia: Work and Lives in a Portuguese Coastal Community* (Princeton, NJ, 1991), pp. 29–37.

38 Cole, *Women of the Praia*, p. 40.

39 J. Cruikshank in collaboration with Angela Sidney, Kitty Smith and Annie Ned, *Life Lived Like a Story: Life Stories of Three Yukon Native Elders* (Lincoln, Nebr., 1990); N. Wachowich, in collaboration with Apphia Agalakto Awa, Rhoda Kaukjak Katsak and Sandra Pikujak Katsak, *Saqiyuq*. A much earlier example is D. Barrios de Chungara with M. Viezzer, *Let Me Speak! Testimony of Domitila, a Woman of the Bolivian Mines* (London, 1978).

40 L. Passerini, *Autobiography of a Generation: Italy, 1968* (Middleton, Conn., 1996).

Self

1 B. Obama, *Dreams from My Father: A Story of Race and Inheritance* (Edinburgh, 2008) and B. Obama, *The Audacity of Hope*: Thoughts on Reclaiming the American Dream (Edinburgh, 2008).

2 See L. L. Langness and G. Frank, *Lives: An Anthropological Approach to Biography* (Novato, Calif., 1981).

3 For a critical survey of this literature see V. Crapanzano, 'Life Histories', *American Anthropologist*, new series, 86 (4) (1984): 953–60.

4 M. Shostak, '"What the Wind Won't Take Away": The Genesis of *Nisa – The Life and Words of a !King Woman*', in T. L. Broughton (ed.), *Autobiography*, Vol. III (London, 2007), pp. 3–15.

5 See, for example, P. Joyce, *Democratic Subjects: The Self and the Social in Nineteenth-Century England* (Cambridge, 1994).

6 C. Steedman, *Landscape for a Good Woman* (London, 1986). See also A. Kuhn, *Family Secrets: Acts of Memory and Imagination* (London, 1995); Diana Gittins, *The Child in Question* (Basingstoke, 1998).

7 J. Flax, *Thinking Fragments: Psychoanalysis, Feminism and Postmodernism in the Contemporary West* (Berkeley, Calif., 1990), p. 8, here cited in P. Summerfield, *Reconstructing Women's Wartime Lives: Discourse and Subjectivity in Oral Histories of the Second World War* (Manchester, 1998), p. 252.

8 For a survey of the development of the modern concept of self, see R. Porter, 'Introduction', in R. Porter (ed.), *Rewriting the Self: Histories from the Renaissance to the Present* (Routledge, 1997), pp. 1–14.

9 C. Geertz cited in N. Rose, 'Assembling the Modern Self', in Porter, *Rewriting the Self*, pp. 224–48; p. 225.

10 A popular example in Britain is the BBC's *Who Do You Think You Are?* television programme which searches for the family roots of famous personalities.

11 G. Gusdorf cited in J. Okely, 'Anthropology and Autobiography: Participatory Experience and Embodied Knowledge', in J. Okely and H. Callaway (eds), *Anthropology and Autobiography* (London, 1992), p. 6.

12 G. Gusdorf cited by S. Stanford Friedman, 'Women's Autobiographical Selves: Theory and Practice', in S. Benstock (ed.), *The Private Self* (London, 1988), p. 34.

13 R. Rosaldo, 'The Story of Tukbaw: "They Listen as He Orates"', in F. Reynolds and D. Capps (eds), *The Biographical Process: Studies in the History and Psychology of Religion* (The Hague, 1976), pp. 121–51; here p. 22.

14 H. D. Wong, *Sending My Heart Back Across the Years: Tradition and Innovation in Native American Autobiography* (Oxford, 1992).

15 K. E. Brustad *et al.*, 'The Fallacy of Western Origins', in T. L. Broughton (ed.), *Autobiography*, Vol. II (London, 2007), pp. 375–93.

16 C. Linde, *Life Stories: The Creation of Coherence* (Oxford, 1993), p. 3.

17 Linde, *Life Stories*, pp. 100 et seq.

18 R. D. Laing, *The Divided Self: A Study of Sanity and Madness* (Chicago, Ill., 1960). Laing writes of the person who 'cannot take the realness, aliveness, autonomy and identity of himself and others for granted' and who consequently contrives strategies to avoid 'losing his self' (p. 44). See S. Sutcliffe, 'After "the Religion of My Fathers": The Quest for Composure in the "Post-Presbyterian" Self', in L. Abrams and C. G. Brown (eds), *Everyday Life in Twentieth Century Scotland* (Edinburgh, 2009), pp. 181–205.

19 Interview with Deborah, conducted by L. Abrams, 20 June 2009.

20 Linde, *Life Stories*, p. 105.

21 Linde, *Life Stories*, p. 105.

22 Interview with Deborah.

23 See I. E. Josephs, 'Talking with the Dead: Self-Construction as Dialogue', in M. G. W. Bamberg (ed.), *Oral Versions of Personal Experience: Three Decades of Narrative Analysis* (London, 1997), pp. 359–68.

24 M.-F. Chanfrault-Duchet, 'Textualisation of the Self and Gender Identity in the Life Story', in T. Cosslett, C. Lury and P. Summerfield (eds), *Feminism and Autobiography* (London, 2000), pp. 61–75; p. 65.

25 Chanfrault-Duchet, 'Textualisation of the Self', p. 65.

26 J. Bruner, 'Life as Narrative', *Social Research*, 54 (1) (1987): 11–32; here p. 31.

27 A. Portelli, 'The Best Garbage Man in Town: Life and Times of Valtèro Peppo-loni, Worker', in *The Death of Luigi Trastulli and Other Stories: Form and Meaning in Oral History* (Albany, NY, 1991), pp. 117–37; p. 118.

28 Linde, *Life Stories*, p. 21.

29 Linde, *Life Stories*, p. 25.

30 Linde, *Life Stories*, p. 221.

31 Note that as a linguist Linde has problems with the Foucauldian definition of discourse as it is not sufficiently precise. Linde, *Life Stories*, pp. 223–4.

32 Edwardians Project, Transcript 2000int142, available online at https://www.esds. ac.uk/qualidata/online/explore/interview.asp?Id=2000int142&keylen=Ronald +walker&check#607 (accessed 2 February 2010). See also C. G. Brown, *The Death of Christian Britain* (London, 2001), pp. 118–22.

33 Linde, *Life Stories*, p. 53.

34 W. L. Andrews, 'The First Century of Afro-American Autobiography: Notes Toward a Definition of a Genre', in Broughton, *Autobiography*, Vol. II, pp. 12–44.

35 See http://newdeal.feri.org/asn/asn12.htm (accessed 20 July 2009). For details of the entire collection of Works Progress Administration slave narratives see http:// memory.loc.gov/ammem/snhtml (accessed 20 July 2009).

36 The notion of 'isolate individualism' is ascribed to Gusdorf. See Friedman, 'Women's Autobiographical Selves', pp. 38–9.

37 M. Gergen, 'Life Stories: Pieces of a Dream', in G. C. Rosenwald and R. L. Ochberg (eds), *Storied Lives: The Cultural Politics of Self-Understanding* (New Haven, Conn., 1992), pp. 127–44; here p. 138.

38 S. N. G. Geiger, 'Women's Life Histories: Method and Content', *Signs*, 11 (2) (1986): 334–51. This article contains a useful overview of a wide range of women's life-history narratives from a variety of cultural contexts.

39 S. Rowbotham, *Woman's Consciousness, Man's World* (Harmondsworth, 1973), p. 27.

40 Summerfield, *Reconstructing Women's Wartime Lives*, pp. 261–9.

41 B. Vasquez Erazo, 'The Stories Our Mothers Tell: Projections-of-Self in the Stor-ies of Puerto Rican Garment Workers', *The Oral History Review*, 16 (2) (1988): 23–8.

42 L. Stanley, *The Auto/biographical I: The Theory and Practice of Feminist Auto/ biography* (Manchester, 1992), p. 62.

43 J. Bruner, 'The "Remembered" Self', in U. Neisser and R. Fivush (eds), *The Remembering Self: Construction and Accuracy in the Self-Narrative* (Cambridge, 1994), pp. 41–54.

44 Bruner, 'The "Remembered" Self', p. 53.

45 P. Lejeune, *On Autobiography* (Minneapolis, Minn., 1989), pp. 131–2.

46 D. Riley, *War in the Nursery: Theories of the Child and Mother* (London, 1983), p. 191.

47 G. Frank, 'Anthropology and Individual Lives: The Story of Life History and the History of the Life Story', *American Anthropologist*, 97 (1) (1995): 145–9; here, p. 145.

48 D. James, *Doña María's Story: Life History, Memory and Political Identity* (London, 2000), p. 136.

49 H. Glassie, *Passing the Time in Ballymenone: Culture and History of an Ulster Community* (Bloomington, Ind., 1995), p. 651.

50 James, *Doña María's Story*, p. 129.

51 James, *Doña María's Story*, p. 130.

52 L. Passerini, *Fascism in Popular Memory: The Cultural Experience of the Turin Working Class* (Cambridge, 1987).

53 Summerfield, *Reconstructing Women's Wartime Lives*, pp. 11–12.

54 P. Summerfield and C. Peniston-Bird, *Contesting Home Defence: Men, Women and the Home Guard in the Second World War* (Manchester, 2007), pp. 206–34.
55 M. Roper, 'Re-remembering the Soldier Hero: The Psychic and Social Construction of Memory in Personal Narratives of the Great War', *History Workshop Journal*, 50 (2000): 181–204.
56 M. Roper, 'Slipping Out of View: Subjectivity and Emotion in Gender History', *History Workshop Journal*, 59 (2005): 57–72; here p. 62.
57 Edwardians Project, Transcript 2000int142, available online at https://www.esds.ac.uk/qualidata/online/explore/interview.asp?Id=2000int142&keylen=Ronald+walker&check#607 (accessed 17 August 2009).
58 For a longer discussion of Walker's testimony, see Brown, *Death of Christian Britain*, pp. 118–21.
59 Portelli, *Death of Luigi Trastulli*, p. 279.
60 Interview with E. Morgan, conducted with L. Abrams, 2009.
61 Interview with Frances (all subsequent quotations from the same source). Transcript in the Scottish Oral History Centre Archive.
62 For a more extensive discussion, see L. Abrams, '"Blood Is Thicker than Water": Family, Fantasy and Identity in the Lives of Scottish Foster Children', in J. Lawrence and P. Starkey (eds), *Child Welfare and Social Action in the Nineteenth and Twentieth Centuries: International Perspectives* (Liverpool, 2001), pp. 195–215.
63 J. Bornat, 'Introduction', in J. Bornat (ed.), *Reminiscence Reviewed: Evaluations, Achievements, Perspectives* (Buckingham, 1994), pp. 1–8. See also P. Coleman, 'Reminiscence Within the Study of Ageing: The Social Significance of the Story', in Bornat (ed.), *Reminiscence Reviewed*, pp. 8–21.
64 A. Portelli, *The Battle of Valle Giulia: Oral History and the Art of Dialogue* (Madison, Wisc., 1997), p. viii.

Subjectivity and intersubjectivity

1 Sherry Ortner defines subjectivity as 'the ensemble of modes of perception, affect, thought, desire, and fear that animate the acting subject', but she continues that she also means 'the cultural and social formations that shape, organise and provoke those modes of affect, thought, and so on'. S. B. Ortner, *Anthropology and Social Theory: Culture, Power and the Acting Subject* (London, 2006), p. 105.
2 P. Summerfield, *Reconstructing Women's Wartime Lives: Discourse and Subjectivity in Oral Histories of the Second World War* (Manchester, 1998), p. 15.
3 Ortner, *Anthropology and Social Theory*, pp. 127–8.
4 P. Bourdieu, *Distinction: A Social Critique of the Judgement of Taste* (London, 1984).
5 Giddens cited by Ortner, *Anthropology and Social Theory*, p. 108.
6 De Lauretis cited in H. Callaway, 'Ethnography and Experience: Gender Implications in Fieldwork and Texts', in J. Okley and H. Callaway (eds), *Anthropology and Autobiography* (London, 1992), pp. 29–49; p. 37.
7 Turner cited in V. Yow, '"Do I Like Them Too Much?" Effects of the Oral History Interview on the Interviewer and Vice Versa', *The Oral History Review*, 24 (1) (1997): 55–79; here p. 63.
8 For a more extensive discussion see C. G. Brown, *Postmodernism for Historians* (London, 2005).
9 E. Stanley, *The Auto/biographical I* (Manchester, 1992), p. 62.
10 J. W. Scott, 'Experience', in J. Butler and J. W. Scott, *Feminists Theorize the Political* (London, 1992).
11 L. Roper, *Oedipus and the Devil: Women, Sexuality and Religion in Early Modern Europe* (London, 1994), p. 3.

12 M. Roper, 'Slipping Out of View: Subjectivity and Emotion in Gender History', *History Workshop Journal*, 59 (2005): 57–72; here p. 62.
13 G. H. Mead, *Mind, Self and Society* (Chicago, Ill., 1934), p. 136.
14 M. Stuart, '"And How Was It For You Mary?"' Self, Identity and Meaning for Oral Historians', *Oral History*, 21 (2) (1993): 80–3, here p. 82.
15 E. Goffman, *The Presentation of Self in Everyday Life* (London, 1990), p. 40.
16 J. Butler, *Gender Trouble* (London, 1990).
17 P. Summerfield, 'Dis/composing the Subject: Intersubjectivities in Oral History', in T. Cosslett, C. Lury and P. Summerfield (eds), *Feminism and Autobiography* (London, 2000), pp. 91–106; p. 102.
18 M. Michielsons, 'Memory Frames: The Role of Concepts and Cognition in Telling Life-Stories', in Cosslett *et al.*, *Feminism and Autobiography*, pp. 183–200; p. 189.
19 D. Patai, 'Ethical Problems of Personal Narratives; or, Who Should Eat the Last Piece of Cake?', *International Journal of Oral History*, 8 (1) (1987): 5–27; here p. 11.
20 K. Blee, 'Evidence, Empathy and Ethics: Lessons from Oral Histories of the Klan', *Journal of American History*, 80 (2) (1993): 596–606.
21 Blee, 'Evidence, Empathy and Ethics', p. 605.
22 E. Harvey, *Women and the Nazi East: Agents and Witnesses of Germanisation* (New Haven, Conn., 2003); and E. Harvey, '"Wir kamen in vollkommenes Neugebiet rein": Der "Einsatz" von Mitgliedern nationalsozialistischer Frauenorganisationen im besetzten Polen', in M. Krauss (ed.), *Sie waren dabei: Mitläuferinnen, Nutzniesserinnen, Täterinnen im Nationalsozialismus* (Göttingen, 2008), pp. 83–102.
23 M. Zukas, 'Friendship as Oral History: A Feminist Psychologist's View', *Oral History*, 21 (2) (1993): 73–9; here p. 78.
24 Zukas, 'Friendship', p. 78. See also J. Finch, 'It's Great to Have Someone to Talk To: The Ethics and Politics of Interviewing Women', in C. Bell and H. Roberts (eds), *Social Researching: Politics, Problems, Practice* (London, 1984); and J. Duncombe and J. Jessop, '"Doing Rapport" and the Ethics of "Faking Friendship"', in M. Mauthner *et al.* (eds), *Ethics in Qualitative Research* (London, 2002), pp. 107–22.
25 H. Young, 'Hard Man, New Man: Re/Composing Masculinities in Glasgow, c. 1950–2000', *Oral History*, 35 (1) (2007): 71–81.
26 Young, 'Hard Man, New Man', p. 73.
27 Young, 'Hard Man, New Man', pp. 77–8.
28 See G. Smith, 'Beyond Individual/Collective Memory: Women's Transactive Memories of Food, Family and Conflict', *Oral History*, 35 (2) (2007): 77–90.
29 S. Cunningham-Burley, '"We Don't Talk About It ... " Issues of Gender and Method in the Portrayal of Grandfatherhood', *Sociology*, 18 (1984): 325–38. I am grateful to Yvonne McFadden for her insights into this kind of scenario.
30 Portelli, 'What Makes Oral History Different?', p. 41.
31 Roper, *Oedipus and the Devil*.
32 L. Stanley, 'From "Self-Made Women" to "Women's Made-Selves"? Audit Selves, Simulation and Surveillance in the Rise of Public Woman', in Cosslett *et al.*, *Feminism and Autobiography*, pp. 41–2.
33 Interview with Robert conducted by L. Abrams, 7 January 1997. Transcript in Scottish Oral History Centre Archive.
34 G. Dawson, *Soldier Heroes, British Adventure, Empire and the Imagining of Masculinities* (London, 1994), p. 22.
35 R. Gagnier, *Subjectivities: A History of Self-Representation in Britain, 1832–1920* (Oxford, 1991), p. 58.
36 J. Ker Conway, *When Memory Speaks: Reflections on Autobiography* (New York, 1998), p. 6.

37 Dawson, *Soldier Heroes*, pp. 22–3.
38 Dawson, *Soldier Heroes*, p. 23.
39 Dawson, *Soldier Heroes*, p. 260.
40 Dawson, *Soldier Heroes*, p. 24.
41 C. K. Riessman, 'Strategic Uses of Narrative in the Presentation of Self and Illness: A Research Note', *Social Science Medicine*, 30 (11) (1999): 1195–200. For a more extensive discussion of this case in the context of narrative see Chapter 6.
42 R. Johnston and A. McIvor, 'Oral History, Subjectivity, and Environmental Reality: Occupational Health Histories in Twentieth-Century Scotland', *Osiris*, 2nd Series, 19 (2004): 234–49; here p. 246.
43 Johnson cited in G.Dawson, *Soldier Heroes*, p. 24.
44 Summerfield, *Reconstructing Women's Wartime Lives*, p. 15.
45 Dawson, *Soldier Heroes*, pp. 25–6.
46 Dawson, *Soldier Heroes*; A. Thomson, *Anzac Memories: Living with the Legend* (Oxford, 1994); Summerfield, *Reconstructing Women's Wartime Lives;* and P. Summerfield and C. Peniston-Bird, *Contesting Home Defence: Men, Women and the Home Guard in the Second World War* (Manchester, 2007).
47 Summerfield, 'Dis/composing the Subject', pp. 94–100.
48 Thomson, *Anzac Memories* and A. Thomson 'Anzac Memories: Putting Popular Memory Theory into Practice in Australia', in R. Perks and A. Thomson (eds), *The Oral History Reader* (2nd edn, London, 2006), pp. 244–54.
49 Thomson, 'Anzac Memories', p. 250.
50 Ortner, *Anthropology and Social Theory*, pp. 126–7.
51 Thomson, 'Anzac Memories', p. 253.
52 Ortner, *Anthropology and Social Theory*, pp. 252–3.
53 For example, see S. Green, 'Individual Remembering and "Collective Memory": Theoretical Presuppositions and Contemporary Debates', *Oral History*, 32 (2) (2004): 35–44.
54 S. B. Gluck, 'What's So Special about Women?', in S. H. Armitage with P. Hart and K. Weathermon (eds), *Women's Oral History* (London, 2002), pp. 3–26; p. 5. See also see J. Sangster, 'Telling Our Stories: Feminist Debates and the Use of Oral History', *Women's History Review*, 3 (1) (1994): 5–28. But as a counter to this see S. Geiger, 'What's So Feminist About Women's Oral History?', *Journal of Women's History*, 2 (1) (1990): 169–82.
55 For a wide range of feminist approaches to the analysis of women's life narratives see The Personal Narratives Group (ed.), *Interpreting Women's Lives: Feminist Theory and Personal Narratives* (Bloomington, Ind., 1989).
56 K. Anderson and D. C. Jack, 'Learning to Listen: Interview Techniques and Analysis', in Perks and Thomson, *Oral History Reader*, pp. 129–42; p. 136.
57 S. H. Armitage, 'The Next Step', in Armitage *et al.*, *Women's Oral History*, pp. 61–74; p. 62.
58 Anderson and Jack, 'Learning to Listen', p. 130.
59 Anderson and Jack, 'Learning to Listen', pp. 16–17; Summerfield, *Reconstructing Women's Wartime Lives*, pp. 28–30.
60 K. Minister, 'A Feminist Frame for the Oral History Interview', in S. B. Gluck and D. Patai (eds), *Women's Words: The Feminist Practice of Oral History* (London, 1991), pp. 27–42; p. 30.
61 Summerfield, *Reconstructing Women's Wartime Lives*, pp. 22–3.
62 A. Oakley, 'Interviewing Women: A Contradiction in Terms?' in H. Roberts (ed.), *Doing Feminist Research* (London, 1981), pp. 30–61; here pp. 31 ff.
63 Anderson and Jack, 'Learning to Listen', p. 136.
64 M.-F. Chanfrault-Duchet, 'Narrative Structures, Social Models and Symbolic Representation in the Life Story', in Gluck and Patai, *Women's Words*, pp. 77–92; p. 78; Summerfield, *Reconstructing Women's Wartime Lives*, pp. 27–8.

65 J. Yung, 'Giving Voice to Chinese American Women', in Armitage *et al.*, *Women's Oral History*, pp. 87–111; p. 87.
66 Minister, 'A Feminist Frame', pp. 31, 35–6.
67 Geiger, 'What's So Feminist?', p. 174.
68 See Finch, 'It's Great to Have Someone to Talk To'; Stacey, 'Can There Be a Feminist Ethnography?' in Gluck and Patai, *Women's Words*, pp. 111–20.
69 Summerfield, *Reconstructing Women's Wartime Lives*, p. 25.
70 C. Borland, '"That's Not What I Said": Interpretive Conflict in Oral Narrative Research', in Gluck and Patai, *Women's Words*, pp. 63–76; p. 64.
71 S. H. Armitage and S. B. Gluck, 'Reflections on Women's Oral History: An Exchange', in Armitage *et al.*, *Women's Oral History*, pp. 75–86; p. 82; and Borland, 'That's Not What I Said'.
72 See Stuart, 'And How Was It for You Mary?' where the author discusses her own experiences of dealing with the issue of reflexivity.
73 Summerfield, *Reconstructing Women's Wartime Lives*, p. 30.
74 Anderson and Jack, 'Learning to Listen', p. 140.
75 Interview with Mary Ellen Odie, Shetland Archives, 3/1/1396. See also. Abrams, *Myth and Materiality in a Woman's World: Shetland 1800–2000* (Manchester, 2005), pp. 24–52.
76 G. Dawson, *Making Peace with the Past: Memory, Trauma, and the Irish Troubles* (Manchester, 2008), p. 123.
77 R. Grele (ed.), *Envelopes of Sound: The Art of Oral History* (New York, 1991), p. 138.

Memory

1 D. Schacter, *Searching for Memory: the Brain, the Mind and the Past* (New York, 1996), p. 71.
2 A. Portelli, 'What Makes Oral History Different?', in A. Portelli, *The Death of Luigi Trastulli and Other Stories: Form and Meaning in Oral History* (New York, 1991), pp. 45–58; here p. 52.
3 A. Kuhn, 'A Journey through Memory', in in T. L. Broughton (ed.), *Autobiography*, Vol. III (London, 2007), p. 264.
4 K. Plummer, *Documents of Life 2: An Invitation to Critical Humanism* (London, 2001), pp. 232–5.
5 A. Thomson, 'Four Paradigm Transformations in Oral History', *The Oral History Review*, 34 (1) (2007): 49–71, here p. 51; D. R. Woolf, 'The Common Voice: History, Folklore and Oral Tradition in Early Modern England', *Past & Present*, 120 (1) (1988): 26–52.
6 J. Marsh, 'A Miraculous Relic?', *The Cambridge Quarterly*, 6 (1) (1972): 70–7; p. 72.
7 P. Thompson, *The Voice of the Past* (3rd edn, Oxford, 2000), pp. 118–28.
8 J. Fentress and C. Wickham, *Social Memory* (Oxford, 1992), p. 2.
9 T. Lummis, *Listening to History: The Authenticity of Oral Evidence* (London, 1988), p. 130.
10 A. Portelli, 'The Death of Luigi Trastulli: Memory and the Event', in *The Death of Luigi Trastulli and Other Stories: Form and Meaning in Oral History* (Albany, NY, 1991), pp. 1–26; p. 26.
11 A. Portelli, *The Order Has Been Carried Out: History, Memory and Meaning of a Nazi Massacre in Rome* (Basingstoke, 2007), p. 16. See Portelli's comment on the 'memory debates', in A. Portelli, *The Battle of Valle Giulia: Oral History and the Art of Dialogue* (Madison, Wisc., 1997), pp. 293–4, note 8.
12 S. Browder, M. H. Frisch, E. F. Loftus and P. Thompson, 'Dialogue I', in P. Thompson *et al.*, *Memory and History: Essays on Recalling and Interpreting Experience* (London, 1994), pp. 63–4.

13 A. M. Hoffman and H. S. Hoffman, 'Reliability and Validity in Oral History: The Case for Memory', in Thompson *et al.*, *Memory and History*, pp. 107–29.
14 Hoffman and Hoffman, 'Reliability and Validity in Oral History', p. 124.
15 U. Eco, *The Mysterious Flame of Queen Loana* (London, 2006).
16 A. L. Stoler with K. Strassler, 'Memory-Work in Java: A Cautionary Tale', in R. Perks and A. Thomson (eds), *The Oral History Reader* (2nd edn, London, 2006), pp. 283–311; p. 288.
17 For an anecdote that suggests it is possible to assemble a workable sense of self without a foundation in the past, see R. Alter's review of Eco's novel at www.slate.com/is/2121402 (accessed 1 September 2009).
18 For an accessible account of this, see Schacter, *Searching for Memory*.
19 Schacter, *Searching for Memory*, p. 17.
20 All this is explained in more depth in Schacter, *Searching for Memory*, Chapter 2.
21 M. Proust, *In Search of Lost Time*, Vol. I: *Swann's Way* (Dover edition, 2002), p. 39.
22 J. Modell and C. Brodsky, 'Envisioning Homestead: Using Photographs in Interviewing (Homestead, Pennsylvania)', in E. M. McMahan and K. L. Rogers (eds), *Interactive Oral History Interviewing* (London, 1994), pp. 141–61; D. Francis, L. Kellaher and G. Neophytou, 'The Cemetery: A Site for the Construction of Memory, Identity and Ethnicity', in J. J. Climo and M. G. Cattell (eds), *Social Memory and History: Anthropological Perspectives* (Walnut Creek, Calif., 2002), pp. 95–110.
23 A. Kuhn, *Family Secrets: Acts of Memory and Imagination* (London, 1995).
24 P. Tinkler, 'Remembering with Photos: Researching Girlhood Photo Albums from the 1950s and 1960s', unpublished paper, 2009. On photographs and memory in relation to family stories, see M. Hirsch, *Family Frames: Photography, Narrative and Memory* (London, 1997).
25 Schacter, *Searching for Memory*, p. 71.
26 J. Ker Conway, cited in D. C. Rubin (ed.), *Remembering our Past: Studies in Autobiographical Memory* (Cambridge, 1995), p. 6.
27 Schacter, *Searching for Memory*, p. 106.
28 Schacter, *Searching for Memory*, p. 106.
29 E. F. Loftus, 'Tricked by Memory', in Thompson *et al*, *Memory and History*, pp. 17–32.
30 R. F. Belli and E. F. Loftus, 'The Pliability of Autobiographical Memory: Misinformation and the False Memory Problem', in Rubin, *Remembering Our Past*, pp. 157–79; here, p. 157.
31 Thompson *et al.* 'Dialogue I', p. 62.
32 E. Winograd, 'The Authenticity and Utility of Memories', in U. Neisser and R. Fivush (eds), *The Remembering Self: Construction and Accuracy in the Self-Narrative* (Cambridge, 1994), pp. 243–51; here p. 246.
33 S. Polishuk, 'Secrets, Lies, and Misremembering: The Perils of Oral History Interviewing', *Journal of Women's Studies*, 19 (3) (1998): 14–23; here p. 21.
34 See L. Fleming, 'Jewish Women in Glasgow c. 1880–1950: Gender, Ethnicity and the Immigrant Experience', unpublished Ph.D. thesis, Glasgow University, 2005.
35 S. J. Dallam, 'Crisis or Creation: A Systematic Examination of False Memory Claims', *Journal of Child Sexual Abuse*, 9 (3/4) (2002): 9–36.
36 W. F. Brewer, cited in C. P. Thompson, J. J. Skowronski, S. F. Larsen and A. L. Betz (eds), *Autobiographical Memory: Theoretical and Applied Perspectives* (London 1998), p. 49. Brewer terms this 'recollective memory', but I have used it in relation to the more familiar autobiographical memory.
37 See G. J. Neimeyer and A. E. Metzler, 'Personal Identity and Autobiographical Recall', in Neisser and Fivush, *The Remembering Self*, pp. 105–35.
38 Lummis, *Listening to History*, p. 120.

39 C. G. Brown and J. D. Stephenson, 'The View from the Workplace: Women's Memories of Work in Stirling *c.* 1910–c. 1950', in E. Gordon and E. Breitenbach (eds), *The World is Ill-Divided: Women's Work in Scotland in the Nineteenth and Early Twentieth Centuries* (Edinburgh, 1990), pp. 7–28.

40 Mrs P.3: Stirling Women's Oral History Collection, Smith Art Gallery and Museum, Stirling, CD-ROM.

41 S.-A. Christianson and M. A. Safer, 'Emotions in Autobiographical Memories', in Rubin, *Remembering Our Past*, pp. 230–1.

42 'Christine', interviewed by Lynn Abrams, 31 January 1997.

43 Mrs J2: Stirling Women's Oral History Collection.

44 Kuhn, *Family Secrets*, p. 4.

45 Kuhn, *Family Secrets*, p. 5.

46 Henry R. J. Pilott, 'WW2 People's War'. 'WW2 People's War' is an online archive of wartime memories contributed by members of the public and gathered by the BBC. The archive can be found at www.bbc.co.uk/ww2peopleswar (accessed 1 September 2009).

47 J. M. Fitzgerald, 'Intersecting Meanings of Reminiscence in Adult Development and Ageing', in Rubin, *Remembering our Past*, pp. 367–8.

48 J. Bornat, 'Reminiscence and Oral History: Parallel Universes or Shared Endeavour?', in Perks and Thomson, *Oral History Reader*, pp. 456–73; p. 460.

49 V. R. Yow, *Recording Oral History: A Guide for the Humanities and Social Sciences* (2nd edn, Walnut Creek, Calif., 2005), pp. 38–9.

50 For an overview of oral history research on this issue, if slightly dated, see S. Leydesdorff, L. Passerini and P. Thompson (eds), *Gender and Memory* (Oxford, 1996).

51 Yvonne McFadden, oral history research for project on gender and home in the Scottish suburbs, University of Glasgow.

52 M. Ross and D. Holmberg, 'Recounting the Past: Gender Differences in the Recall of Events in the History of a Close Relationship', in J. M. Olson and M. P. Zanna (eds), *Self-Inference Processes: The Ontario Symposium* (1990), pp. 135–52.

53 G. Daniel and P. Thompson, 'Stepchildren's Memories of Love and Loss: Men's and Women's Narratives', in Leydesdorff *et al.*, *Gender and Memory*, pp. 165–86.

54 R. Ely and A. McCabe, 'Gender Differences in Memories for Speech', in Leydesdorff *et al.*, *Gender and Memory*, pp. 17–30; p. 28.

55 D. Tannen cited in Ely and McCabe, 'Gender Differences', p. 28.

56 I. Bertaux-Wiame, 'The Life-History Approach to the Study of Internal Migration: How Women and Men Came to Paris between the Wars', in P. Thompson (ed.), *Our Common History* (London, 1982), pp. 186–200.

57 M. Cohen, '"It Wasn't a Woman's World": Memory Construction and the Culture of Control in a North of Ireland Parish', in Climo and Cattell, *Social Memory and History*, pp. 53–64; E. Roberts, *A Woman's Place: An Oral History of Working-Class Women, 1890–1940* (Oxford, 1984), pp. 187–92.

58 S. Sloan, 'Oral History and Hurricane Katrina: Reflections on Shouts and Silences', *The Oral History Review*, 35 (2) (2008): 176–86, here p. 178.

59 For a wide-ranging collection of studies engaging with the relationship between trauma and life stories see K. L. Rogers and S. Leydesdorff (eds), *Trauma: Life Stories of Survivors* (London, 2004).

60 A. Parr, 'Breaking the Silence: Traumatised War Veterans and Oral History', *Oral History*, 35 (1) (2007): 61–70; p. 62.

61 D. Laub cited in M. Klempner, 'Navigating Life Review Interviews with Survivors of Trauma', in Perks and Thomson, *Oral History Reader*, pp. 198–210; p. 200.

62 C. Vegh, cited in Thompson, *Voice of the Past*, pp. 182–3.

63 See C. J. Colvin, '"Brothers and Sisters So Not Be Afraid of Me": Trauma, History and the Therapeutic Imagination in the New South Africa', in K. Hodgkin

and S. Radstone (eds), *Contested Pasts: The Politics of Memory* (London, 2003), pp. 153–68.

64 L. Langer cited in M. Roseman, 'Surviving Memory: Truth and Inaccuracy in Holocaust Testimony', in Perks and Thomson, *Oral History Reader*, pp. 230–43; p. 231.

65 Roseman, 'Surviving Memory', p. 241.

66 Klempner, 'Navigating Life Review Interviews', pp. 202–3.

67 W. James, cited in Christianson and Safer, 'Emotions in Autobiographical Memories', p. 230.

68 Cited in Parr, 'Breaking the Silence', p. 62.

69 C. R. Barclay, 'Autobiographical Remembering: Narrative Constraints on Objectified Selves', in Rubin, *Remembering Our Past*, pp. 94–128; p. 96.

70 Barclay, 'Autobiographical Remembering', p. 97.

71 M. Halbwachs, *On Collective Memory* (London, 1992), p. 53.

72 Halbwachs, *On Collective Memory*.

73 W. Kansteiner, cited in A. Green, 'Individual Remembering and "Collective Memory": Theoretical Presuppositions and Contemporary Debates', *Oral History*, 32 (2) (2004): 35–44; here p. 37.

74 Fentress and Wickham, *Social Memory*, p. ix.

75 Halbwachs, *On Collective Memory*, p. 53.

76 Popular Memory Group, 'Popular Memory: Theory, Politics, Method', in Perks and Thomson, *Oral History Reader*, pp. 43–53; p. 44.

77 Popular Memory Group, 'Popular Memory', p. 46.

78 A. Thomson 'Anzac Memories: Putting Popular Memory Theory into Practice in Australia', in Perks and Thomson, *Oral History Reader*, pp. 244–54.

79 T. Martin, 'Memory, Gender and Class: Counter-Memories of the Winter of Discontent', unpublished paper presented at conference on Modern British History, University of Strathclyde, 2008.

80 Examples of feminist memoirs include S. Rowbotham, *Promise of a Dream: Remembering the Sixties* (London, 2000); M. Roberts, *Paper Houses: A Memoir of the 70s and Beyond* (London, 2007). Oral history research on rank-and-file feminists has been conducted under the auspices of The Women's Liberation Research Network at the Women's Library in London.

81 Thomson, 'Anzac Memories'.

82 See www.wartimememories.co.uk/bevinboys.html (accessed 27 October 2009).

83 M. Phillips and T. Phillips, *Windrush: The Irresistible Rise of Multi-racial Britain* (London, 1998).

84 P. Summerfield and C. Peniston-Bird, *Contesting Home Defence: Men, Women and the Home Guard in the Second World War* (Manchester, 2007), Chapter 7; here pp. 232–4.

85 A. Confino, 'Collective Memory and Cultural History: Problems of Method', *The American Historical Review*, 102 (5) (1997): 1386–403; here p. 1387.

86 Confino, 'Collective Memory and Cultural History', p. 1387.

87 P. Hamilton, 'The Oral Historian as Memorist', *The Oral History Review*, 32 (1) (2005): 11–18; here p. 17.

88 Fentress and Wickham, *Social Memory*, p. x.

89 J. Cruikshank, *The Social Life of Stories: Narrative and Knowledge in the Yukon Territory* (Lincoln, Nebr., 2000).

90 Green, 'Individual Remembering and Collective Memory', p. 36.

91 Green, 'Individual Remembering and Collective Memory', p. 40.

92 Green, 'Individual Remembering and Collective Memory', p. 40.

93 M. Roper, 'Re-remembering the Soldier Hero: The Psychic and Social Construction of Memory in Personal Narratives of the Great War', *History Workshop Journal*, 50 (2000): 181–204.

94 Browder *et al.*, 'Dialogue I', p. 65.

95 The BBC drama was *Housewife 49* based on *Nella Last's War: The Second World War Diaries of 'Housewife 49'* (London, 2006).

96 S. A. Crane, 'Writing the Individual Back into Collective Memory', *The American Historical Review*, 102 (5) (1997): 1372–85; here p. 1378.

97 G. Dawson, 'Trauma, Place and the Politics of Memory', *History Workshop Journal*, 59 (2005): 151–78; p. 167.

98 G. Dawson, *Making Peace with the Past: Memory, Trauma and the Irish Troubles* (Manchester, 2007), p. 197.

99 J. Bodnar, *Remaking America: Public Memory, Commemoration, and Patriotism in the Twentieth Century* (Princeton, NJ, 1999), p. 14.

100 John Gillis (ed.), *Commemorations: The Politics of National Identity* (Princeton, NJ, 1994), p. 5.

101 L. Passerini, 'Introduction', in L. Passerini (ed.), *Memory and Totalitarianism* (Oxford, 1992), pp. 1–20; p. 3.

102 O. Figes, 'Private Life in Stalin's Russia: Family Narratives, Memory and Oral History', *History Workshop Journal*, 65 (2008): 117–37; and O. Figes, *The Whisperers: Private Life in Stalin's Russia* (London, 2007).

103 See D. Khubova, A. Ivankiev and T. Sharova, 'After Glasnost: Oral History in the Soviet Union', in Passerini, *Memory and Totalitarianism*, pp. 89–102; and I. Sherbakova, 'The Gulag in Memory', in Passerini, *Memory and Totalitarianism*, pp. 103–24.

104 A. Portelli, *The Order Has Been Carried Out: History, Memory and Meaning of a Nazi Massacre in Rome* (Basingstoke, 2003), especially pp. 232–76; and A. Portelli, 'The Massacre at the Fosse Ardeatine: History, Myth, Ritual and Symbol', in K. Hodgkin and S. Radstone (eds), *Memory, History, Nation* (London, 2006), pp. 29–41.

105 Rebecca Clifford, 'The Limits of National Memory: Anti-Fascism, the Holocaust and the Fosse Ardeatine Memorial in 1990s Italy', *Forum for Modern Language Studies*, 44 (2) (2008): 1–12; here p. 10.

106 G. Smith, 'Beyond Individual Collective Memory: Women's Transactive Memories of Food, Family and Conflict', *Oral History*, 35 (2) (2007): 77–90.

107 Smith, 'Beyond Individual/Collective Memory', p. 79.

108 A. Portelli, 'The Massacre at Civitella Val Di Chiana', in Portelli, *The Battle of Valle Giulia*, pp. 140–60; p. 157.

109 V. Yow, 'Review', *Oral History Review*, 28 (2) (2001): 151–4; p. 154.

110 Portelli, 'Massacre at Civitella Val di Chiana', p. 158.

111 L. Passerini, 'Work, Ideology and Consensus under Italian Fascism', *History Workshop Journal*, 8 (1979): 82–108; here p. 91.

112 L. Passerini, 'Memories between Silence and Oblivion', in Hodgkin and Radstone, *Memory, History, Nation*, pp. 238–54; here pp. 241–3.

113 J. Zar, 'Remembering and Forgetting: Guatemalan War-Widows' Forbidden Memories', in K. L. Rogers and S. Leydesdorff (eds), *Trauma: Life Stories of Survivors* (New York, 2004), pp. 45–59.

114 G. Dawson, 'Trauma, Place and the Politics of Memory: Bloody Sunday, Derry, 1972–2004', *History Workshop Journal*, 59 (2005): 151–78, here p. 169.

Narrative

1 S. E. Chase, 'Taking Narrative Seriously: Consequences for Method and Theory in Interview Studies', in Y. S. Lincoln and N. K. Denzin (eds), *Turning Points in Qualitative Research* (New York, 2003), pp. 273–96; p. 273.

2 H. White, 'The Value of Narrativity in the Representation of Reality', *Critical Inquiry*, 7 (1) (1980): 5–27; here p. 5.

3 B. Hardy, 'Towards a Poetics of Fiction: An Approach through Narrative', *Novel*, 2 (1) (1968): 5–14; here p. 5.

4 For a classic study of the storied nature of modern life, see R. Finnegan, *Tales of the City: A Study of Narrative and Urban Life* (Cambridge, 1998).

5 See K. M. Langellier and R. E. Peterson, *Storytelling in Everyday Life: Performing Narrative* (Philadelphia, Pa., 2004), pp. 1–5.

6 Interview 2000int007: Mrs Clara Wilson, ESDS Qualidata, available online at www.esds.ac.uk/qualidata/online/explore/interview.asp?id=2000int007 (accessed 10 February 2010).

7 A. Portelli, 'What Makes Oral History Different?', in A. Portelli, *The Death of Luigi Trastulli and Other Stories: Form and Meaning in Oral History* (New York, 1991), pp. 45–58; p. 35.

8 See M. Chamberlain, 'Narrative Theory', in T. L. Charlton, L. E. Myers and R. Sharpless (eds), *Handbook of Oral History* (Altamira, Calif., 2006), pp. 384–410.

9 C. K. Riessman, *Narrative Analysis* (London, 1993), p. 4.

10 J. Brockmeier and R. Harré, 'Narrative: Problems and Promises of an Alternative Paradigm', in J. Brockmeier and D. Carbaugh (eds), *Narrative and Identity: Studies in Autobiography, Self and Culture* (Amsterdam, 2001), pp. 39–58; here p. 41.

11 For a very clear example of this approach see N. Fabb, 'Narrative', in *Linguistics and Literature* (Oxford, 1997), pp. 193–220.

12 Mrs I1 (born 1894): Stirling Women's Oral History Collection, Smith Art Gallery and Museum, Stirling, CD-ROM.

13 K. M. Langellier, cited in Riessman, *Narrative Analysis*, p. 20.

14 W. Labov and J. Waletzky, 'Narrative Analysis: Oral Versions of Personal Experience', in J. Helm (ed.), *Essays on the Verbal and Visual Arts: Proceedings of the 1966 Annual Spring Meeting of the American Ethnological Society* (Seattle, Wash., 1967), pp. 12–44.

15 For a clear example of this in practice see C. Linde, *Life Stories: The Creation of Coherence* (Oxford, 1993), pp. 67–84.

16 Mrs I1 (born 1894).

17 J. Brockmeier and D. Carbaugh, 'Introduction', in J. Brockmeier and D. Carbaugh (eds), *Narrative and Identity* (Amsterdam, 2001), pp. 6–7.

18 Brockmeier and Harré, 'Narrative', p. 40.

19 Riessman, *Narrative Analysis*, p. 20.

20 U. Eco, *The Role of the Reader* (Bloomington, Ind., 1979).

21 See C. G. Brown, *The Death of Christian Britain* (London, 2001), pp. 69–79.

22 J. Dixon, *The Romance Fiction of Mills & Boon, 1909–1990s* (London, 1999).

23 See Fabb, *Linguistics and Literature*, for a wide range of examples of linguistic forms from different cultures and languages.

24 R. Grele, 'Movement without Aim: Methodological and Theoretical Problems in Oral History', in R. Grele (ed.), *Envelopes of Sound* (Chicago, Ill., 1975), pp. 126–55; here p. 136.

25 Grele, 'Movement without Aim pp. 135–8.

26 Finnegan, *Tales of the City*.

27 Finnegan, *Tales of the City*, p. 100.

28 A. Portelli, 'There's Gonna Always Be a Line: History-Telling as a Multi-Vocal Art', in A. Portelli, *The Battle of Valle Giulia: Oral History and the Art of Dialogue* (Madison, Wisc., 1997), pp. 24–39; here p. 27.

29 M.-F. Chanfrault-Duchet, 'Narrative Structures, Social Models, and Symbolic Representation in the Life Story', in S. B. Gluck and D. Patai (eds), *Women's Words: the Feminist Practice of Oral History* (London, 1991), pp. 77–92; here p. 84.

30 Chanfrault-Duchet, 'Narrative Structures', p. 79.

31 H. White, 'The Fictions of Factual Representation', in A. Green and K. Troup (eds), *The Houses of History: A Critical Reader in Twentieth Century History and Theory* (Manchester, 1999), pp. 214–29.
32 Chanfrault-Duchet, 'Narrative Structures', p. 80.
33 Chanfrault-Duchet, 'Narrative Structures', p. 89.
34 Chanfrault-Duchet, 'Narrative Structures', here p. 77.
35 Chanfrault-Duchet, 'Narrative Structures', p. 79.
36 C. Kohler Riessman, 'Strategic Uses of Narrative in the Presentation of Self and Illness: A Research Note', *Social Science Medicine*, 30 (11) (1990): 1195–200.
37 Riessman, 'Strategic Uses', p. 1197.
38 Riessman 'Strategic Uses', p. 1195.
39 Riessman, 'Strategic Uses', p. 1198.
40 Riessman, 'Strategic Uses', p. 1195.
41 See, for example, D. Tannen, *You Just Don't Understand: Men and Women in Conversation* (London, 1991); D. Tannen, *Talking from 9 to 5: How Men's and Women's Conversational Styles Affect Who Gets Heard, Who Gets Credit and What Gets Done at Work* (London, 1995).
42 On men's conversation styles see J. Coates, *Men Talk: Stories in the Making of Masculinities* (Oxford, 2003).
43 Baldwin cited in K. M. Langellier and E. E. Peterson, 'Spinstorying: An Analysis of Women Storytelling', in E. C. Fine and J. H. Speer (eds), *Performance, Culture, Identity* (London, 1992), p. 164.
44 Langellier and Peterson, 'Spinstorying', pp. 165–6.
45 K. Langellier and E. E. Peterson, *Storytelling in Daily Life: Performing Narrative* (Philadephia, Pa., 2004), pp. 108–9.
46 G. Bennett, '"And I Turned Round to Her and Said … "': A Preliminary Analysis of Shape and Structure in Women's Storytelling', *Folklore*, 100 (2) (1989): 167–83; here p. 168.
47 Bennett, 'And I Turned Round', pp. 168, 170.
48 Bennett, 'And I Turned Round', p. 176.
49 Langellier and Peterson, 'Spinstorying', p. 174.
50 K. Minister, 'A Feminist Frame for the Oral History Interview', in Gluck and Patai, *Women's Words*, pp. 27–42; p. 31.
51 C. K. Riessman, 'When Gender Is Not Enough: Women Interviewing Women', *Gender and Society*, 1 (2) (1987): 172–207.
52 Riessman, 'When Gender Is Not Enough', p. 183.
53 For examples, see Fabb, *Linguistics and Literature*.
54 See R. Finnegan, *Oral Traditions and the Verbal Arts* (London, 1992), pp. 167–9. See also R. Finnegan, *Oral Literature in Africa* (Oxford, 1970).
55 See J. Cruikshank, *The Social Life of Stories: Narrative and Knowledge in the Yukon Territory* (Lincoln, Nebr., 1998) and N. Wachowich, *Saqiyuq: Stories from the Lives of Three Inuit Women* (Montreal, 1999).
56 Riessman, *Narrative Analysis*, p. 4.
57 J. A. Robinson, 'Personal Narratives Reconsidered', *Journal of American Folklore*, 94 (371) (1981): 58–85; p. 63.
58 See the collection of articles in K. L. Rogers and S. Leydesdorff (eds), *Trauma: Life Stories of Survivors* (London, 2004).
59 Walter Benjamin, *The Storyteller* (1936) in *The Chicago Review* 16 (1) (1963): 80–101.
60 Martine N. quoted in M. Klempner, 'Navigating Life-Review Interviews with Survivors of Trauma', *The Oral History Review*, 27 (2) (2000): 67–83; here p. 76.
61 C. R. Barclay, 'Autobiographical Remembering: Narrative Constraints on Objectified Selves', in David C. Rubin (ed.), *Remembering Our Past: Studies in Autobiographical Memory* (Cambridge, 1995), pp. 96–7.

62 See www.traumaresearch.net/net2/forum2/laub.htm. Dori Laub founded the Holocaust Survivors' Film Project in 1979 which collected 3,800 videotaped interviews.
63 Barclay, 'Autobiographical Remembering', p. 113.
64 P. Levi, *If This Is a Man* (London, 1959), p. 144. And see N. Rosh White, 'Marking Absences: Holocaust Testimony and History', in R. Perks and A. Thomson (eds), *The Oral History Reader* (London, 1998), pp. 172–82.
65 Klempner, 'Navigating Life-Review Interviews', p. 73.
66 A. Parr, 'Breaking the Silence: Traumatised War Veterans and Oral History', *Oral History*, 35 (1) (2007): 61–70; p. 62.
67 Cited in Parr, 'Breaking the Silence', p. 62.
68 S. Field, 'Beyond "Healing": Trauma, Oral History and Regeneration', *Oral History*, 34 (1) (2006): 31–42.
69 A. Krog, *Country of My Skull* (London, 1999), p. 55.
70 S. E. Chase, 'Taking Narrative Seriously: Consequences for Method and Theory in Interview Studies', in Y. S. Lincoln and N. K. Denzin (eds), *Turning Points in Qualitative Research* (New York, 2003), pp. 273–96.
71 Chase, 'Taking Narrative Seriously', pp. 275–6. She is citing K. B. Sacks, *Caring by the Hour: Women, Work, and Organizing at Duke Medical Center* (Chicago, Ill., 1988).
72 Mrs X1 (born 1897): Stirling Women's Oral History Collection.
73 Mrs X1 (born 1897): Stirling Women's Oral History Collection.
74 Shetland Archive, 3/1/162/1: interview with Agnes Leask, 1986.
75 Interview by L. Abrams with Agnes Leask, 2002.
76 For an extended discussion of this see. Abrams, *Myth and Materiality in a Woman's World: Shetland 1800–2000* (Manchester, 2005), pp. 38–47.
77 R. Grele cited in D. James, *Doña María's Story: Life History, Memory and Political Identity* (London, 2000), p. 135.

Performance

1 R. Blythe, *Akenfield: Portrait of an English Village* (London, 1969), p. 21.
2 'Oracy' is a term coined by Ruth Finnegan in *Oral Traditions and the Verbal Arts* (London, 1992), pp. 3–4.
3 G. Ewart Evans, *Spoken History* (London, 1987), p. xv.
4 G. Ewart Evans, *Spoken History* (London, 1987), p. xv.
5 Finnegan, *Oral Traditions*, pp. 48–9.
6 A. Haley, *Roots: The Saga of an American Family* (London, 1976) and the 1977 US TV dramatisation of the same name.
7 A. Haley, 'Black History, Oral History and Genealogy', *The Oral History Review*, 1 (1973): 1–25; here p. 15.
8 R. Bauman, 'Performance', in R. Bauman (ed.), *Folklore, Cultural Performances, and Popular Entertainments: A Communication-centred Handbook* (Oxford, 1992), p. 41.
9 R. Bauman, *Verbal Art as Performance* (Prospect Heights, Ill., 1977), p. 11.
10 Bauman, 'Performance', p. 44.
11 Bauman, 'Performance', p. 44.
12 Bauman, *Verbal Art*, p. 11.
13 Bauman, *Verbal Art*, p. 11.
14 For an analysis of joke-telling as a distinctive speech act, see H. Sacks, 'An Analysis of the Course of a Joke's Telling in Conversation', in R. Bauman and J. Scherzer (eds), *Explorations in the Ethnography of Speaking*, 2nd edn (Cambridge, 1989), pp. 337–53.

15 R. D. Abrahams, 'Black Talking on the Streets', in Bauman and Scherzer, *Explorations in the Ethnography of Speaking*, pp. 240–62.

16 J Goody, *Representations and Contradictions: Ambivalence towards Images, Theatre, Fiction, Relics and Sexuality* (Oxford, 1997), p. 67.

17 R. D. Abrahams, 'A Performance-Centred Approach to Gossip', *Man*, new series, 5 (2) (1970): 290–301.

18 R. Bauman, *Let Your Words Be Few: Symbolism of Speaking and Silence among Seventeenth-Century Quakers* (Cambridge, 1983), pp. 43–7.

19 E. Goffman, *Frame Analysis: An Essay on the Organisation of Experience* (New York, 1974).

20 Bauman, *Verbal Art*, pp. 15–24. See also N. Fabb, *Linguistics and Literature* (Oxford, 1997), pp. 222–7.

21 Henry Allen, 'His Way with Words: Cadence and Credibility', *The Washington Post*, 20 January 2009, available online at www.washingtonpost.com/wp-dyn/content/video/2009/01/20/VI2009012001475.html (accessed 10 August 2009).

22 W. M. Kabira, *The Oral Artist* (Nairobi, 1983), p. 16.

23 E. Tonkin, *Narrating Our Pasts: The Social Construction of Oral History* (Cambridge, 1992), pp. 18–37.

24 H. Glassie, *Passing the Time in Ballymenone: Culture and History of an Ulster Community* (Bloomington, Ind., 1995), p. 37.

25 J. Cruikshank, 'Oral Tradition and Oral History: Reviewing Some Issues', *Canadian Historical Review 1994*, 75 (3): 403–18.

26 J. Butler, *Gender Trouble* (London, 1990), especially Chapter 3, pp. 101–80 Butler further states: 'That the speech act is a bodily act means that the act is redoubled in the moment of speech: there is what is said, and then there is the kind of saying that the bodily "instrument" of the utterance performs.' J. Butler, *Excitable Speech: A Politics of the Performance* (New York, 1997), p. 11.

27 K. M. Langellier and E. E. Peterson, *Storytelling in Daily Life: Performing Narrative* (Philadelphia, Pa., 2004), p. 2.

28 Langellier and Peterson, *Storytelling*, p. 51.

29 Derrida has articulated a theoretical position on voice, but this has yet to be translated into useful practical theory for the oral historian. See J. Derrida, 'The Voice That Keeps Silence', in *Speech and Phenomena* (Evanston, Ill., 1973), pp. 70–87.

30 A. Karpf, *The Human Voice: The Story of a Remarkable Talent* (London, 2006), p. 4.

31 Karpf, *The Human Voice*, p. 20.

32 L. Dégh, *Narratives in Society: A Performer-Centred Study of Narration* (Helsinki, 1995), p. 9.

33 Dégh, *Narratives in Society*, p. 9.

34 J. Shaw, 'Storytellers in Scotland: Context and Function', in J. Beech (ed.), *Scottish Life and Society*, 14 vols (Edinburgh, 2007), vol. X, pp. 28–41.

35 J. Cruikshank, *The Social Life of Stories: Narrative and Knowledge in the Yukon Territory* (Lincoln, Nebr., 1998), p. 41.

36 B. Kirschenblatt-Gimblett, 'The Concept and Varieties of Narrative Performance in East European Jewish Culture', in R. Bauman and J. Sherzer (eds), *Explorations in the Ethnography of Speaking*, 2nd edn (Cambridge, 1989), pp. 283–308; here 284.

37 Cruikshank, *Social Life of Stories*, p. 28. See also Cruikshank, 'Claiming Legitimacy: Prophecy Narratives from Northern Aboriginal Women', *American Indian Quarterly*, 18 (2) (1994): 147–67.

38 Cruikshank, *Social Life of Stories*, pp. 26–8.

39 D. Pollock, 'Introduction: Remembering', in D. Pollock (ed.), *Remembering: Oral History Performance* (Basingstoke, 2005), p. 1.

40 Pollock, 'Remembering', p. 1.
41 Pollock, 'Remembering', p. 2.
42 For examples of projects that seek to keep memory stories active, see A. Green, 'The Exhibition That Speaks for Itself: Oral History in Museums', in R. Perks and A. Thomson (eds), *The Oral History Reader*, 2nd edn (London, 2006), pp. 416–24; and T. Butler and G. Miller, 'Linked: A Landmark in Sound, a Public Walk of Art', in Perks and Thomson, *The Oral History Reader*, pp. 425–33.
43 B. Meyerhoff 'Life History Among the Elderly: Performance, Visibility, and Remembering', in B. Meyerhoff (ed.), *Remembered Lives: The Work of Ritual, Storytelling, and Growing Older* (Ann Arbor, Mich., 1992), pp. 231–47, here p. 233.
44 A. Portelli, *The Battle of Valle Giulia: Oral History and the Art of Dialogue* (Madison, Wisc., 1997), p. 6.
45 A. Howkins, 'The Voice of the People: The Social Meaning and Context of Country Song', *Oral History*, 3 (1) (1975): 50–75. See also R. Colls, *The Collier's Rant: Song and Culture in the Industrial Village* (London, 1977).
46 R. G. O'Meally, 'On Burke and the Vernacular: Realph Ellison's Boomerang of History', in R. G. O'Meally and G. Fabre (eds), *History and Memory in African-American Culture* (Oxford, 1994), pp. 244–60; here p. 248.
47 A. Impey, 'Sound, Memory and Dis/Placement: Exploring Sound, Song and Performance as Oral History in the Southern African Borderlands', *Oral History*, 36 (1) (2008): 33–55; here pp. 37–8.
48 Impey, 'Sound, Memory and Dis/Placement', pp. 37–8.
49 M. Vaughan, *The Story of an African Famine: Gender and Famine in Twentieth Century Malawi* (Cambridge, 1987).
50 R. Y. Williams, '"I'm a Keeper of Information": History-Telling and Voice', *The Oral History Review*, 28 (1) (2001): 41–63; here p. 53.
51 Williams, 'I'm a Keeper of Information', p. 53.
52 K. Minister, 'Rehearsing for the Ultimate Audience', in E. C. Fine and J. H. Speer (eds), *Performance, Culture, Identity* (Westport, Conn., 1992), pp. 249–77.
53 Meyerhoff, 'Life History among the Elderly'.
54 P. Schweitzer, 'Dramatizing Reminiscences', in J. Bornat (ed.), *Reminiscence Reviewed: Evaluations, Achievements, Perspectives* (Buckingham, 1994), pp. 105–15.
55 Pollock, 'Remembering', p. 1.
56 J. Dowd Hall, J. Leloudis, R. Korstad, M. Murphy, L. Jones, C. B. Daly, *Like a Family: The Making of a Southern Cotton Mill World* (Chapel Hill, NC, 1987).
57 D. Pollock, 'Telling the Told: Performing *Like a Family*', *The Oral History Review*, 18 (2) (1990): 1–36; p. 35.
58 N. M. Fousekis, 'Experiencing History: A Journey from Oral History to Performance', in Pollock, *Remembering*, pp. 167–86.
59 J. Deller, *The English Civil War Part II: Personal Accounts of the 1984–85 Miners' Strike* (Artangel, 2001). The re-enactment event was made into a film *The Battle of Orgreave* (2001).
60 See www.akenfield. com.
61 Interview with Craig Taylor, available online at www.bbc.co.uk/suffolk/content/articles/2009/04/16/craig_taylor_feature.shtml (accessed 10 September 2009).
62 L. Abrams, 'Akenfield: Forty Years of an Iconic Text', *Oral History*, 37 (1) (2009): 33–42.
63 See www.ourstoryscotland.org.uk/drama/seXshunned/index.htm (accessed 10 September 2009).
64 Butler and Miller, 'Linked'. See also A. Marchant, 'Treading the Traces of Discarded History: Oral History Installations', in S. H. Armitage and P. Hart (eds), *Women's Oral History: The Frontiers Reader* (London, 2002), pp. 183–95.
65 Finnegan, *Oral Traditions*, p. 92.

66 D. Sipe, 'The Future of Oral History and Moving Images', *The Oral History Review*, 19 (1/2) (1991): 75–87.
67 *The Oral History Review* has regularly reviewed oral history and film productions. For a wide-ranging discussion of one such see '*One Village in China:* A Review Symposium', *The Oral History Review*, 15 (2) (1988): 115–35.
68 D. Hymes, 'Models of the Interaction of Language and Social Life', in J. J. Gumperz and D. Hymes (eds), *Directions in Sociolinguistics: The Ethnography of Communication* (Oxford, 1986), pp. 35–71.
69 E. C. Fine, *The Folklore Text: From Performance to Print* (Bloomington, Ind., 1984), pp. 166–203.
70 D. Tedlock, 'On the Translation of Style in Oral Narrative', *Journal of American Folklore*, 84 (1) (1971): 114–33.
71 Tedlock, 'On the Translation of Style', p. 124.
72 D. Soyini Madison, 'That Was My Occupation: Oral Narrative, Performance and Black Feminist Thought', in D. Pollock (ed.), *Exceptional Spaces: Essays in Performance and History* (Chapel Hill, NC, 1998), pp. 319–42; here p. 322.
73 Madison, 'That Was My Occupation', p. 324.
74 Madison, 'That Was My Occupation', p. 325.
75 P. Morrow, 'On Shaky Ground: Folklore, Collaboration and Problematic Outcomes', in P. Morrow and W. Schneider (eds), *When Our Words Return: Writing, Hearing and Remembering Oral Traditions of Alaska and the Yukon* (Logan, Utah, 1995), pp. 27–51.
76 F. Good, 'Voice, Ear and Text: Words, Meaning and Transcription', in Perks and Thomson, *Oral History Reader*, pp. 362–73; here p. 365.
77 Shetland Archive, 3.1.77.2: interview with Mary Manson.
78 My analysis of this narrative is heavily indebted to the observations of literary-linguist Nigel Fabb, University of Strathclyde.
79 Cruikshank, *Social Life of Stories*, p. 155.

Power and empowerment

1 P. Thompson, *The Voice of the Past* (3rd edn, Oxford, 2000), p. 3.
2 M. Frisch, 'Introduction', in M. Frisch, *A Shared Authority: Essays on the Craft and Meaning of Oral and Public History* (New York, 1989), pp. xv–xxiv; p. xviii.
3 R. Grele, 'History and the Languages of History in the Oral History Interview: Who Answers Whose Questions and Why?', in E. M. McMahan and K. L. Rogers (eds), *Interactive Oral History Interviewing* (Hillsdale, NJ, 1994), pp. 1–18; p. 1.
4 The main gateway is at www.yadvashem.org (accessed 11 February 2010).
5 See, for instance, the federally supported United States Holocaust Museum at www.ushmm.org/research/collections/oralhistory and the Voice/Vision Holocaust Survivor Oral History Archive at University of Michigan, http://holocaust.umd. umich.edu (accessed 13 November 2009). Many other projects can be found online.
6 From the Mission Statement of the Voice/Vision Holocaust Survivor Oral History Archive.
7 See, for example, S. Terkel, *Hard Times: An Oral History of the Great Depression* (New York, 1970); *The Good War: An Oral History of World War II* (New York, 1984), and *Hope Dies Last: Keeping the Faith in Troubled Times* (New York, 2003).
8 R. Samuel, 'Unofficial Knowledge', in R. Samuel (ed.), *Theatres of Memory* (London, 1994), pp. 3–48.
9 R. Samuel, 'Headington Quarry: Recording a Labouring Community', *Oral History*, 1 (4) (1973): 107–22; p. 119.

10 Samuel, 'Headington Quarry', 119.
11 For instance, R. Samuel, *Village Life and Labour* (London, 1975); *Miners, Quarrymen and Saltworkers* (London, 1977); *People's History and Socialist Theory* (London, 1981).
12 P. Thompson, 'Playing at Being Skilled Men: Factory Culture and Pride in Work Skills Among Coventry Car Workers', *Social History*, 13 (1) (1988): 45–69. The Tamiment Library at New York University holds the archives of the Oral History of the American Left, established in 1976. See http://dlib.nyu.edu/findingaids/html/tamwag/ohal.html (accessed 13 November 2009).
13 Examples include: J. J. Gier-Viskovatoff and A. Porter, 'Women of the British Coalfields on Strike in 1926 and 1984', in S. H. Armitage and P. Hart (eds), *Women's Oral History: The Frontiers Reader* (London, 2002), pp. 338–70; G. Hutton, *Coal not Dole: Memories of the 1984/85 Miners' Strike* (Catrine, 2005); D. Bell, *The Dirty Thirty: Heroes of the Miners' Strike* (Nottingham, 2009). T. Holden, *Queen Coal: Women of the Miners' Strike* (Stroud, 2005).
14 L. Niethammer, 'Oral History as a Channel of Communication Between Workers and Historians', in P. Thompson (ed.), *Our Common History: The Transformation of Daily Life* (London, 1982), pp. 23–37; here p. 28. See also D. Peukert, *Die KPD in Widerstand* (Wuppertal, 1980).
15 The Scottish Working People's History Trust has published a large number of books based largely on oral history mostly edited and written by I. MacDougall including I. MacDougall, *Through the Mill: Personal Recollections by Veteran Men and Women Penicuik Paper Workers* (Edinburgh, 2008); *Voices from the Hunger Marches* (Edinburgh, 1990).
16 Frisch, *A Shared Authority*, p. 2.
17 Frisch, 'Oral History and the Presentation of Class Consciousness: The *New York Times* v. the Buffalo Unemployed', in Frisch, *A Shared Authority*, pp. 59–80; p. 70.
18 Frisch, 'Oral History and the Presentation of Class Consciousness', p. 71.
19 'Introduction', in S. B. Gluck and D. Patai (eds), *Women's Words: The Feminist Practice of Oral History* (London, 1991), pp. 1–5; p. 2.
20 J. Stacey, 'Can There Be a Feminist Ethnography?', in Gluck and Patai, *Women's Words*, pp. 111–20; p. 112.
21 L. Davidoff and B. Westover (eds), *Our Work, Our Lives, Our Words: Women's History and Women's Work* (London, 1986).
22 J. McCrindle and S. Rowbotham (eds), *Dutiful Daughters* (Harmondsworth, 1979).
23 S. B. Gluck, 'What's So Special about Women?', in S. Armitage (ed.), *Women's Oral History: The Frontiers Reader* (London, 2002), pp. 3–26, originally published in *Frontiers: A Journal of Women Studies*, 2 (2) (1977): 3–17.
24 J. Sangster, 'Telling Our Stories: Feminist Debates and the Use of Oral History', *Women's History Review*, 3 (1) (1994): 5–28; here, p. 11.
25 S. Armitage and. B. Gluck, 'Reflections on Women's Oral History: An Exchange', in S. H. Armitage (ed.), *Women's Oral History* (London, 2002), pp. 75–86; p. 77.
26 Popular Memory Group, 'Popular Memory: Theory, Politics, Method', in R. Perks and A. Thomson (eds), *The Oral History Reader*, 2nd edn (London, 2006), pp. 43–53; p. 47.
27 Some notable examples in these fields include: E. Marcus, *Making History: The Struggle for Gay and Lesbian Equal Rights, 1945–1990* (New York, 1992); B. Blauner, *Black Lives, White Lives: Three Decades of Race Relations in America* (Berkeley, Calif., 1989); E. Genovese, *Roll Jordan Roll: The World the Slaves Made* (London, 1974). For an overview of oral history and disability history, see K. Hirsch, 'Culture and Disability: The Role of Oral History', *Oral History Review*, 22 (1) (1995): 1–27.

28 See www.history.ufl.edu/oral/index.html (accessed 2 November 2009).
29 See www.wsulibs.wsu.edu/holland/masc/xblackoralhistory.html (accessed 2 November 2009). The interviews undertaken in the 1970s on cassette recorders have been digitised and are available to listen to on the website.
30 Hirsch, 'Culture and Disability', p. 6.
31 R. R. Martin, *Oral History in Social Work: Research, Assessment and Intervention* (London, 1995), p. 9.
32 See J. Bornat, '"Oral History as a Social Movement": Reminiscence and Older People', *Oral History*, 17 (2) (1989): 16–20, for a survey of the origins of the reminiscence movement.
33 See P. G. Coleman, *Ageing and Reminiscence Processes: Social and Clinical Implications* (Chichester, 1986).
34 See P. Thane, *Old Age in English History: Past Experiences, Present Issues* (London, 2000); and P. Stearns, *Old Age in European Society* (London, 1977), but neither of these use oral history methodology.
35 For a summary of the development of reminiscence work in Britain, see J. Bornat, 'Introduction', in J. Bornat (ed.), *Reminiscence Reviewed* (Buckingham, 1994), pp. 1–7, and the contributions to this volume.
36 C. Archibald, 'Hearing the Voices of Older Lesbians: Exploring Residential Care and Other Needs', University of Stirling Research Report, 2003; D. Rosenfeld, 'Identity Work among Lesbian and Gay Elderly', *Journal of Aging Studies*, 13 (2) (1999): 121–44.
37 I. Sherbakova, 'The Gulag in Memory', in Perks and Thomson, *The Oral History Reader*, pp. 521–30.
38 O. Figes, *The Whisperers: Private Life in Stalin's Russia* (London, 2007).
39 Figes, *The Whisperers*, p. xxxi.
40 For example, P. Molloy, *The Lost World of Communism: An Oral History of Daily Life behind the Iron Curtain* (London, 2009); A. Funder, *Stasiland: Stories from behind the Berlin Wall* (London, 2003); and see the chapters in L. Passerini (ed.), *Memory and Totalitarianism* (Oxford, 1992).
41 See www.restorativejustice.org (accessed 4 June 2009).
42 I. de Kok, 'Cracked Heirlooms: Memory on Exhibition', in S. Nuttall and C. Coetzee (eds), *Negotiating the Past: The Making of Memory in South Africa* (Oxford, 1998), pp. 57–71; here p. 58.
43 A. Seldon and J. Papworth, *By Word of Mouth: Elite Oral History* (London, 1983).
44 E. M. McMahan, *Elite Oral History: A Study of Cooperation and Coherence* (Tuscaloosa, Ala., 1989).
45 McMahan, *Elite Oral History*, pp. 24–53.
46 McMahan, *Elite Oral History*, pp. 54–79.
47 Information provided by Ulrike Thieme.
48 Information provided by Angela Bartie.
49 L. Passerini, 'Work, Ideology and Consensus in Italian Fascism', *History Workshop Journal*, 8 (1979), pp. 82–108; p. 84.
50 Popular Memory Group, 'Popular Memory', p. 52.
51 See A. Oakley, 'Interviewing Women: A Contradiction in Terms', in H. Roberts (ed.), *Doing Feminist Research* (London, 1981), pp. 30–61; and K. Minister, 'A Feminist Frame for the Oral History Interview', in Gluck and Patai, *Women's Words*, pp. 27–41.
52 Sangster, 'Telling Our Stories', p. 11.
53 Stacey, 'Can There Be a Feminist Ethnography?', p. 113.
54 D. Reay, 'Insider Perspectives or Stealing the Words Out of Women's Mouths', *Feminist Review*, 53 (1996): 57–73; here p. 63.
55 S. Hale, 'Feminist Method, Process and Self-Criticism: Interviewing Sudanese Women', in Gluck and Patai, *Women's Words*, pp. 121–36; p. 133.

56 Hale, 'Feminist Method, Process and Self-Criticism', p. 133.
57 K. Borland, '"That's Not What I Said": Interpretive Conflict in Oral Narrative Research', in Gluck and Patai, *Women's Words*, pp. 63–76; p. 63.
58 P. Summerfield, *Reconstructing Women's Wartime Lives: Discourse and Subjectivity in Oral Histories of the Second World War* (Manchester, 1998), p. 26.
59 Summerfield, *Reconstructing Women's Wartime Lives*, p. 26.
60 D. Patai, 'US Academics and Third World Women: Is Ethical Research Possible?', in Gluck and Patai, *Women's Words*, pp. 137–53.
61 Patai, 'US Academics and Third World Women', p. 150.
62 D. Patai, 'Ethical Problems of Personal Narratives, or Who Should Eat the Last Piece of Cake?', *International Journal of Oral History*, 8 (1) (1987): 5–27; and Patai, 'US Academics and Third World Women', pp. 140–2.
63 Frisch, *Shared Authority*, p. xx.
64 Frisch, *Shared Authority*, p. xxii.
65 Frisch, *Shared Authority*, p. xxiii.
66 L. Shopes, 'Commentary: Sharing Authority', *The Oral History Review*, 30 (1) (2003): 103–10. See also the other articles in this special issue.
67 J. Walmsley, 'Life History Interviews with People with Learning Disabilities', in Perks and Thomson, *Oral History Reader*, pp. 184–97; here p. 186.
68 M. McCarthy, 'Interviewing People with Learning Disabilities about Sensitive Topics: A Discussion of Ethical Issues', *British Journal of Learning Disabilities*, 26 (1998): 140–5.
69 L. Brigham, 'Representing the Lives of Women with Learning Difficulties: Ethical Dilemmas in the Research Process', *British Journal of Learning Disabilities*, 26 (1998): 146–50.
70 Brigham, 'Representing the Lives', p. 149.
71 See www.peoplefirstltd.com/index.php (accessed 13 June 2009).
72 L. Sitzia, 'A Shared Authority: An Impossible Goal?', *The Oral History Review*, 30 (1) (2003): 87–101.
73 T. E. K'Meyer and A. Glenn Crothers, '"If I See Some of This in Writing, I'm Going to Shoot You": Reluctant Narrators, Taboo Topics, and the Ethical Dilemmas of the Oral Historian', *The Oral History Review*, 34 (1) (2007): 71–93.
74 K'Meyer and Crothers, 'If I See Some of This in Writing', p. 92.
75 K'Meyer and Crothers, 'If I See Some of This in Writing', p. 93.
76 S. B. Gluck, 'Advocacy Oral History: Palestinian Women in Resistance', in Gluck and Patai, *Women's Words*, pp. 205–19; p. 206.
77 N. Cross and R. Barker, 'The Sahel Oral History Project', in Perks and Thomson, *Oral History Reader*, pp. 538–48. See also www.panos.org.uk/?lid=317 and *At the Desert Edge: Oral Histories from the Sahel* (London, 1991).
78 See www.panos.org.uk (accessed 4 June 2009).
79 Chuqulisa: edited narrative, available online at www.panos.org.uk/?lid=469 (accessed 5 June 2009).
80 See www.panos.org.uk/?lid=3791 (accessed 5 June 2009).
81 See www.npach.org/k-r.htm (accessed 17 June 2009).
82 See D. Allan, 'Mythologising *al-Nakba*: Narratives, Collective Identity and Cultural Practice Among Palestinian Refugees in Lebanon', *Oral History*, 33 (1) (1995): 47–56.
83 See www.palestineremembered.com/OralHistory/index.html#Introduction (accessed 16 June 2009).
84 R. Farah, 'Palestinian Refugees and Their Oral Histories: History's Silence, Memory's Burden', available online at www.zmag.org/znet/viewArticle/20757 (accessed 16 June 2009).
85 Allan, 'Mythologising *al-Nakba*', p. 48.
86 Yusif, quoted in Allan, 'Mythologising *al-Nakba*', pp. 52–3.

87 See www.icar.org.uk/2763/research-directory/every-tree-has-its-roots-refugees-from-vietnam-and-their-children-speak-about-here-and-there.html (accessed 16 June 2009).
88 A. Thomson, 'Moving Stories: Oral History and Migration Studies', *Oral History*, 27 (1) (1999): 24–37; here, p. 31.
89 See J. Cruikshank, *The Social Life of Stories: Narrative and Knowledge in the Yukon* (Lincoln, Nebr., 1998). On the equivalent process in New Zealand, see A. Erueti and A. Ward, 'Maori Land Law and the Treaty Claims Process', in B. Attwood and F. Magowan (eds), *Telling Stories: Indigenous History and Memory in Australia and New Zealand* (Crows Nest, NSW, 2001), pp. 161–82.
90 D. McNab, *Circles of Time: Aboriginal Land Rights and Resistance in Ontario* (Waterloo, Ontario, 1999), p. 3
91 Cruikshank, *Social Life of Stories*, pp. 63–4.
92 J. Finlayson and A. Curthoys, 'The Proof of Continuity of Native Title', *Australian Institute of Aboriginal and Torres Strait Islander Studies*, Issues Paper Series, No. 18 (1997). Available online at http://ntru.aiatsis.gov.au/ntpapers/ntip18.pdf (accessed 17 September 2009).
93 D. Rose, 'Histories and Rituals: Land Claims in the Territory', cited in Finlayson and Curthoys, 'The Proof of Continuity of Native Title', p. 11.
94 See www.panos.org.uk/?lid=23124 (accessed 17 September 2009).
95 See www.patientvoices.co.uk (accessed 17 September 2009).
96 See www.healthtalkonline.org (accessed 5 October 2009).
97 P. Thompson and B. Corti, 'Whose Community? The Shaping of Collective Memory in a Volunteer Project', *Oral History*, 36 (2) (2008): 89–98.
98 H. Glassie, *Passing the Time in Ballymenone: Culture and History of an Ulster Community* (Bloomington, Ind., 1995), p. 34.

Further reading

This list represents just a small selection of the available material. Readers should refer to the endnotes to each chapter for full bibliographical details of all the works consulted. For an extensive guide to publications on oral history method and theory see the 'Recommended Reading' sections in V. Yow's *Recording Oral History*, 2nd edn (Walnut Creek, Calif. and Oxford, 2005) and the bibliography in R. Perks and A. Thomson (eds), *The Oral History Reader*, 2nd edn (London, 2006). For up-to-date information on the most recent oral history studies see the book-review sections in the journals *Oral History* and *The Oral History Review*.

Practical guides to oral history method

Perks, R., *Oral History: Talking about the Past*, 2nd edn, (London, 1995).
Ritchie, D., *Doing Oral History: A Practical Guide* (New York, 2003).
Thompson, P., *The Voice of the Past: Oral History*, 3rd edn (Oxford, 2000).
Yow, V. R., *Recording Oral History: A Guide for the Humanities and Social Sciences*, 2nd edn (Walnut Creek, Calif., and Oxford, 2005).
Oral History, www.oralhistory.org.uk. The website of the UK Oral History Society, which contains a section with advice on interviewing.
Oral History, www.oralhistory.org. The website of the US Oral History Association.

Oral history theory and method

Armitage, S. H. with P. Hart and K. Weatherman (eds), *Women's Oral History: The Frontiers Reader* (Lincoln, Nebr., 2002).
Attwood, B. and Magowan, F. (eds), *Telling Stories: Indigenous History and Memory in Australia and New Zealand* (Crows Nest, NSW, 2001).
Bornat, J. (ed.), *Reminiscence Reviewed: Perspectives, Evaluations, Achievements* (Buckingham, 1994).
Charlton, T. L., Myers, L. E. and Sharpless, R. (eds), *Handbook of Oral History* (Walnut Creek, Calif., 2006).
Cruikshank, J., *The Social Life of Stories: Narrative and Knowledge in the Yukon Territory* (Lincoln, Nebr., 2000).
Dunaway, D. K. and Baum, W. K. (eds), *Oral History: An Interdisciplinary Anthology* (Walnut Creek, Calif., 1996).
Frisch, M., *A Shared Authority: Essays on the Craft and Meaning of Oral and Public History* (New York, 1990).

Gluck, S. B. and Patai, D. (eds), *Women's Words: The Feminist Practice of Oral History* (London, 1991).

Grele, R. (ed.), *Envelopes of Sound: The Art of Oral History* (New York, 1991).

Hamilton, P. and Shopes, L. (eds), *Oral History and Public Memories* (Philadelphia, Pa., 2008).

James, D., *Doña María's Story: Life History, Memory and Political Identity* (Durham, NC, 2000).

Lincoln, Y. S. and Denzin, N. K. (eds), *Turning Points in Qualitative Research* (New York, 2003).

Lummis, T., *Listening to History: The Authenticity of Oral Evidence* (London, 1987).

McMahan, E. and Rogers, K. L. (eds), *Interactive Oral History Interviewing* (Hillsdale, NJ, 1994).

Perks, R. and Thomson, A. (eds), *The Oral History Reader* (London, 1998); 2nd edn (London, 2006). The two editions are substantially different. The second edition is much extended but does not contain all of the same articles as the first edition.

Passerini, L., 'Work, Ideology and Consensus under Italian Fascism', *History Workshop Journal*, 8 (1979): 82–108.

——*Fascism in Popular Memory: The Cultural Experiences of the Turin Working Class* (Cambridge, 1987).

——*Autobiography of a Generation: Italy, 1968* (Middleton, Conn., 1996).

Personal Narratives Group (eds), *Interpreting Women's Lives: Feminist Theory and Personal Narratives* (Bloomington, Ind., 1989).

Portelli, A., *The Death of Luigi Trastulli and Other Stories: Form and Meaning in Oral History* (New York, 1991).

——*The Battle of Valle Giulia: Oral History and the Art of Dialogue* (Madison, Wisc., 1997).

——*The Order Has Been Carried Out: History, Memory and Meaning of a Nazi Massacre in Rome* (Basingstoke, 2007).

Sangster, J., 'Telling Our Stories: Feminist Debates and the Use of Oral History', *Women's History Review*, 3 (1) (1994): 5–28.

Summerfield, P., *Reconstructing Women's Wartime Lives: Discourse and Subjectivity in Oral Histories of the Second World War* (Manchester, 1998).

Thomson, A., *Anzac Memories: Living with the Legend* (Oxford, 1994).

——'Fifty Years On: An International Perspective on Oral History', *Journal of American History*, 85 (2) (1998): 581–95.

——'Four Paradigm Transformations in Oral History', *The Oral History Review*, 34 (1) (2007): 49–71.

Tonkin, E., *Narrating Our Pasts: The Social Construction of Oral History* (Cambridge, 1992).

Vansina, J., *Oral Tradition: A Study in Historical Methodology* (London, 1965).

——*Oral Tradition as History* (Madison, Wisc., 1985).

White, L., Miescher, S. F. and Cohen, D. W. (eds), *African Words, African Voices: Critical Practices in Oral History* (Bloomington, Ind., 2001).

Self

Broughton, T. L. (ed.), *Autobiography: Critical Concepts in Literary and Cultural Studies*, 4 vols (London, 2007). Readers would do well to start with this multivolume edited collection of short pieces addressing all conceivable aspects of auto-biographical narratives.

Bertaux, D. (ed.), *Biography and Society: The Life History Approach in the Social Sciences* (Beverly Hills, Calif., 1981).

Chamberlayne, P., Bornat, J. and Wengraf, T. (eds), *The Turn to Biographical Methods in the Social Sciences* (London, 2000).

Cosslett, T., Lury, C. and Summerfield, P. (eds), *Feminism and Autobiography* (London, 2000).

Goffman, E., *The Presentation of Self in Everyday Life* (London, 1990). First published 1959.

Ker Conway, J., *When Memory Speaks: Reflections on Autobiography* (New York, 1998).

Langness, L. L. and Frank, G., *Lives: An Anthropological Approach to Biography* (Novato, Calif., 1981).

Neisser, U. and Fivush, R. (eds), *The Remembering Self: Construction and Accuracy in the Self-Narrative* (Cambridge, 1994).

Okely, J. and Callaway, H. (eds), *Anthropology and Autobiography* (London, 1992).

Plummer, K., *Documents of Life 2: An Invitation to Critical Humanism* (London, 2001).

Porter, R. (ed.), *Rewriting the Self: Histories from the Renaissance to the Present* (Routledge, 1997).

Roberts, B., *Biographical Research* (Buckingham, 2002).

Rosenwald, G. C. and Ochberg, R. L. (eds), *Storied Lives: The Cultural Politics of Self-Understanding* (New Haven, Conn., 1992).

Stanley, L., *The Auto/biographical I: The Theory and Practice of Feminist Auto/biography* (Manchester, 1992).

Stuart, M., '"And How Was It for You Mary?" Self, Identity and Meaning for Oral Historians', *Oral History,* 21 (2) (1993): 80–3.

Subjectivity and intersubjectivity

Cotterill, P., 'Interviewing Women: Issues of Friendship, Vulnerability and Power', *Women's Studies International Forum,* 15 (5–6) (1992): 593–606.

Dawson, G., *Soldier Heroes: British Adventure, Empire and the Imagining of Masculinities* (London, 1994).

Ellis, C. and Flaherty, M. G. (eds), *Investigating Subjectivity: Research on Lived Experience* (London, 1992).

Geiger, S., 'What's So Feminist About Women's Oral History?', *Journal of Women's History,* 2 (1) (1990): 169–82.

Gluck, S. B. and Patai, D. (eds), *Women's Words: The Feminist Practice of Oral History* (London, 1991).

Oakley, J., 'Interviewing Women: A Contradiction in Terms', in H. Roberts (ed.), *Doing Feminist Research* (London, 1981), pp. 30–61.

Ortner, S. B., *Anthropology and Social Theory: Culture, Power and the Acting Subject* (London, 2006).

Summerfield, P., 'Dis/composing the Subject: Intersubjectivities in Oral History', in T. Cosslett, C. Lury and P. Summerfield (eds), *Feminism and Autobiography* (London, 2000), 91–106.

Yow, V., '"Do I Like Them Too Much?" Effects on the Oral History Interview of the Interviewer and Vice Versa', *The Oral History Review,* 24 (1) (1997): 55–79.

Memory

Ashplant, T. G., Dawson, G. and Roper, M. (eds), *The Politics of War Memory and Commemoration* (New Brunswick, NJ, 2004).

Climo, J. J. and Cattell, M. G. (eds), *Social Memory and History: Anthropological Perspectives* (Walnut Creek, Calif., 2002).

Crane, S. A., 'Writing the Individual Back into Collective Memory', *American Historical Review,* 102 (5) (1997): 1372–85.

Fentress, J. and Wickham, C., *Social Memory* (Oxford, 1992).

Green, A., 'Individual Remembering and "Collective Memory": Theoretical Presuppositions and Contemporary Debates', *Oral History,* 32 (2) (2004): 35–44.

Halbwachs, M., *On Collective Memory* (London, 1992).

Hodgkin, K. and Radstone, S. (eds), *Contested Pasts: The Politics of Memory* (London, 2003).

——(eds), *Memory, History, Nation: Contested Pasts* (New Brunswick, NJ, 2006).

Leydesdorff, S., Passerini, L. and Thompson, P. (eds), *Gender and Memory* (Oxford, 1996).

Neisser, U. and Fivush, R. (eds), *The Remembering Self: Construction and Accuracy in the Self-Narrative* (Cambridge, 1994).

Nuttall, S. and Coetzee, C. (eds), *Negotiating the Past: The Making of Memory in South Africa* (Cape Town, 1998).

Passerini, L. (ed.), *Memory and Totalitarianism* (Oxford, 1992).

Popular Memory Group, 'Popular Memory: Theory, Politics, Method', in R. Perks and A. Thomson (eds), *The Oral History Reader,* 2nd edn (London, 2006), pp. 43–53.

Rogers, K. L. and Leydesdorff, S. (eds), *Trauma: Life Stories of Survivors* (London, 2004).

Rubin, D. C. (ed.), *Remembering our Past: Studies in Autobiographical Memory* (Cambridge, 1995).

Schacter, D., *Searching for Memory* (New York, 1996).

Smith, G., 'Beyond Individual/Collective Memory: Women's Transactive Memories of Food, Family and Conflict', *Oral History,* 35 (2) (2007): 77–90.

Thompson, C. P., Skowronski, J. J., Larsen, S. F., Betz, A. L. (eds), *Autobiographical Memory: Theoretical and Applied Perspectives* (London 1998).

Thompson, P. *et al.*, *Memory and History: Essays on Recalling and Interpreting Experience* (London, 1994).

Narrative

Bennett, G., '"And I Turned Round to Her and Said … " A Preliminary Analysis of Shape and Structure in Women's Storytelling', *Folklore,* 100 (2) (1989): 167–83.

Brockmeier, J. and Carbaugh, D. (eds), *Narrative and Identity: Studies in Autobiography, Self and Culture* (Amsterdam, 2001).

Chamberlain, M. and Thompson, P. (eds), *Narrative and Genre: Contexts and Types of Communication* (London, 2004).

Chanfrault-Duchet, M.-F., 'Narrative Structures, Social Models, and Symbolic Representation in the Life Story', in S. B. Gluck and D. Patai (eds), *Women's Words: The Feminist Practice of Oral History* (London, 1991), pp. 77–92.

Chase, S. E., 'Taking Narrative Seriously: Consequences for Method and Theory in Interview Studies', in Y. S. Lincoln and N. K. Denzin (eds), *Turning Points in Qualitative Research* (New York, 2003), pp. 273–96.

Clandinin, D. J. and Connelly, F. M., *Narrative Inquiry: Experience and Story in Qualitative Research* (San Francisco, Calif., 2000).

Fabb, N., *Linguistics and Literature* (Oxford, 1997).

Finnegan, R., *Tales of the City: A Study of Narrative and Urban Life* (Cambridge, 1998).

Langellier, K. M. and Peterson, E. E., 'Spinstorying: An Analysis of Women Story-telling', in E. C. Fine and J. H. Speer (eds), *Performance, Culture, Identity* (London, 1992), pp. 157–80.

——*Storytelling in Everyday Life: Performing Narrative* (Philadelphia, Pa., 2004).

Linde, C., *Life Stories: The Creation of Coherence* (Oxford, 1983).

Riessman, C. K., 'When Gender Is Not Enough: Women Interviewing Women', *Gender & Society,* 1 (1987): 172–207.

——'Strategic Uses of Narrative in the Presentation of Self and Illness: A Research Note', *Social Science Medicine,* 30 (11) (1990): 1195–200.

——*Narrative Analysis* (London, 1993).

White, H., 'The Value of Narrativity in the Representation of Reality', *Critical Inquiry,* 7 (1) (1980): 5–27.

Performance

Bauman, R., *Verbal Art as Performance* (Prospect Heights, Ill., 1977).

——(ed.), *Folklore, Cultural Performances, and Popular Entertainments: A Commu-nication-centred Handbook* (Oxford, 1992).

Bauman, R. and Scherzer, J. (eds), *Explorations in the Ethnography of Speaking,* 2nd edn (Cambridge, 1989).

Dégh, L., *Narratives in Society: A Performer-Centred Study of Narration* (Helsinki, 1995).

Fabb, N., *Linguistics and Literature* (Oxford, 1997).

Fine, E. C., *The Folklore Text: From Performance to Print* (Bloomington, Ind., 1984).

Fine, E. C. and Speer, J. H. (eds), *Performance, Culture, Identity* (Westport, Conn., 1992).

Finnegan, R., *Oral Traditions and the Verbal Arts* (London, 1992).

Karpf, A., *The Human Voice: The Story of a Remarkable Talent* (London, 2006).

Pollock, D., 'Telling the Told: Performing Like a Family', *The Oral History Review,* 18 (2) (1990): 1–36.

——(ed.), *Exceptional Spaces: Essays in Performance and History* (Chapel Hill, NC, 1998).

——(ed.), *Remembering: Oral History Performance* (Basingstoke, 2005).

Tedlock, D., 'On the Translation of Style in Oral Narrative', *Journal of American Folklore,* 84 (1) (1971): 114–33.

Williams, R. Y., '"I'm a Keeper of Information": History-Telling and Voice', *The Oral History Review,* 28 (1) (2001): 41–63.

Power and empowerment

Frisch, M. (ed.), *A Shared Authority: Essays on the Craft and Meaning of Oral and Public History* (New York, 1990).

McMahan, E. M., *Elite Oral History: A Study of Cooperation and Coherence* (Tusca-loosa, Ala., 1989).

Niethammer, L., 'Oral History as a Channel of Communication Between Workers and Historians', in P. Thompson (ed.), *Our Common History: The Transformation of Daily Life* (London, 1982), pp. 23–37.

Patai, D., 'Ethical Problems of Personal Narratives, or Who Should Eat the Last Piece of Cake?', *International Journal of Oral History,* 8 (1) (1987): 5–27.

Popular Memory Group, 'Popular Memory: Theory, Politics, Method', in R. Perks and A. Thomson (eds), *The Oral History Reader,* 2nd edn (London, 2006), pp. 43–53.

Seldon, A. and Papworth, J., *By Word of Mouth: Elite Oral History* (London, 1983).

Sitzia, L., 'A Shared Authority: An Impossible Goal?', *The Oral History Review,* 30 (1) (2003): 87–101.

Index

Wickham, Chris 96, 99
Williams, Rhonda 141
Winter of Discontent 97
women: Chinese–American 72;
  communication styles of 119–21;
  emancipation 39, 60–61, 96, 103;
  history of 8, 44, 74, 75–76, 124–25,
  144, 156–57; liberation of 51; motifs
  used by 28; oral history of 4, 30–31,
  79, 87; self narration 38–39, 44–45;
  and subjectivity 71; working class 8
women's movement 98, 156

Wong, Hertha Dawn 37
working class 7, 8
World Trade Centre Attacks
  92, 122
world wide web 30, 89, 173

Young, Hilary 62
Yow, Valerie 103
Yukon 99, 121, 38–39
Yung, Judy 72

Zukas, Miriam 61–62

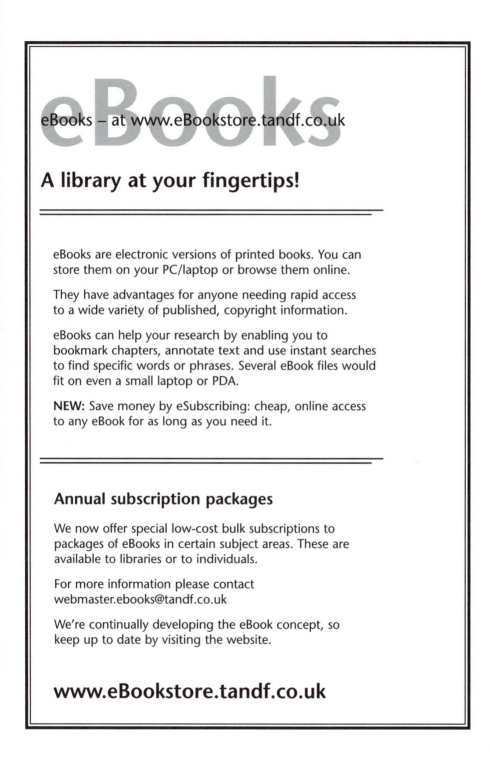